A-Z LEICESTER

CONTENTS

Key to Map Pages	2-3	Road Map (3.	
Large Scale City Centre	4-5	Index to Stree.	
Map Pages	6-65	Villages, Hospitals etc. and	70-104
Postcode Map	66-67	selected Places of Interest	

REFERENCE

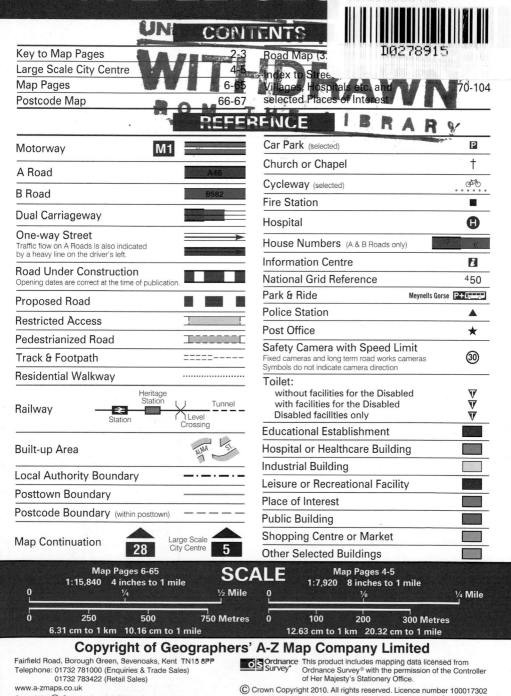

Motorway	M1	Car Park (selected)	P
A Road	A46	Church or Chapel	†
B Road	B582	Cycleway (selected)	
Dual Carriageway		Fire Station	■
One-way Street		Hospital	H
Traffic flow on A Roads is also indicated by a heavy line on the driver's left.		House Numbers (A & B Roads only)	
Road Under Construction		Information Centre	i
Opening dates are correct at the time of publication.		National Grid Reference	450
Proposed Road		Park & Ride	Meynells Gorse P+
Restricted Access		Police Station	▲
Pedestrianized Road		Post Office	★
Track & Footpath		Safety Camera with Speed Limit	30
Residential Walkway		Fixed cameras and long term road works cameras Symbols do not indicate camera direction	

Railway — Heritage Station, Station, Tunnel, Level Crossing

Toilet:	
without facilities for the Disabled	▽
with facilities for the Disabled	▽
Disabled facilities only	▽
Built-up Area	
Local Authority Boundary	— · — · —
Educational Establishment	■
Hospital or Healthcare Building	■
Posttown Boundary	
Industrial Building	■
Postcode Boundary (within posttown)	— — —
Leisure or Recreational Facility	■
Place of Interest	■
Map Continuation	28	Large Scale City Centre	5
Public Building	■
Shopping Centre or Market	■
Other Selected Buildings	■

SCALE

Map Pages 6-65	Map Pages 4-5
1:15,840 4 inches to 1 mile	1:7,920 8 inches to 1 mile
0 ¼ ½ Mile	0 ⅛ ¼ Mile
0 250 500 750 Metres	0 100 200 300 Metres
6.31 cm to 1 km 10.16 cm to 1 mile	12.63 cm to 1 km 20.32 cm to 1 mile

Copyright of Geographers' A-Z Map Company Limited

Fairfield Road, Borough Green, Sevenoaks, Kent TN15 8PP
Telephone: 01732 781000 (Enquiries & Trade Sales)
01732 783422 (Retail Sales)
www.a-zmaps.co.uk
Copyright © Geographers' A-Z Map Co. Ltd.
Edition 7 2011

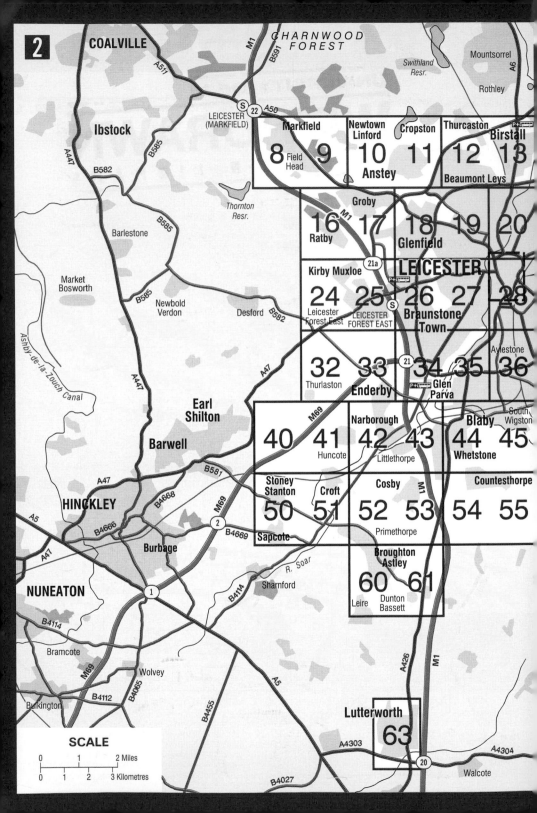

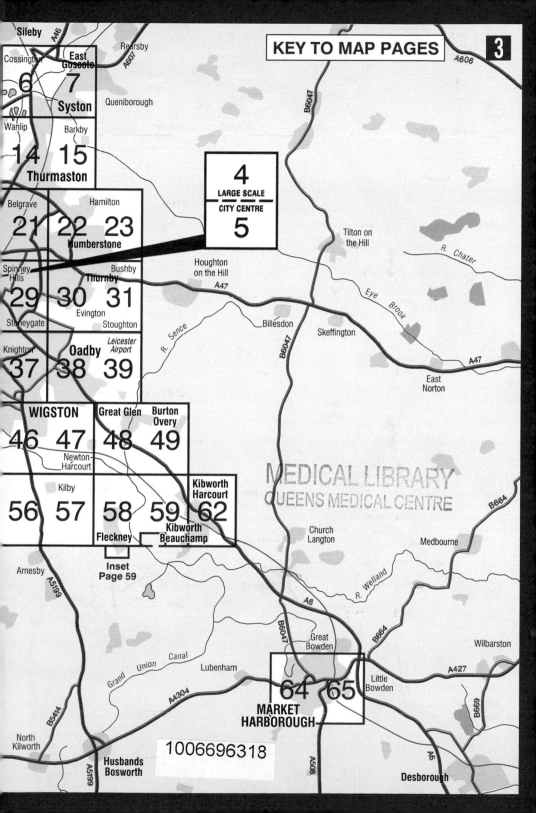

Sileby
A46
East
Goscote
Cossington
Rearsby
A607
6   7
Syston
Queniborough
B6047
A606

Wanlip
Barkby

14   15
Thurmaston

4
LARGE SCALE
CITY CENTRE
5

Belgrave
Hamilton

21   22   23
Humberstone

Tilton on
the Hill
R. Chater

Spinney
Hills
Bushby
Thurnby
Houghton
on the Hill
A47

29   30   31
Evington
Stoughton

Stoneygate

R. Sence
Billesdon
B6047
Skeffington
Eye
Brook
A47

Knighton

37   38   39
Oadby
Leicester
Airport

East
Norton

WIGSTON
Great Glen
Burton
Overy

46   47   48   49
Newton
Harcourt

MEDICAL LIBRARY
QUEENS MEDICAL CENTRE
B664

Kilby
Kibworth
Harcourt

56   57   58   59   62
Fleckney
Kibworth
Beauchamp

Church
Langton
Medbourne

Arnesby
A5199
Inset
Page 59

R. Welland

Grand
Union
Canal
Lubenham

B6047
Great
Bowden
B664
Wilbarston

North
Kilworth
B5414
A4304

64   65
Little
Bowden
A427
B669

MARKET
HARBOROUGH

A5199
Husbands
Bosworth
A508
Desborough
A6

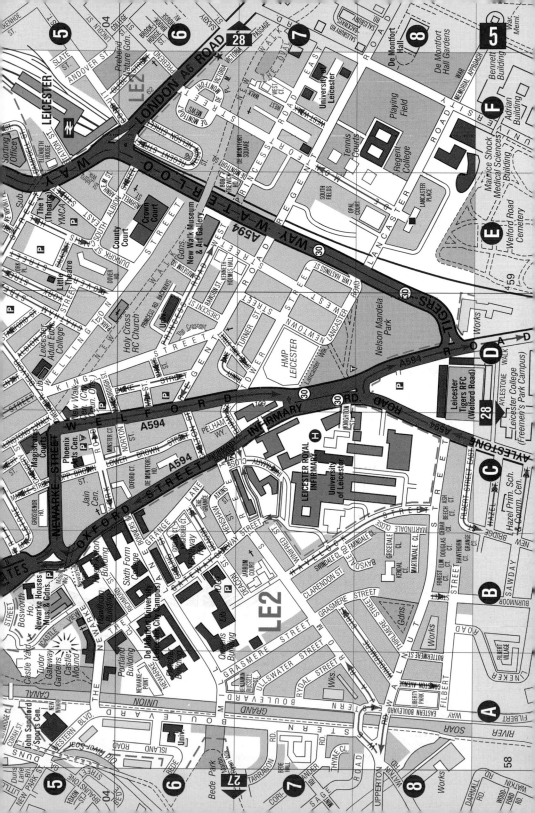

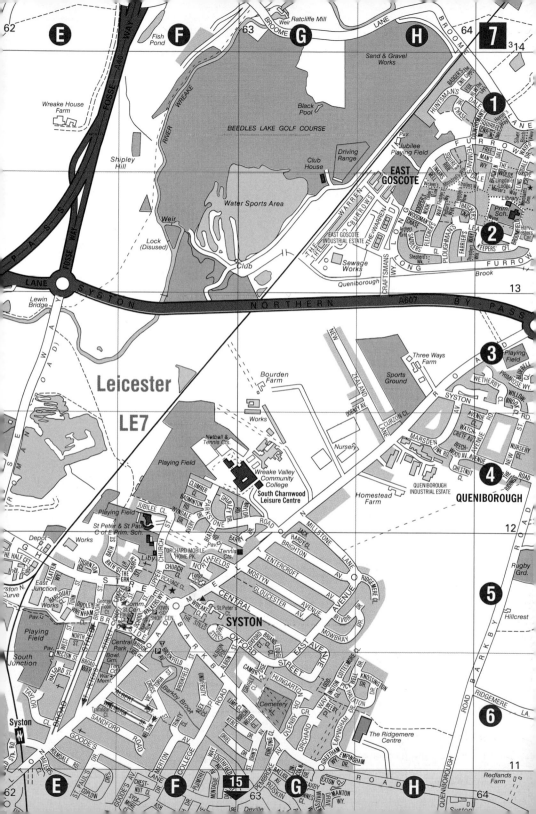

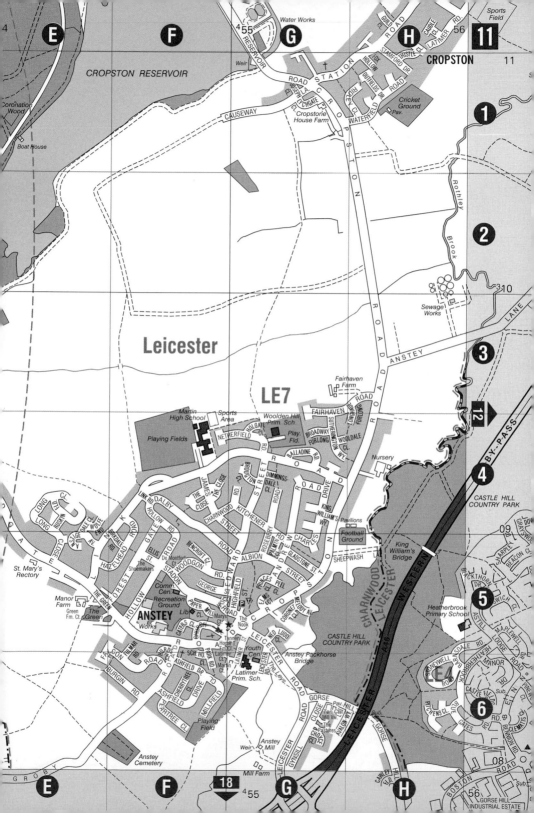

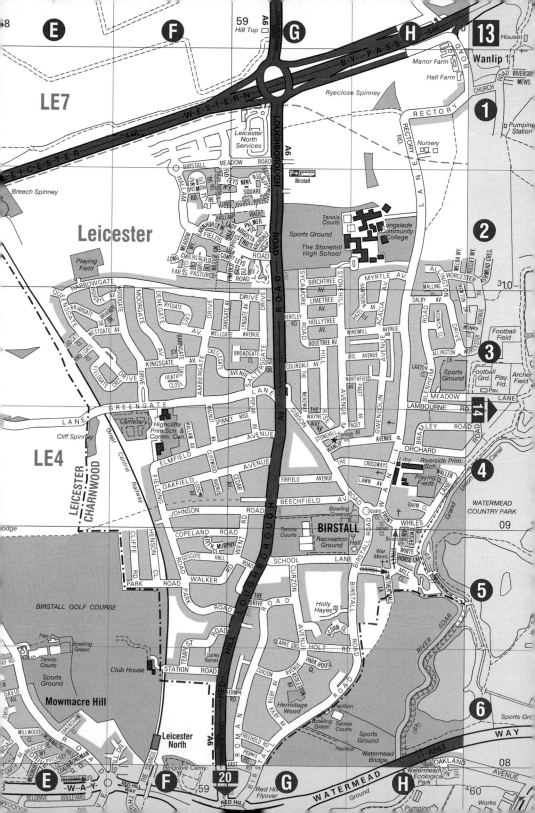

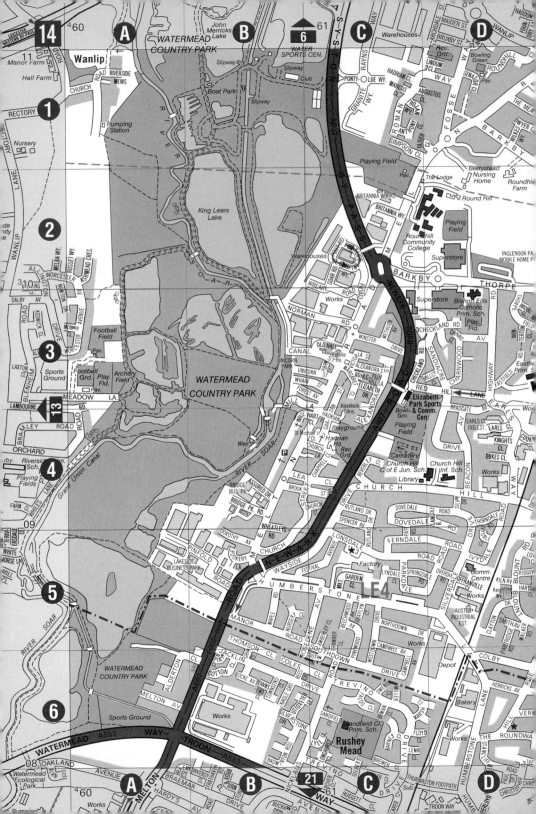

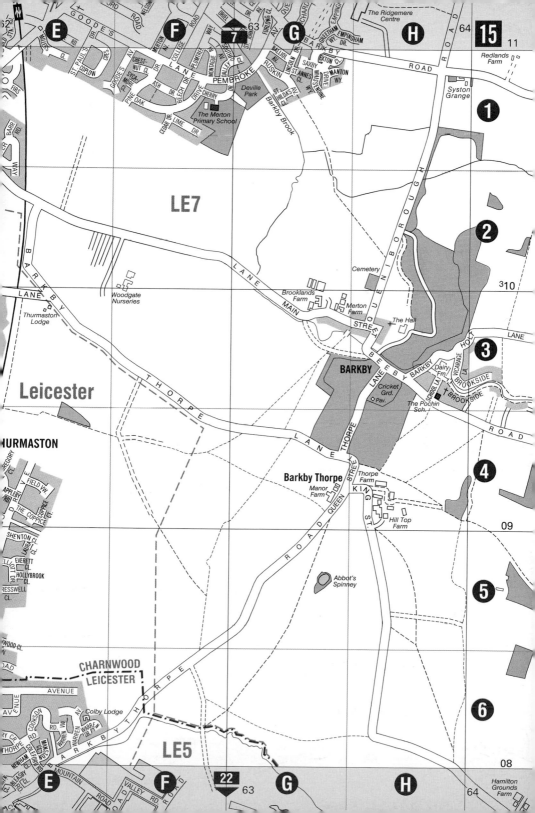

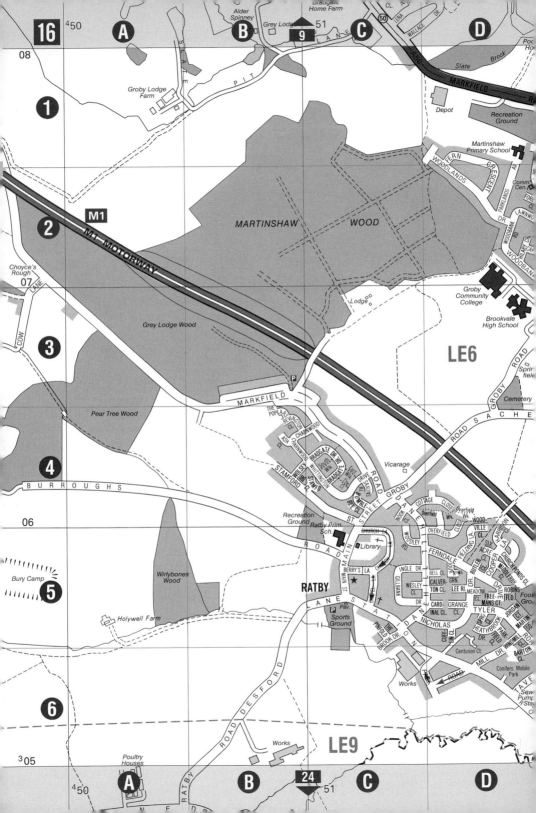

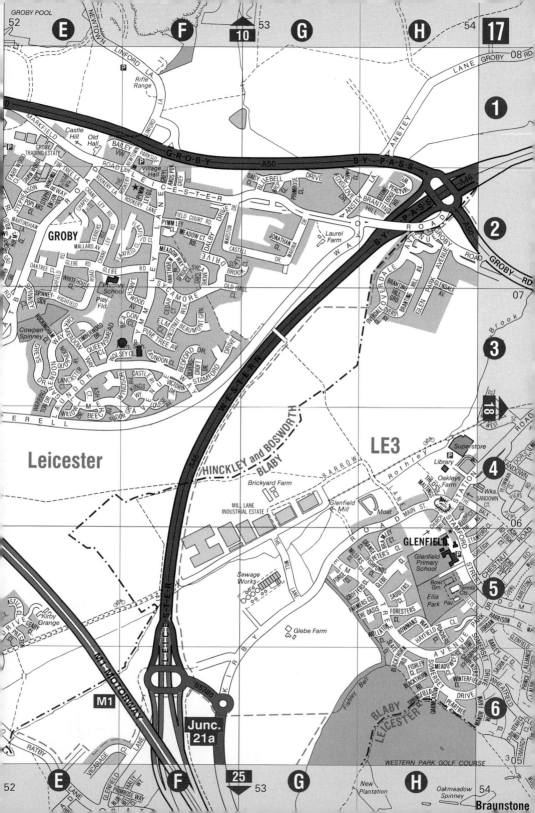

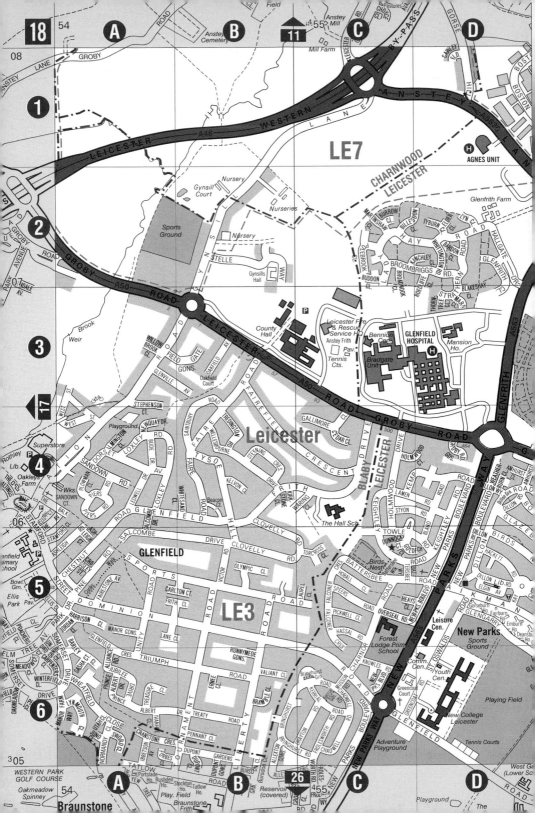

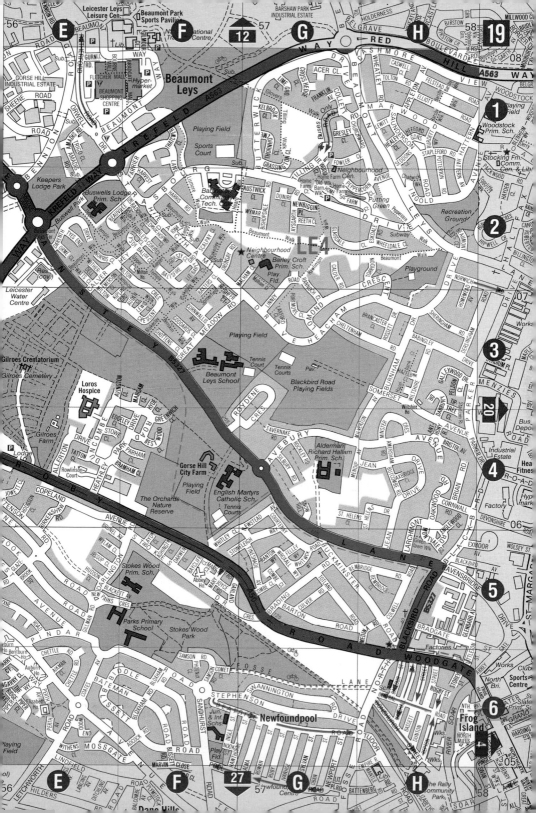

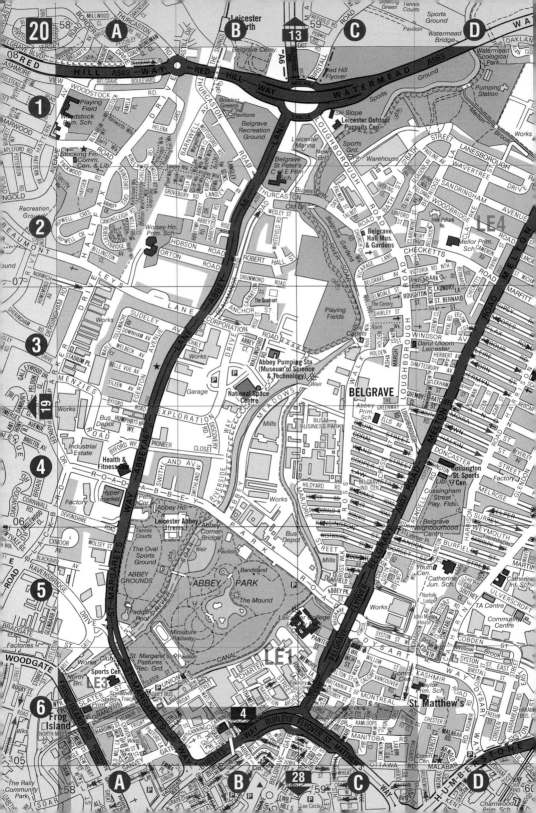

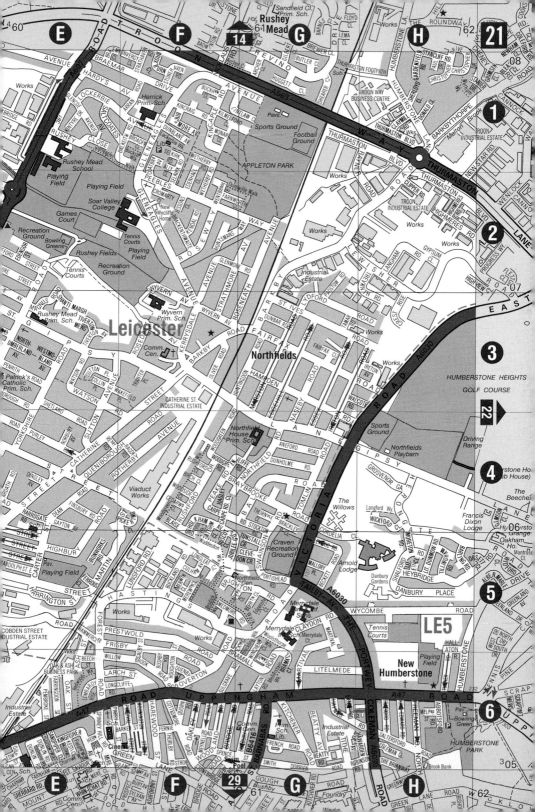

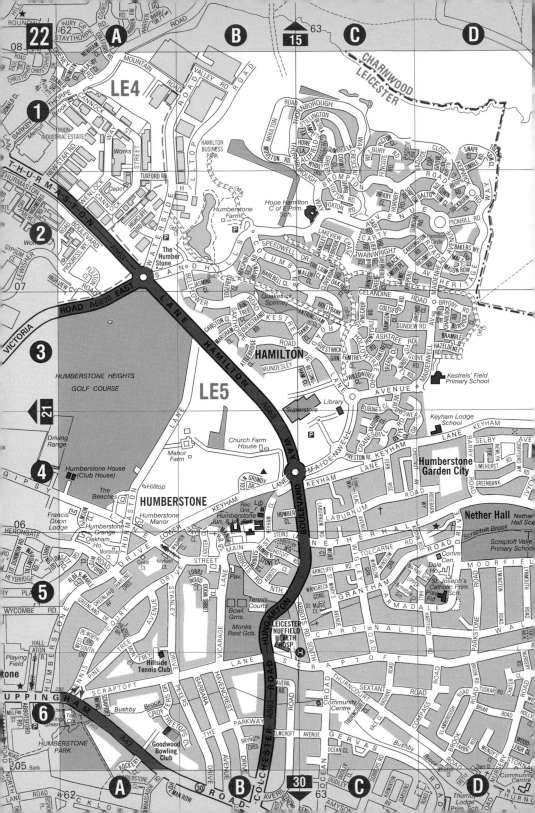

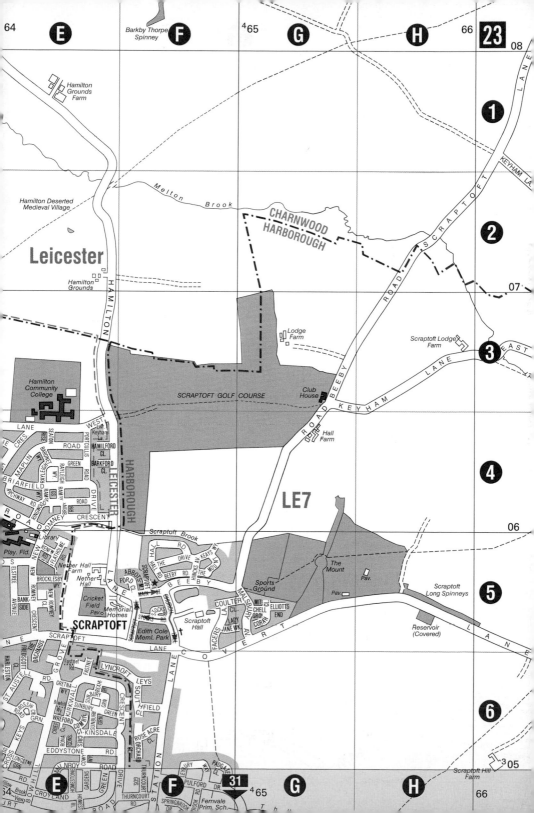

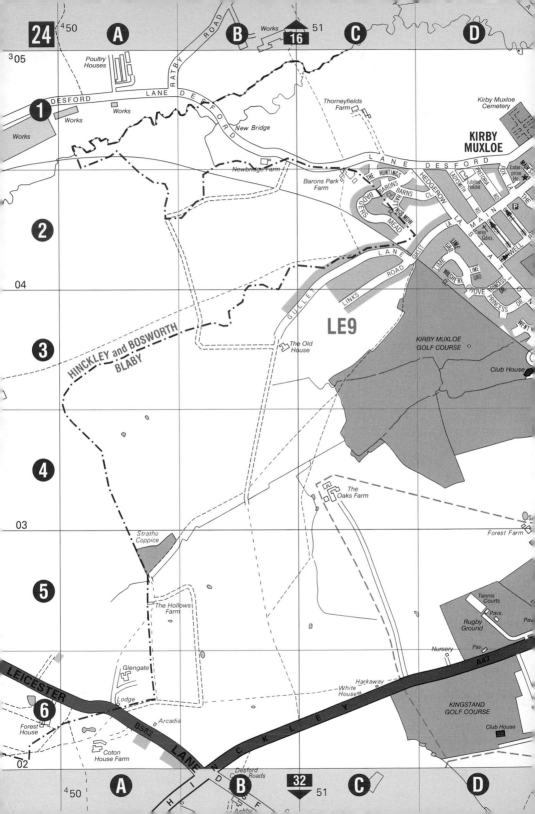

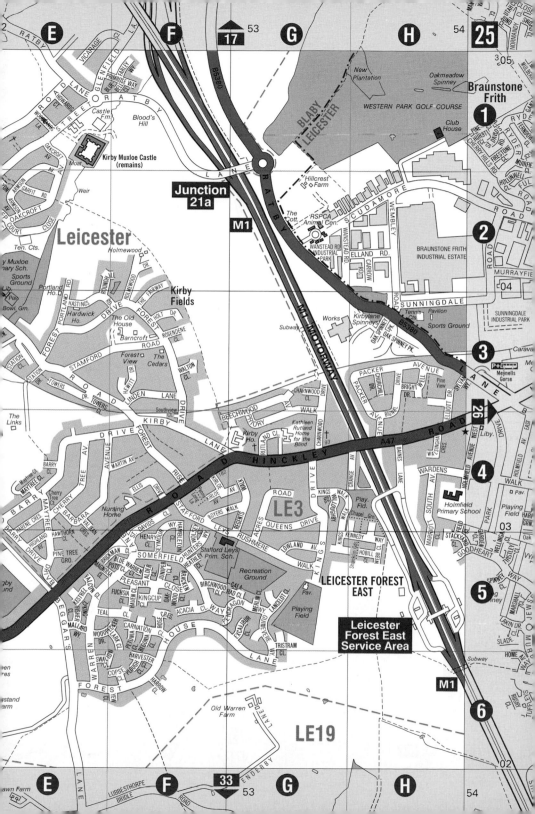

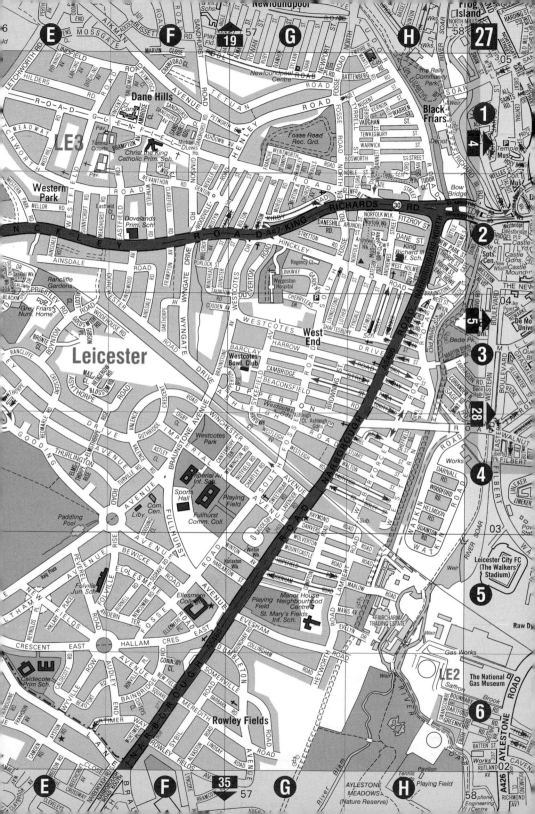

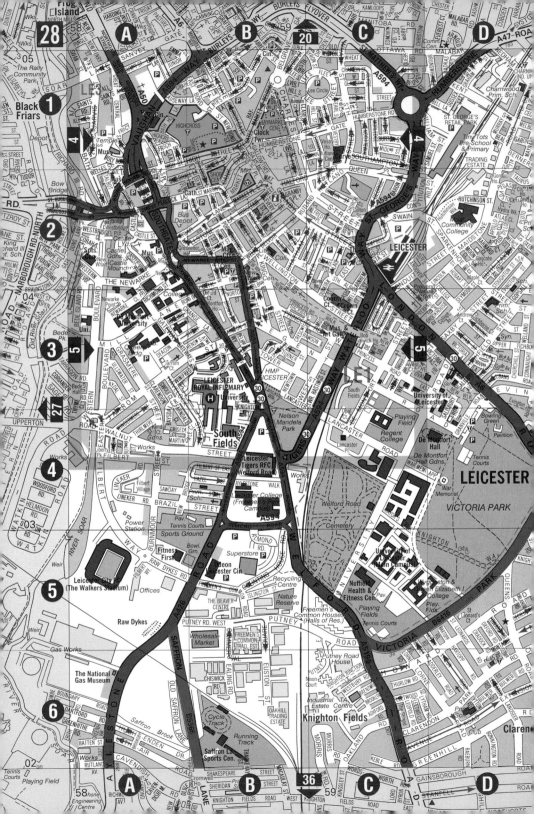

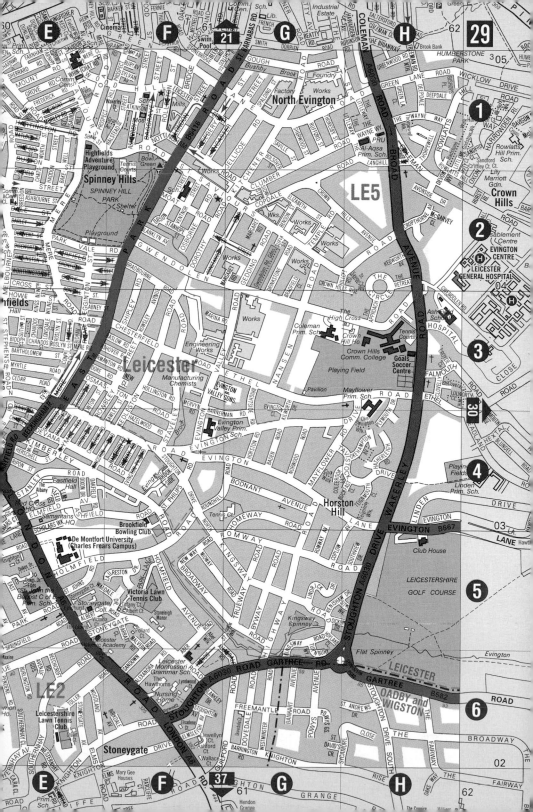

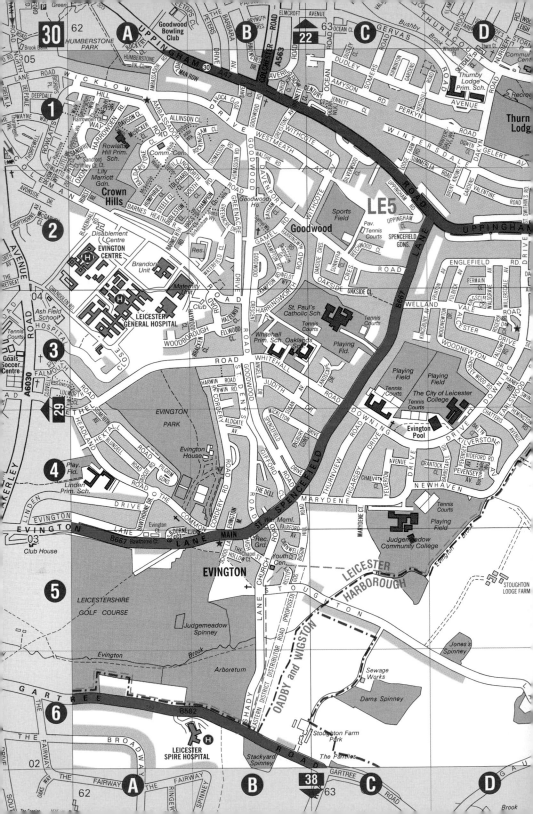

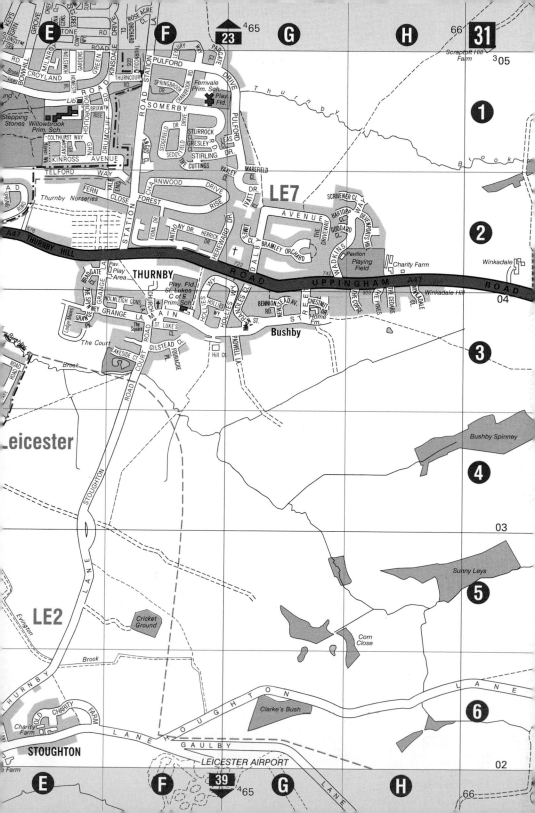

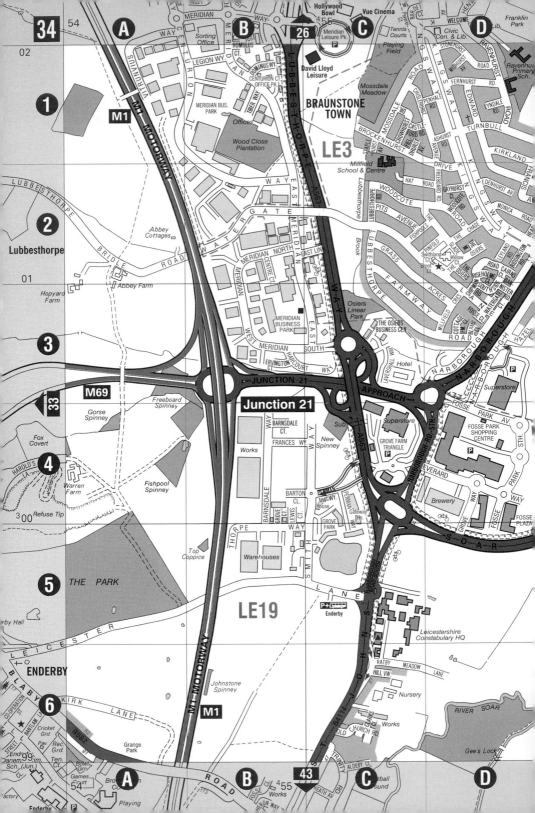

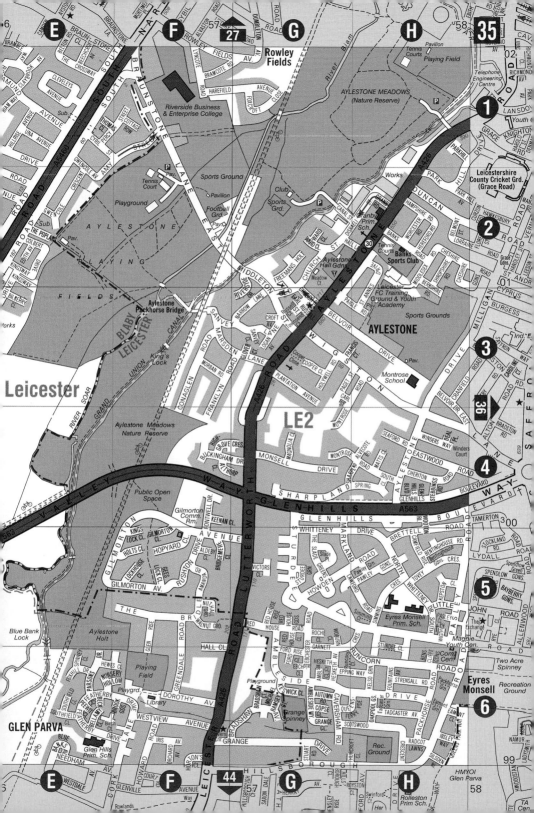

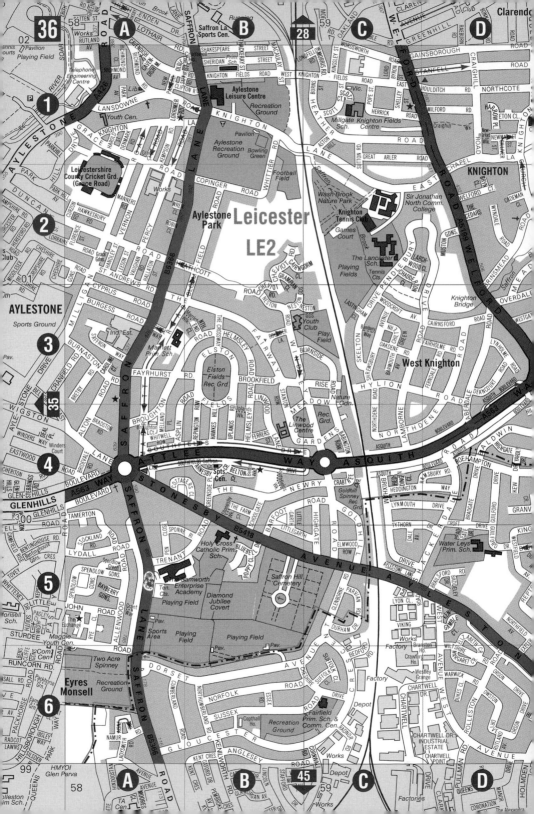

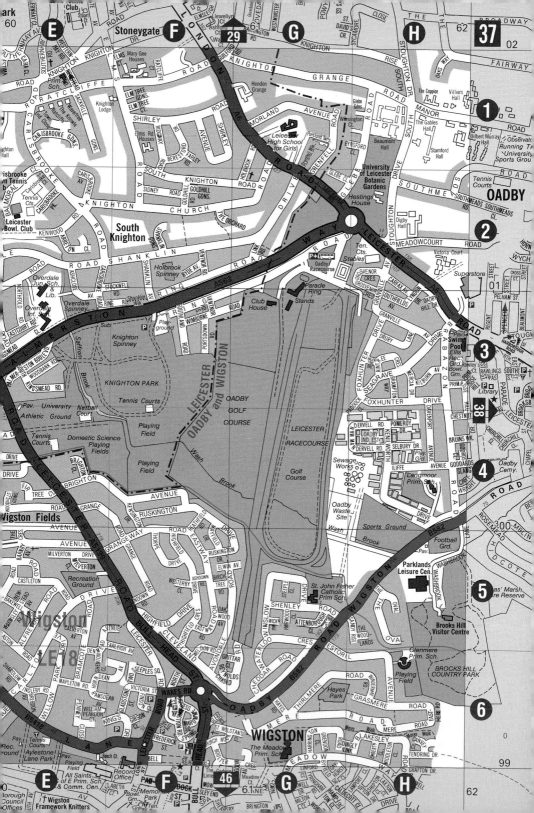

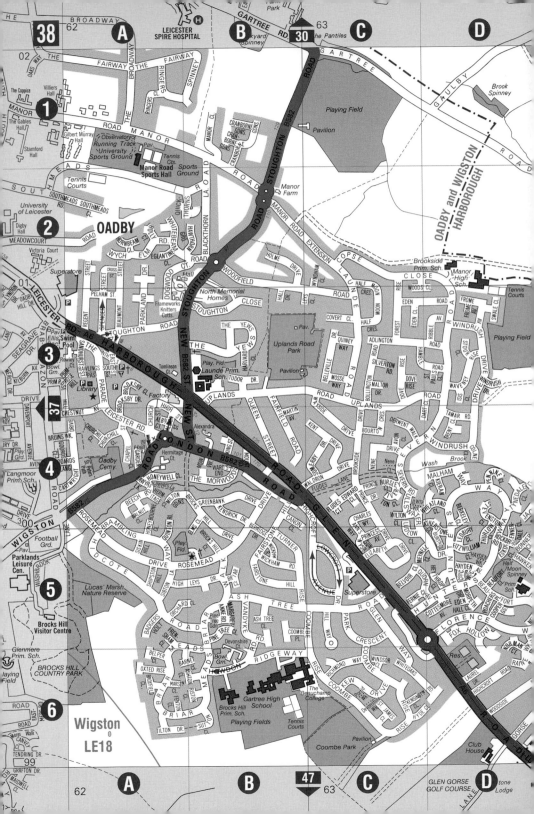

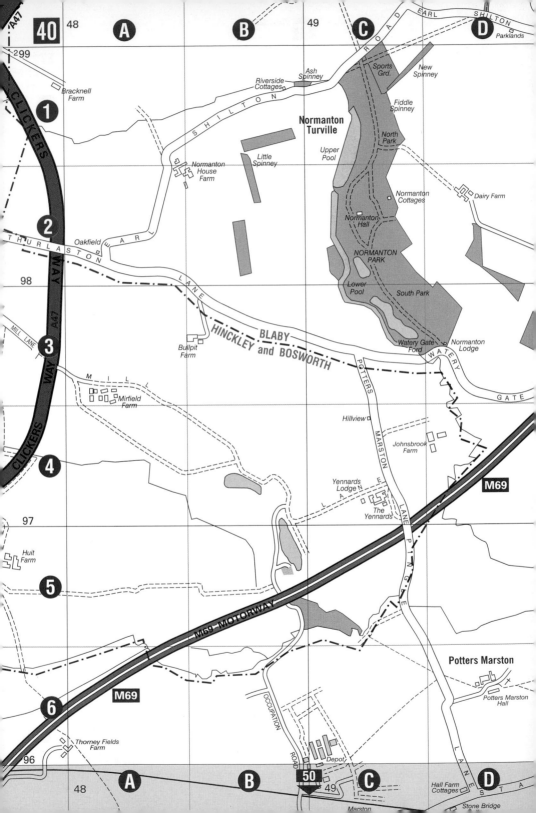

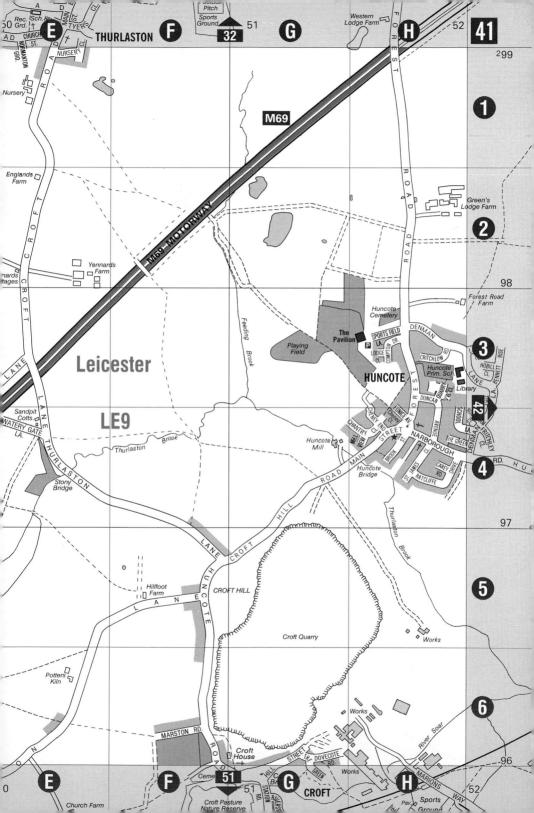

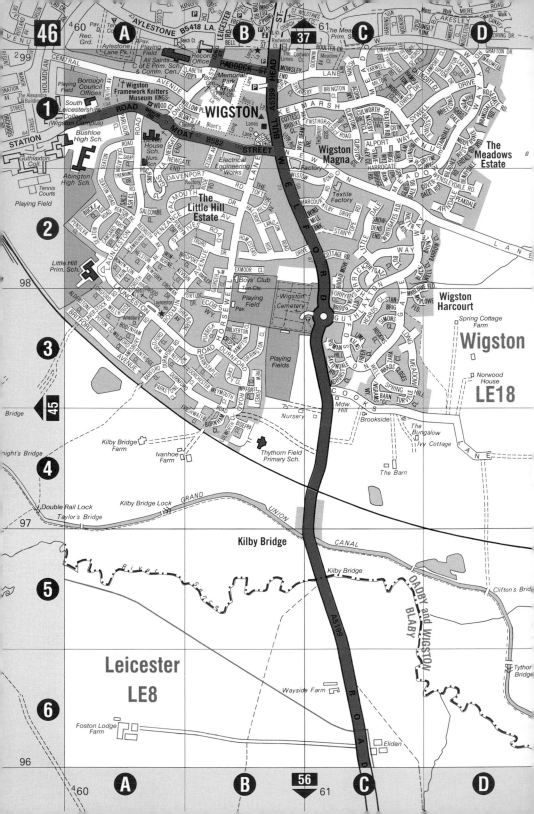

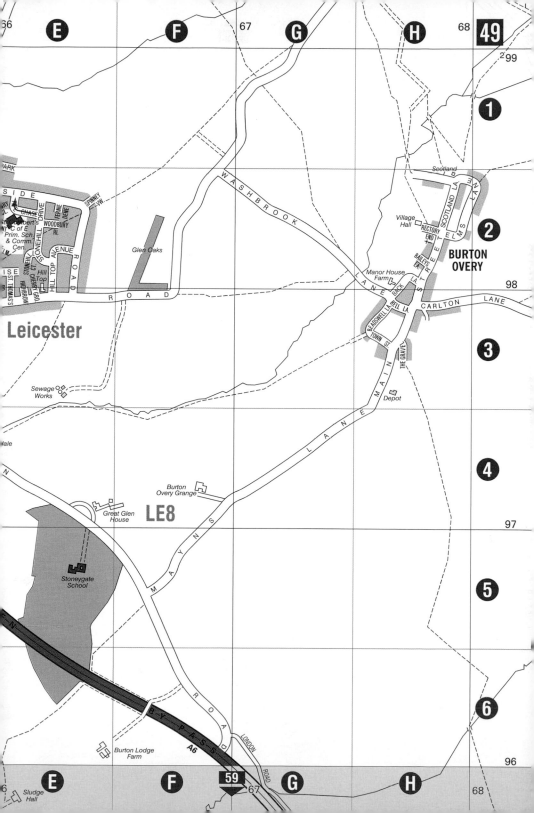

66

299

1

Scotland

Scotland La

Elms

Village
Hall

RECTORY
END

STREET

WASHBROOK

2

**BURTON
OVERY**

BAILEYS LA

CHASE

SPINNEY VW

FERNIE
DENE

WOODBURY
RI

STONEHILL CT

HILL TOP

CHERRY GRO

WOMBROOK

AVENUE

DRIVE

Hill
Top

Robert's
C of E
Prim. Sch.
& Comm.
Cen.

SIDE

PARK

RISE

S.

ST. ALBANS

ST. JOHN'S

Glen Oaks

ROAD

LANE

Manor House
Farm

BACK

BELL LA

CARLTON   LANE

98

Leicester

BEADSWELL LA

TOWN ST

MAIN

THE GRAVE

3

Sewage
Works

Depot

dale

LANE

4

Burton
Overy Grange

97

LE8

Great Glen
House

5

Stoneygate
School

MAYNS

ROAD

6

E   **F**   BY-PASS

Burton Lodge
Farm

A6

LONDON

ROAD

B-Y-P-A-S-S

59

67

G

96

H

68

Sludge
Hall

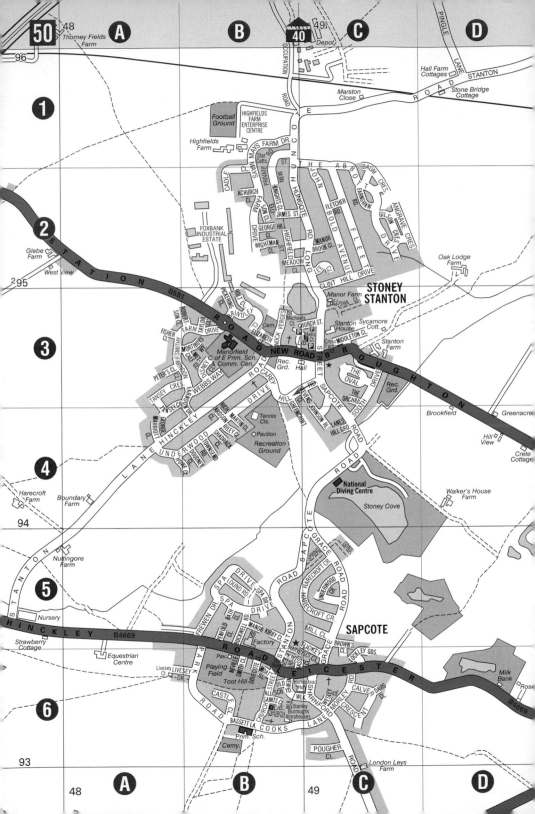

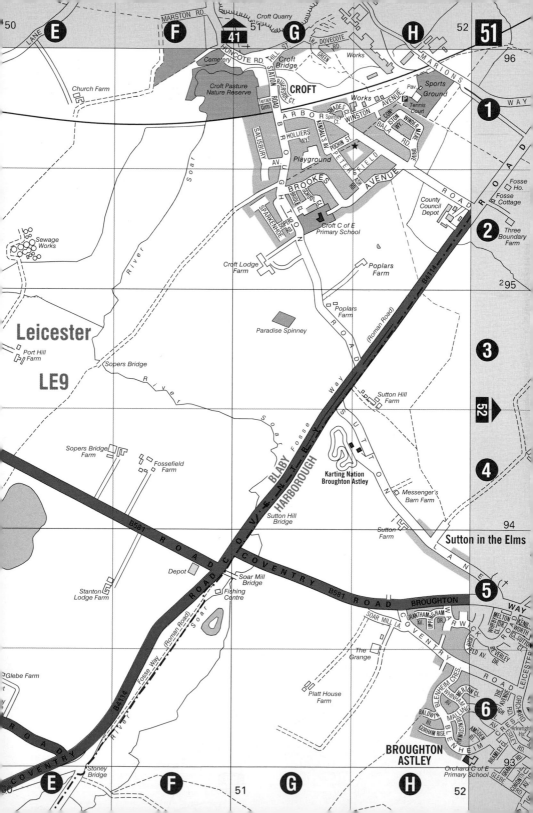

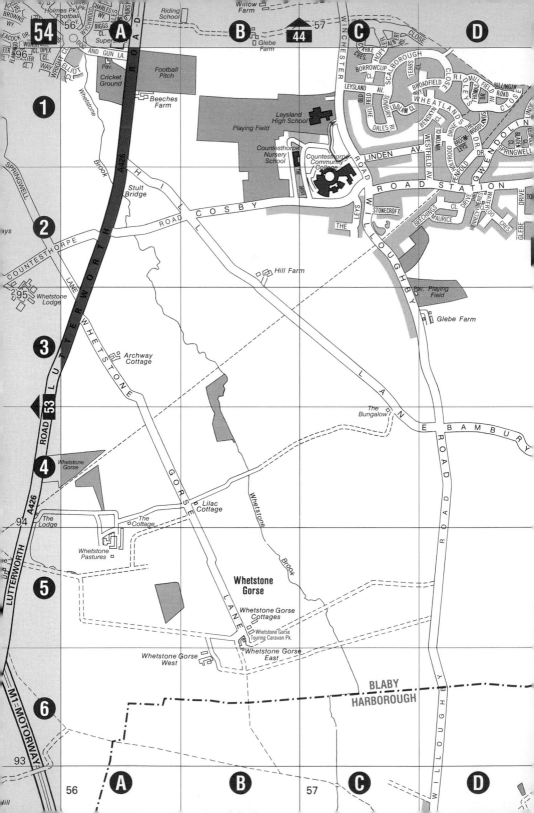

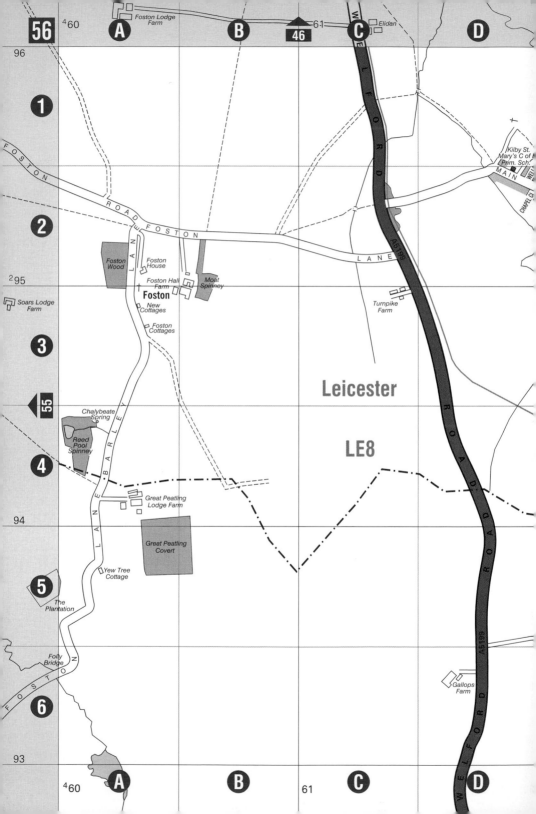

⁴60   ⒶА   Ⓑ   ▲61   Ⓒ   Ⓓ

96

1

2

3

4

94

5

6

93

Foston Lodge Farm

▲ 46

Elidan

Kilby St. Mary's C of Prim. Sch.

MAIN

CHAPEL CL.

Foston Wood

Foston House

Foston Hall Farm

Moat Spinney

Foston

New Cottages

Foston Cottages

Soars Lodge Farm

Turnpike Farm

Leicester

LE8

55

Chalybeate Spring

Reed Pool Spinney

Great Peatling Lodge Farm

Great Peatling Covert

Yew Tree Cottage

The Plantation

Folly Bridge

Gallops Farm

FOSTON ROAD FOSTON

FOSTON LANE

WELFORD LANE

A5199

BARLEY LANE

FOSTON

WELFORD ROAD

A5199

²95

²95

⁴60   ⒶА   Ⓑ   61   Ⓒ   Ⓓ

Turnover Bridge

WISTOW RD.

Wistow Maze

R O A D   KIBWORTH   96 RD.

The Nooks

Wistow Rural Centre

Wistow

Wistow Hall

1

River   Sence

ROAD KILBY

Brackland Farm

Sunnyside Farm

Kilby Lodge

e Glebe ouse

KILBY

Play Fld

Steeple Chase Farm

WISTOW

STREET

GODDARDS CL.

Halford Farm

FLECKNEY

ROAD

WISTOW CL.

Amberdale Spinney

2

2 95

Wistow Lodge Farm

Wigston

LE18

FLECKNEY

3

Coal Pit La.

Fox Covert

Waterman's Spinney

58

Kilby Grange Farm

Kilby Grange Farm Cottages

ROAD KILBY

4

Fleckney Grange

BLABY
HARBOROUGH

94

KILBY

R O A D

SH

The Meadows Riding Centre

The Bungalow

Lyndon Lodge Farm

5

Arnesby Lodge Farm

rnesby Lodge Cottage

6

93

The Grange

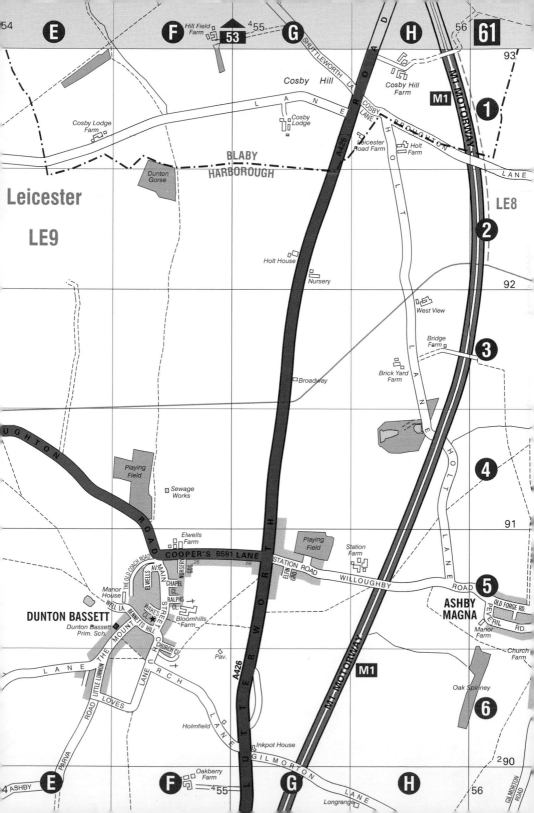

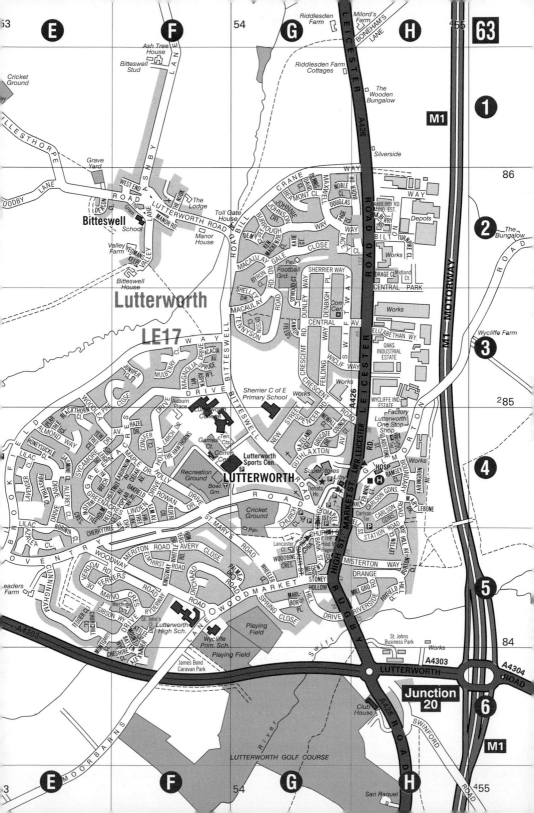

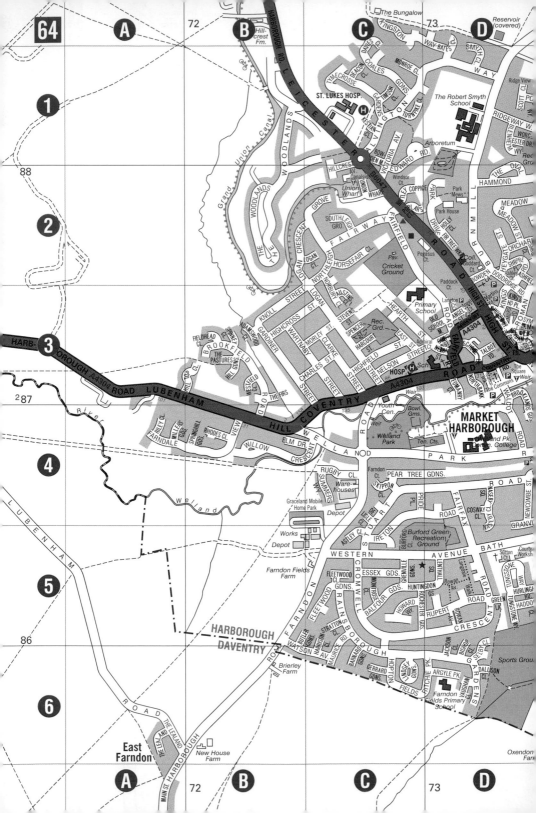

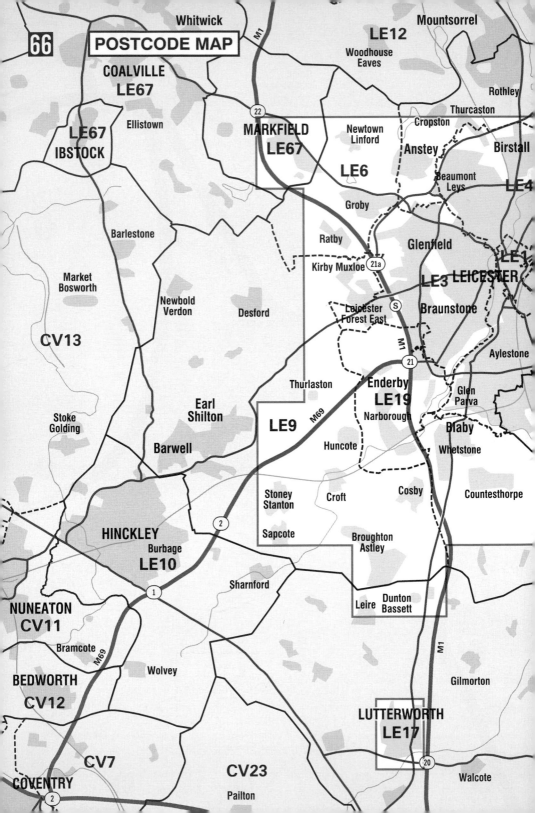

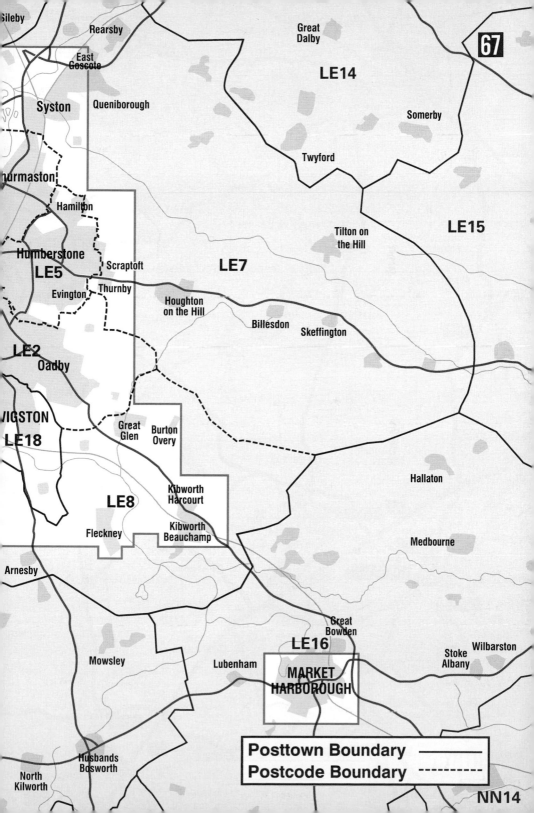

Sileby

Rearsby

Great
Dalby

67

East
Goscote

LE14

Syston

Queniborough

Somerby

urmaston

Twyford

Hamilton

LE15

Humberstone

Scraptoft

Tilton on
the Hill

LE5

Thurnby

LE7

Evington

Houghton
on the Hill

Billesdon

Skeffington

LE2

Oadby

WIGSTON

Great
Glen

Burton
Overy

Hallaton

LE18

Kibworth
Harcourt

LE8

Fleckney

Kibworth
Beauchamp

Medbourne

Arnesby

Great
Bowden

LE16

Wilbarston

Mowsley

Lubenham

MARKET
HARBOROUGH

Stoke
Albany

Posttown Boundary

Postcode Boundary

Husbands
Bosworth

North
Kilworth

NN14

INDEX

Including Streets, Places & Areas, Hospitals etc., Industrial Estates,
Selected Flats & Walkways, Service Areas, Stations and Selected Places of Interest.

HOW TO USE THIS INDEX

1. Each street name is followed by its Postcode District, then by its Locality abbreviation(s) and then by its map reference;
   e.g. **Abbey La.** LE4: Leic . . . .4A **20** is in the LE4 Postcode District and the Leicester Locality and is to be found in square 4A on page **20**.
   The page number is shown in bold type.

2. A strict alphabetical order is followed in which Av., Rd., St., etc. (though abbreviated) are read in full and as part of the street name;
   e.g. **Ashclose Av.** appears after **Ash Cl.** but before **Ash Ct.**

3. Streets and a selection of flats and walkways that cannot be shown on the mapping, appear in the index with the thoroughfare to which
   they are connected shown in brackets; e.g. **Aldwinckles Yd.** LE16: Mkt H . . . .3D **64** (off Church Sq.)

4. Addresses that are in more than one part are referred to as not continuous.

5. Places and areas are shown in the index in **BLUE TYPE** and the map reference is to the actual map square in which the town centre or
   area is located and not to the place name shown on the map; e.g. **ANSTEY 5G 11**

6. An example of a selected place of interest is **Belgrave Hall Mus. & Gardens 2C 20**

7. An example of a station is **Market Harborough Station (Rail) . . . .3F 65**, also included is **Park & Ride**.
   e.g. **Birstall (Park & Ride) 2G 13**

8. Service Areas are shown in the index in **BOLD CAPITAL TYPE**; e.g. **LEICESTER FOREST EAST SERVICE AREA 5H 25**

9. An example of a Hospital or Hospice is **FEILDING PALMER HOSPITAL 4H 63**

10. Map references for entries that appear on large scale pages **4** & **5** are shown first, with small scale map references shown in brackets;
    e.g. **Abbey St.** LE1: Leic 1D **4** (6B **20**)

GENERAL ABBREVIATIONS

App. : Approach	**Fld.** : Field	**Mus.** : Museum
Arc. : Arcade	**Flds.** : Fields	**Nth.** : North
Av. : Avenue	**Gdn.** : Garden	**Pde.** : Parade
Blvd. : Boulevard	**Gdns.** : Gardens	**Pk.** : Park
Bri. : Bridge	**Ga.** : Gate	**Pas.** : Passage
Bldgs. : Buildings	**Gt.** : Great	**Pl.** : Place
Bus. : Business	**Grn.** : Green	**Ri.** : Rise
Cvn. : Caravan	**Gro.** : Grove	**Rd.** : Road
C'way. : Causeway	**Hgts.** : Heights	**Rdbt.** : Roundabout
Cen. : Centre	**Ho.** : House	**Shop.** : Shopping
Chu. : Church	**Ho's.** : Houses	**Sth.** : South
Circ. : Circle	**Ind.** : Industrial	**Sq.** : Square
Cl. : Close	**Info.** : Information	**St.** : Street
Comn. : Common	**Junc.** : Junction	**Ter.** : Terrace
Cnr. : Corner	**La.** : Lane	**Twr.** : Tower
Cotts. : Cottages	**Lit.** : Little	**Trad.** : Trading
Ct. : Court	**Lwr.** : Lower	**Up.** : Upper
Cres. : Crescent	**Mnr.** : Manor	**Va.** : Vale
Cft. : Croft	**Mkt.** : Market	**Vw.** : View
Dr. : Drive	**Mdw.** : Meadow	**Vis.** : Visitors
E. : East	**Mdws.** : Meadows	**Wlk.** : Walk
Ent. : Enterprise	**M.** : Mews	**W.** : West
Est. : Estate	**Mt.** : Mount	**Yd.** : Yard

LOCALITY ABBREVIATIONS

Anst : **Anstey**	Crof : **Croft**	Hun : **Huncote**
Arne : **Arnesby**	Crop : **Cropston**	Keyh : **Keyham**
Ash M : **Ashby Magna**	Des : **Desford**	Kib B : **Kibworth Beauchamp**
Bark : **Barkby**	Din : **Dingley**	Kib H : **Kibworth Harcourt**
Bark T : **Barkby Thorpe**	D Bas : **Dunton Bassett**	Kilby : **Kilby**
Beau L : **Beaumont Leys**	Earl S : **Earl Shilton**	K Mux : **Kirby Muxloe**
Bee : **Beeby**	E Farn : **East Farndon**	Leic : **Leicester**
Birs : **Birstall**	E Gos : **East Goscote**	Leic E : **Leicester Forest East**
Bitt : **Bitteswell**	Elm : **Elmesthorpe**	Leire : **Leire**
Bla : **Blaby**	End : **Enderby**	L Bow : **Little Bowden**
Brau : **Braunstone**	Flec : **Fleckney**	Litt : **Littlethorpe**
Bray : **Braybrooke**	Fost : **Foston**	Lub : **Lubenham**
B Ast : **Broughton Astley**	Glen : **Glenfield**	Lut : **Lutterworth**
Bur O : **Burton Overy**	G Par : **Glen Parva**	Mkt H : **Market Harborough**
Bush : **Bushby**	G Bow : **Great Bowden**	Mark : **Markfield**
Carl C : **Carlton Culieu**	G Gle : **Great Glen**	Mist : **Misterton**
C Oak : **Copt Oak**	G Ox : **Great Oxendon**	Nar : **Narborough**
Cosb : **Cosby**	Gt Stret : **Great Stretton**	New H : **Newton Harcourt**
Coss : **Cossington**	Groby : **Groby**	New L : **Newtown Linford**
C'ach : **Cotesbach**	Ham : **Hamilton**	New U : **Newtown Unthank**
Count : **Countesthorpe**	Hou H : **Houghton on the Hill**	Oad : **Oadby**

Peat M : **Peatling Magna**
Pott M : **Potters Marston**
Quen : **Queniborough**
Ratby : **Ratby**
Rat W : **Ratcliffe on the Wreake**
R'ley : **Rothley**
Sad : **Saddington**
Sap : **Sapcote**
Scra : **Scraptoft**

Sileby : **Sileby**
Smee W : **Smeeton Westerby**
S Bar : **Stanton under Bardon**
S Stan : **Stoney Stanton**
S'ton : **Stoughton**
Sys : **Syston**
Thurc : **Thurcaston**
Thurl : **Thurlaston**
Thurm : **Thurmaston**

Thurn : **Thurnby**
Ulv : **Ulverscroft**
Wan : **Wanlip**
Whet : **Whetstone**
Wig : **Wigston**
Will W : **Willoughby Waterleys**
Wist : **Wistow**

A

Abbey Bus. Pk. LE1: Leic 1B 4 (6A 20)
Abbey Ct. LE4: Leic 3B 20
Abbeycourt Rd. LE4: Leic 2B 20
Abbey Dr. LE4: Leic 2B 20
Abbey Ga. LE4: Leic 6A 20
Abbey Ho. LE3: Leic 5F 19
Abbey La. LE4: Leic 4A 20
Abbey Mdws. LE4: Leic 4B 20
Abbeymead Rd. LE4: Leic 2B 20
Abbey Pk. Rd. LE4: Leic 4A 20
Abbey Pk. St. LE4: Leic 5C 20
Abbey Pumping Station 3B 20
Abbey Ri. LE4: Leic 2B 20
Abbey Rd. LE19: End 2F 43
Abbey St. LE1: Leic 1D 4 (6B 20)
    LE16: Mkt H 3D 64
Abbey Wlk. LE1: Leic 1C 4 (6B 20)
Abbots Cl. LE5: Leic 5B 22
Abbots Ct. LE5: Leic 5B 22
Abbotsford Cl. LE7: Scra 5F 23
Abbotsford Rd. LE5: Leic 6H 21
Abbots Rd. Nth.
    LE5: Leic .5B 22
Abbots Rd. Sth. LE5: Leic 5C 22
Abbott Dr. LE9: S Stan 2C 50
Abbotts Cl. LE7: Sys 6D 6
Aberdale Rd. LE2: Leic 4D 36
Aber Rd. LE2: Leic 5F 29
Aber Wlk. LE2: Leic 5F 29
Abingdon Rd. LE2: Leic 3D 28
Abingdon Wlk. LE2: Leic 4D 28
Abney St. LE5: Leic 3E 29
Acacia Av. LE4: Birs 3H 13
    LE17: Lut .3F 63
Acacia Cl. LE3: Leic E 5F 25
Acan Way LE19: Nar 4C 42
Acer Cl. LE4: Leic 1G 19
    LE19: Nar .4C 42
Achurch Cl. LE9: S Stan 2B 50
Acorn Cl. LE4: Birs 5G 13
Acorn St. LE4: Leic 3D 20
Acorn Way LE18: Wig 1C 46
    (not continuous)
Acres Rd. LE3: Leic E 4G 25
Adam & Eve St. LE16: Mkt H 3D 64
Adamswood Cl. LE16: Mkt H 3B 64
Adcock Rd. LE3: Leic 6F 19
Adderley Rd. LE2: Leic 5C 28
Adelaide Cl. LE4: Beau L 4C 12
Adlington Rd. LE2: Oad 3C 38
Admiral Ct. LE16: Mkt H 3C 64
Agar St. LE4: Leic 4D 20
AGNES UNIT 1D 18
Aikman Av. LE3: Leic 5D 18
Aikman Cl. LE3: Leic 6E 19
Ainsdale LE8: Flec 6C 58
Ainsdale Rd. LE3: Leic 2E 27
Ainsworth Wlk. LE3: Leic 6F 19
Aintree Cl. LE5: Leic 3D 30
Aintree Cres. LE2: Oad 3H 37
Airedale Cl. LE17: Leire 6B 60
Aisne Rd. LE18: Wig 6A 36
Alan Cl. LE4: Leic 1D 20
Aland Gdns. LE9: B Ast 1C 60
Albany, The LE2: Leic 4E 29
Albany Cl. LE16: Mkt H 1F 65
Albany Rd. LE16: Mkt H 2E 65
Albemarle Cl. LE5: Leic 5A 22
Alberta St. LE5: Leic 1D 28

Albert Ct. LE2: Leic 5F 29
    LE8: Whet .3H 43
Albert Rd. LE2: Leic 5E 29
    LE8: Count 6C 44
    LE16: Mkt H 3E 65
Albert St. LE7: Sys 6F 7
    LE8: Flec .5B 58
    LE8: Kib H 3A 62
Albion Ct. LE2: Oad 4A 38
Albion Pde. LE7: Sys 6F 7
Albion St. LE1: Leic 5D 5 (2B 28)
    LE2: Oad .4A 38
    LE7: Anst .5G 11
    LE7: Sys 6F 7
    LE18: Wig .1F 45
Alcester Dr. LE5: Leic 3D 30
Alcott Cl. LE3: Leic 3E 27
Aldeby Cl. LE2: Leic 5F 35
    LE19: End .1G 43
Alder Cl. LE3: Leic E 5F 25
Alder Cres. LE17: Lut 4F 63
Alder Gro. Est. LE19: Nar 1B 42
Alderleigh Rd. LE2: G Par 2E 45
Alderstone Cl. LE18: Wig 3A 46
Alderton Cl. LE4: Leic 6A 14
Aldfield Grn. LE5: Ham 1C 22
Aldgate Av. LE5: Leic 4B 30
Aldwinckles Yd. *LE16: Mkt H* 3D 64
    (off Church Sq.)
Alexander Av. LE19: End 6G 33
Alexander Dr. LE17: Lut 6F 63
Alexander St. LE3: Leic 3A 4 (1A 28)
Alexandra Bldg., The LE18: Wig 1H 45
Alexandra Ct. LE2: Oad 4B 38
Alexandra Rd. LE2: Leic 6F 29
Alexandra St. LE4: Thurm 3C 14
    LE19: Nar .3E 43
Alfred Pl. LE1: Leic 4E 4 (2C 28)
Alfreton Rd. LE18: Wig 5E 37
Alice Gdns. LE8: Whet 6H 43
Allandale Rd. LE2: Leic 6G 29
Allenson Rd. LE2: Leic 5A 36
Allerton Dr. LE3: Leic 4E 19
Allexton Gdns. LE3: Leic 6B 18
Allfrey Cl. LE17: Lut 4E 63
Alliance Rd. LE3: Glen 6A 18
Allington Dr. LE4: Birs 2H 13
Allington St. LE4: Leic 5D 20
Allinson Cl. LE5: Leic 1A 30
Alloway Cl. LE4: Leic 1F 21
All Saints Cl. LE9: Sap 6B 50
All Saints Open LE1: Leic . . .2A 4 (1A 28)
All Saints Rd. LE3: Leic 3A 4 (1A 28)
    (not continuous)
    LE7: Thurc 1B 12
Alma St. LE3: Leic 6G 19
Almond Cl. LE8: Count 1E 55
Almond Rd. LE2: Leic 4B 28
Almond Way LE17: Lut 4E 63
Alport Way LE18: Wig 1C 46
Altar Stones La. LE67: Mark 1A 8
Althorp Cl. LE2: Leic 4F 35
    LE16: L Bow 3G 65
Alton Rd. LE2: Leic 4A 36
Alvaston Rd. LE3: Leic 6F 27
Alvecote Rd. LE4: Leic 4H 35
Alvington Way LE16: Mkt H 1C 64
Alyssum Way LE19: Nar 2B 42
Amadis Rd. LE4: Beau L 1E 19
Amanda Rd. LE2: Leic 5F 35
Ambassador Rd. LE5: Leic 1A 30
Ambassador Wlk. LE5: Leic 1A 30

Ambergate Cl. LE9: B Ast 2C 60
Ambergate Dr. LE4: Birs 3F 13
Amberley Cl. LE4: Thurm 5C 14
Ambler Cl. LE18: Wig 2B 46
Ambleside Cl. LE2: Leic 6G 35
Ambleside Dr. LE2: Leic 5G 35
Ambleside Way LE2: Leic 6G 35
Ambrose Cl. LE3: Leic 1F 27
Amersham Rd. LE4: Leic 4H 19
Amesbury Ct. LE18: Wig 3A 46
Amesbury Rd. LE18: Wig 3A 46
Amhurst Cl. LE3: Leic 4D 18
Amos Rd. LE3: Leic 1B 26
Ampleforth La. LE5: Ham 1C 22
Amsden Ri. LE9: B Ast 6A 52
Amyson Rd. LE5: Leic 1C 30
Amy St. LE3: Brau 2E 35
Anchor St. LE1: Leic 3B 20
Andover St. LE2: Leic 5F 5 (2C 28)
Andrew Av. LE9: Cosb 1F 53
Andrew Ct. LE3: Leic 3D 28
Andrewes Cl. LE3: Leic 2H 27
Andrewes St. LE3: Leic 2H 27
Andrewes Wlk. LE3: Leic 2H 27
Andrew Macdonald Cl.
    LE16: Mkt H 3E 65
Andrew Rd. LE7: Anst 5G 11
Andrews Cl. LE17: Leire 5B 60
Aneford Rd. LE4: Leic 4G 21
Angela Dr. LE5: Leic 3B 30
Angel Cl. LE16: Mkt H 3D 64
Angel St. LE16: Mkt H 3D 64
Anglesey Rd. LE18: Wig 6B 36
Angrave Cres. LE9: S Stan 2C 50
Angus Cl. LE7: Thurn 1F 31
Anna's Way LE8: Whet 4H 43
Ann St. LE1: Leic 3F 4 (1C 28)
Ann's Way LE2: Oad 5C 38
ANSTEY 5G 11
Anstey Frith LE3: Glen 3C 18
Anstey La. LE4: Leic 2E 19
    LE6: Groby 2G 17
    (not continuous)
    LE7: Anst .1C 18
    LE7: Thurc 3H 11
Anstige Av. LE7: Anst 5E 11
Anthony Cl. LE7: Sys 1C 14
Anthony Dr. LE7: Thurn 2F 31
Anthony Rd. LE4: Leic 4H 19
Antringham Cl. LE5: Ham 3C 22
Apollo Cl. LE2: Leic 2D 28
Apollo Ct. LE2: Leic 2D 28
Appleby Cl. LE3: Leic 2A 26
Appleby Rd. LE4: Thurm 4E 15
Applegate LE1: Leic 4B 4 (2A 28)
Appleton Av. LE4: Leic 1H 19
Approach, The LE5: Leic 3H 29
Aquitaine Cl. LE19: End 6G 33
Arbor Ct. LE2: Leic 3D 28
Arbor Rd. LE9: Crof 1G 51
Arbour Rd. LE4: Leic 3D 20
Arcade, The LE18: Wig 6F 37
Archdale Cl. LE4: Birs 2G 13
Archdale St. LE7: Sys 6D 6
Archdeacon La. LE1: Leic 1D 4 (6B 20)
Archer Cl. LE4: Leic 1F 21
Archers Grn. LE7: E Gos 2H 7
Archers Rdbt. LE8: G Gle 4C 48
Archery Cl. LE8: Count 1F 55
Archway Rd. LE5: Leic 4E 23
Ardath Rd. LE4: Leic 4E 21
Arden Av. LE3: Brau 6D 26

Arden Cl.—Barkby Thorpe

Arden Cl. LE16: Mkt H 2F **65**
Arden Way LE16: Mkt H 1E **65**
Ardern Ter. LE3: Leic 5F **27**
Argyle Pk. LE16: Mkt H 6D **64**
Arkwright Cotts. LE9: B Ast 2B **60**
Arkwright Ho. LE9: B Ast 6A **52**
Armadale Dr. LE5: Leic 5C **22**
Armadale Grn. LE5: Leic 5C **22**
Armson Av. LE9: K Mux 2E **25**
Armston Rd. LE9: Cosb 2F **53**
Arncliffe Rd. LE5: Leic 5C **22**
Arndale LE18: Wig 2D **46**
Arnesby Cres. LE2: Leic 4B **36**
Arnesby Rd. LE8: Flec 6A **58**
Arnhem St. LE1: Leic 5E **5** (2C **28**)
Arnold Av. LE18: Wig 2G **45**
Arnold Cl. LE9: Cosb 3F **53**
Arnold St. LE1: Leic 6D **20**
Arran Rd. LE4: Leic 1F **21**
Arran Way LE8: Count 2F **55**
Arreton Cl. LE2: Leic 2E **37**
Arum Way LE3: Leic 1B **26**
Arundel St. LE3: Leic 2H **27**
Ascot Rd. LE4: Leic 3D **20**
Asfordby St. LE5: Leic 1F **29**
Asha Margh LE4: Leic 3C **20**
Ashbourne Rd. LE18: Wig 5E **37**
Ashbourne St. LE2: Leic 2E **29**
Ashby La. LE17: Bitt 2F **63**
ASHBY MAGNA **5H 61**
Ashby Parva Rd. LE17: D Bas 6E **61**
Ashby Ri. LE8: G Gle 2D **48**
Ashby Rd. LE67: Mark 1B **8**
Ash Cl. LE6: Ratby 4B **16**
Ashclose Av. LE2: Leic 2E **37**
Ash Ct. LE2: Leic 8C **5**
LE6: Groby 3E **17**
Ashdown Av. LE3: Leic 1F **27**
Ashdown Rd. LE18: Wig 5F **37**
Ash Dr. LE7: Sys 1F **15**
Ashfield Dr. LE7: Anst 6F **11**
Ashfield Rd. LE2: Leic 4E **29**
LE4: Thurm 3D **14**
LE16: Mkt H 2D **64**
Ashford Ct. LE2: Leic 6F **29**
Ashford Rd. LE2: Leic 6C **28**
Ash Gro. LE8: Bla 3B **44**
Ashington Cl. LE3: Leic 5F **19**
Ashlands Way LE19: Nar 2B **42**
Ashleigh Ct. LE3: Glen 5A **18**
LE3: Leic 4G **27**
Ashleigh Dr. LE17: Lut 4E **63**
Ashleigh Gdns. LE3: Leic 4G **27**
Ashleigh Rd. LE3: Glen 5A **18**
LE3: Leic 3F **27**
Ashley Ct. LE16: Mkt H 2D **64**
Ashley Way LE16: L Bow 2G **65**
Ashlyns Ri. LE3: Leic 2C **26**
Ashmead Cres. LE4: Birs 2A **14**
Ashover Cl. LE9: Cosb 1F **53**
Ashover Rd. LE5: Leic 3F **29**
Ash Rd. LE9: Crof 2H **51**
Ash St. LE5: Leic 6E **21**
Ashthorpe Rd. LE3: Leic 3E **27**
Ashton Cl. LE2: Oad 6A **38**
LE4: Leic 5D **12**
LE18: Wig 2A **46**
Ash Tree Cl. LE2: Oad 5B **38**
Ash Tree Rd. LE2: Oad 5B **38**
Ashtree Rd. LE5: Ham 3C **22**
LE9: Cosb 2F **53**
Ashurst Cl. LE18: Wig 3C **46**
Ashurst Rd. LE3: Brau 1D **34**
Ashville Trad. Est. LE8: Whet 1G **53**
Ashville Way LE8: Whet 6G **43**
Ashwell St. LE1: Leic 6E **5** (3C **28**)
Askrigg Way LE18: Wig 1C **46**
Aspen Dr. LE8: Count 1E **55**
Aspen Way LE17: Lut 3F **63**
Asplin Rd. LE2: Leic 4A **36**
Asquith Blvd. LE2: Leic 4C **36**
(not continuous)
Asquith Way LE2: Leic 4C **36**
Assured Dr. LE4: Thurm 4B **14**
Astill Cl. LE6: Ratby 5E **17**
Astill Dr. LE4: Leic 1B **20**
Astill Lodge Rd. LE4: Beau L 5A **12**
Astley Cl. LE3: Leic 4F **27**
LE16: Mkt H 5C **64**
Aston Hill LE2: Leic 1C **36**
Atherstone Cl. LE2: Oad 4D **38**
Atkinson St. LE5: Leic 1F **29**
(not continuous)
Atkins St. LE2: Leic 6C **5** (3B **28**)
Atlas Cl. LE2: Leic 2D **28**
Atrium, The LE1: Leic 3F **4**
Attenborough Cl. LE3: Brau 6B **26**
LE18: Wig 5G **37**
Attfield Dr. LE8: Whet 4H **43**
Attingham Cl. LE4: Leic 4F **21**
Attlebridge Cl. LE5: Ham 3B **22**
Attlee Cl. LE17: Lut 5F **63**
Attlee Way LE2: Leic 4A **36**
Auburn Ho. LE3: Leic 6E **19**
LE8: Bla .3A **44**
Auburn Pl. LE17: Lut 3F **63**
Auburn Rd. LE8: Bla 3A **44**
Auden Cl. LE4: Leic 3F **19**
Audley Cl. LE16: L Bow 4G **65**
Audley End LE3: Leic 6F **27**
Augusta Cl. LE3: Leic 1A **26**
Augustus Cl. LE7: Sys 1D **14**
Auriga St. LE16: Mkt H 4E **65**
Auster Ind. Est. LE4: Thurm 5D **14**
Austin Ri. LE5: Leic 4C **22**
Austins Cl. LE16: Mkt H 3C **64**
Austrey La. LE8: Count 3F **55**
Austwick Cl. LE4: Leic 2G **19**
Autumn Rd. LE2: Leic 6G **35**
Avalon Way LE7: Anst 6G **11**
Avebury Av. LE4: Leic 4G **19**
Avenue, The LE2: Leic 5E **29**
LE2: Oad 5G **39**
LE3: Glen 4H **17**
LE8: Bla .3A **44**
LE9: B Ast 6A **52**
Avenue Cl. LE7: Quen 4H **7**
Avenue Gdns. LE2: Leic 6E **29**
Avenue Rd. LE2: Leic 6E **29**
LE7: Quen 4H **7**
Avenue Rd. Extension LE2: Leic 6C **28**
Averil Rd. LE5: Leic 6B **22**
Avery Cl. LE17: Lut 5F **63**
Avery Dr. LE7: Sys 4F **7**
LE67: Mark 2B **8**
Avery Hill LE3: Leic 3B **26**
Avington Cl. LE3: Leic 3E **19**
Avoca Cl. LE5: Leic 1B **30**
Avon Cl. LE2: Oad 4C **38**
Avondale Rd. LE18: Wig 6F **37**
Avon Dr. LE8: Whet 4H **43**
Avon Ho. LE16: Mkt H 3F **65**
Avon Rd. LE3: Brau 5C **26**
Avonside Dr. LE5: Leic 2H **29**
Avon St. LE2: Leic 3D **28**
Axbridge Cl. LE4: Leic 4H **19**
AYLESTONE **3G 35**
Aylestone Dr. LE2: Leic 4H **35**
Aylestone La. LE18: Wig 5C **36**
Aylestone Leisure Cen. **1B 36**
Aylestone Meadows Nature Reserve
. . . .**4F 35**
Aylestone Packhorse Bridge **3F 35**
AYLESTONE PARK **2B 36**
Aylestone Rd. LE2: Leic 8C **5** (3G **35**)
Aylestone Wlk. LE2: Leic 8D **5** (4B **28**)
Aylmer Rd. LE3: Leic 3D **26**
Aysgarth Rd. LE4: Leic 2G **19**
Ayston Rd. LE3: Brau 6E **27**
Azalea Cl. LE17: Lut 5E **63**

B

Babingley Dr. LE4: Leic 3H **19**
Babington Row LE2: Leic 4C **36**
Back La. LE7: Coss 2B **6**
LE8: Bur O 3H **49**
LE17: Leire 6A **60**
Backway, The LE16: Mkt H 4E **65**
Badcock Way LE8: Flec 6F **59**
Baddeley Dr. LE18: Wig 5D **36**
Baden Rd. LE5: Leic 4G **29**
Badger Cl. LE8: Flec 6F **59**
Badger Dr. LE8: Whet 6H **43**
Badgers Cl. LE4: Leic 2F **19**
LE19: Nar 4C **42**
Badger's Cnr. LE7: E Gos 1H **7**
Badgers Holt LE2: Oad 5A **38**
Badgers Mead LE9: K Mux 2C **24**
Badminton Rd. LE4: Leic 6B **14**
LE7: Sys .4F **7**
Baggrave St. LE5: Leic 1F **29**
Baileys La. LE8: Bur O 2H **49**
Bailey Vw. LE6: Groby 1E **17**
Bainbridge Rd. LE3: Leic 6F **27**
LE18: Wig 2C **46**
Baines La. LE3: Leic E 4H **25**
Baker St. LE17: Lut 5G **63**
Bakers Way LE5: Ham 2D **22**
Bakery Cl. LE9: Cosb 3F **53**
Bakewell Rd. LE18: Wig 5E **37**
Bakewell St. LE2: Leic 2E **29**
Bala Rd. LE9: Crof 1H **51**
Balcombe Av. LE3: Leic 1F **27**
Balderstone Cl. LE5: Leic 2A **30**
Baldwin Av. LE18: Wig 2G **45**
Baldwin Ri. LE9: B Ast 6H **51**
Baldwin Rd. LE2: Leic 4D **36**
Bale Rd. LE4: Leic 4G **21**
Balfour Gdns. LE16: Mkt H 5C **64**
Balfour St. LE3: Leic 6H **19**
Balisfire Gro. LE4: Leic 2F **19**
Balk, The LE3: Glen 4H **17**
Balladine Rd. LE7: Anst 4G **11**
Ballards Cl. LE4: Leic 2F **19**
Ballater Cl. LE5: Leic 4D **30**
Balliol Av. LE7: Sys 1G **15**
Balmoral Cl. LE2: Leic 2E **37**
LE16: L Bow 4G **65**
Balmoral Dr. LE3: Brau 5C **26**
Bamburgh Cl. LE16: L Bow 3G **65**
Bambury La. LE8: Count 4D **54**
LE8: Peat M 6G **55**
Bambury Way LE2: Leic 3C **36**
Bampton Cl. LE18: Wig 3B **46**
Bank, The LE8: Count 1F **55**
LE8: Kib B 5A **62**
Bankart Av. LE2: Leic 6G **29**
Bankfield Dr. LE16: G Bow 1F **65**
Banks, The LE9: Cosb 3F **53**
Bankside LE5: Leic 5E **23**
Banks Rd. LE2: Leic 2H **35**
Banks Sports Club **2H 35**
Bank St. LE17: Lut 5G **63**
Bannerman Rd. LE5: Leic 4F **29**
Bannister Rd. LE3: Brau 3D **34**
Bantlam La. LE19: End 6H **33**
Baptist Mews, The
LE8: Bla .2C **44**
Barbara Av. LE5: Leic 6B **22**
LE9: Leic E 4E **25**
Barbara Cl. LE19: End 6G **33**
Barbara Rd. LE3: Leic 6F **27**
Barclay St. LE3: Leic 3G **27**
Bardolph St. LE4: Leic 5D **20**
Bardolph St. E. LE4: Leic 5E **21**
Bardon Cl. LE3: Leic 2D **18**
Barfoot Cl. LE8: Flec 4A **58**
Barfoot Rd. LE2: Leic 4B **36**
Barford Cl. LE18: Wig 3A **46**
Barge Cl. LE18: Wig 3G **45**
BARKBY **3H 15**
Barkby Holt La. LE7: Bark 3H **15**
Barkby La. LE7: Sys 1D **14**
Barkby Rd. LE4: Leic 3F **21**
LE7: Quen 6H **7**
LE7: Sys .5F **7**
BARKBY THORPE **4G 15**

Barkby Thorpe La. LE4: Thurm 2C **14**
  LE7: Bark T 2E **15**
Barkbythorpe Rd. LE4: Leic 1H **21**
  LE7: Bark T 1H **21**
Barker St. LE5: Leic 6F **21**
Barkford Cl. LE7: Scra 4E **23**
Barley Cl. LE3: Glen 5A **18**
Barley La. LE8: Fost 4A **56**
Barleyman Cl. LE5: Ham 2C **22**
Barling Rd. LE5: Leic 5H **21**
Barmouth Av. LE2: Leic 3C **36**
Barnard Cl. LE2: Leic 2D **28**
Barnard Gdns. LE16: Mkt H 6C **64**
Barnards Way LE8: Kib H 4G **59**
Barnby Av. LE18: Wig 5E **37**
Barn Cl. LE18: Wig 3C **46**
Barnes Cl. LE4: Leic 6C **14**
  LE8: Kib B 5H **59**
Barnes Heath Rd. LE5: Leic 2A **30**
Barnet Cl. LE2: Oad 6A **38**
Barnett Cl. LE7: Coss 2B **6**
Barnfield Cl. LE8: G Gle 2D **48**
Barngate Cl. LE4: Birs 3F **13**
Barnley Cl. LE8: Count 1E **55**
Barn Mdw. Rd. LE4: Wan 2F **13**
Barns Cl. LE9: K Mux 2C **24**
Barnsdale Ct. LE19: End 4B **34**
Barnsdale Rd. LE4: Beau L 6H **11**
Barnsdale Way LE19: End 4B **34**
Barnstaple Cl. LE18: Wig 3B **46**
Barnstaple Rd. LE5: Leic 4D **30**
Barn Way LE67: Mark 3C **8**
Barnwell Av. LE4: Leic 1B **20**
Baronet Way LE5: Leic 4E **23**
Barons Cl. LE9: K Mux 2C **24**
Baron St. LE1: Leic 4F **4** (2C **28**)
Barratt Cl. LE2: Leic 5F **29**
Barrington Pk. Ind. Est.
  LE4: Beau L 6B **12**
Barrington Rd. LE2: Leic 6G **29**
Barrow La. LE3: Glen 4G **17**
Barr Rd. LE7: Sys 1E **15**
Barry Cl. LE9: Leic E 4E **25**
Barry Dr. LE7: Sys 5F **7**
  LE9: Leic E 4E **25**
Barry Rd. LE5: Leic 4D **22**
Barsby Wlk. LE4: Leic 1H **19**
Barshaw Pk. Ind. Est.
  LE4: Beau L 6C **12**
Bartholomew St. LE2: Leic 3E **29**
Barton Cl. LE6: Ratby 6D **16**
  LE18: Wig 2A **46**
  LE19: End 4B **34**
Barton Rd. LE3: Leic 5G **19**
Barwell Rd. LE9: K Mux 2D **24**
Baslow Rd. LE5: Leic 3F **29**
Bassett Av. LE8: Count 2E **55**
Bassett La. LE9: Sap 6B **50**
Bassett St. LE3: Leic 6H **19**
  LE18: Wig 2F **45**
Batchelor Rd. LE8: Flec 5B **58**
Bateman Rd. LE3: Leic 6E **19**
Bates Cl. LE16: Mkt H 1D **64**
Bates Ct. LE18: Wig 2G **45**
Bath Cl. LE9: Sap 5B **50**
Bath Ho. La. LE1: Leic 3B **4** (1A **28**)
Bath La. LE3: Leic 3A **4** (1A **28**)
Bath St. LE4: Leic 2C **20**
  (not continuous)
  LE7: Sys 5E **7**
  LE16: Mkt H 5D **64**
Bathurst Rd. LE5: Leic 3D **30**
Batten St. LE2: Leic 6A **28**
Battenberg Rd. LE3: Leic 1G **27**
Battersbee Rd. LE3: Leic 5C **18**
Battersbee Wlk. LE3: Leic 5C **18**
Battersbee Way LE3: Leic 5C **18**
Baum Cres. LE9: S Stan 2C **50**
Baxters Cl. LE4: Leic 2F **19**
Bayberry Gdns. LE2: Leic 5A **36**
Baycliff Cl. LE3: Leic 5F **19**
Bayham Cl. LE5: Leic 2B **30**
Baysdale LE18: Wig 1D **46**

Baysdale Rd. LE2: Leic 8B **5** (4A **28**)
Bay St. LE1: Leic 1B **4** (6A **20**)
Bayswater Dr. LE2: G Par 2D **44**
Beacon Av. LE4: Thurm 4D **14**
Beacon Cl. LE4: Beau L 5A **12**
  LE6: Groby 3F **17**
  LE67: Mark 2C **8**
Beacon Ct. LE3: Glen 4B **18**
Beaconsfield Rd. LE3: Leic 3G **27**
Beadswell La. LE8: Bur O 3H **49**
Beal St. LE2: Leic 1D **28**
Beamont Cl. LE17: Lut 2G **63**
Beatrice Rd. LE3: Leic 6F **19**
Beatty Av. LE5: Leic 6G **21**
Beatty Rd. LE5: Leic 6G **21**
  LE7: Sys 5F **7**
Beauchamp Gdns. LE8: Kib B 6A **62**
Beauchamp Rd. LE8: Kib B 5H **59**
Beaufort Cl. LE2: Oad 5D **38**
Beaufort Rd. LE3: Leic 6E **27**
Beaufort Way LE2: Oad 5D **38**
Beaumanor Rd. LE4: Leic 3B **20**
Beaumont Grn. LE6: Groby 3F **17**
Beaumont Hall LE2: Leic 1H **37**
BEAUMONT LEYS 1E **19**
Beaumont Leys Cl. LE4: Leic 2H **19**
Beaumont Leys La.
  LE4: Beau L, Leic 6C **12**
Beaumont Leys Ter. LE4: Leic 2E **19**
Beaumont Lodge Rd. LE4: Beau L 5B **12**
Beaumont Pk. Sports Pavilion 6B **12**
Beaumont Rd. LE5: Leic 1E **29**
Beaumont Shop. Cen. LE4: Beau L 1E **19**
Beaumont St. LE2: Oad 3A **38**
Beaumont Wlk. LE4: Leic 2E **19**
Beaumont Way LE4: Beau L 6A **12**
Beauville Dr. LE4: Leic 2E **19**
Beaver Cen., The LE2: Leic 5B **28**
Beaver Cl. LE8: Whet 6H **43**
Beck Cl. LE2: G Par 6E **35**
Beckett Rd. LE5: Leic 5G **21**
Beckingham Rd. LE2: Leic 4E **29**
Bedale Dr. LE4: Leic 6C **12**
Bede Hall LE2: Leic 7A **5** (3A **28**)
Bede Island Rd. LE2: Leic 6A **5** (3A **28**)
Bede St. LE3: Leic 6A **5** (2H **27**)
Bedford Dr. LE6: Groby 3F **17**
Bedford Rd. LE18: Wig 6C **36**
Bedford St. Nth. LE1: Leic 1E **4** (6C **20**)
Bedford St. Sth. LE1: Leic 2D **4** (1B **28**)
Beeby Cl. LE7: Sys 6G **7**
Beeby Rd. LE5: Leic 1F **29**
  LE7: Bark, Bee 3H **15**
  LE7: Scra 5F **23**
  (not continuous)
Beech Av. LE6: Groby 4E **17**
  LE17: Lut 4E **63**
Beech Cl. LE67: Mark 3C **8**
Beech Ct. LE2: Leic 8C **5**
  LE18: Wig 6E **37**
Beechcroft Av. LE3: Brau 1E **35**
Beechcroft Rd. LE2: Leic 6E **29**
Beech Dr. LE3: Brau 4B **26**
  LE7: Sys 1F **15**
Beechfield Av. LE4: Birs 4G **13**
Beechfield Cl. LE8: G Gle 2D **48**
Beechings Cl. LE8: Count 2D **54**
Beech Rd. LE2: Oad 4A **38**
  LE8: Bla 4B **44**
Beech St. LE5: Leic 6E **21**
Beech Tree Cl. LE8: Kib H 3A **62**
Beech Wlk. LE67: Mark 3C **8**
Beechwood Av. LE3: Leic E 4G **25**
  LE4: Thurm 5C **14**
  LE7: Quen 4H **7**
Beechwood Cl. LE5: Leic 2C **30**
Beechwood Rd. LE19: Litt 5D **42**
Beggar's La. LE3: End, Leic E 5E **25**
  LE19: End 2E **33**
Begonia Cl. LE3: Leic E 5F **25**
Belfry Dr. LE3: Leic 2A **26**
BELGRAVE 4D **20**
Belgrave Av. LE4: Leic 2C **20**

Belgrave Blvd. LE4: Leic 6C **12**
  (not continuous)
Belgrave Circ. LE1: Leic 5C **20**
Belgrave Flyover LE1: Leic 6C **20**
  LE4: Leic 6C **20**
Belgrave Ga. LE1: Leic 3D **4** (1B **28**)
Belgrave Hall Mus. & Gardens 2C **20**
Belgrave Ind. Cen. LE4: Leic 4C **20**
Belgrave Rd. LE4: Leic 5C **20**
Bellamy Cl. LE2: G Par 6E **35**
Bell Cl. LE6: Ratby 5D **16**
  LE9: B Ast 3C **60**
Belleville Dr. LE2: Oad 3C **38**
Belle Vue Av. LE4: Leic 3A **20**
Belle-Vue Cinema 1D **4** (1B **28**)
Bellfields La. LE16: L Bow 4F **65**
Bellfields St. LE16: L Bow 4F **65**
Bellflower Rd. LE5: Ham 2B **22**
Bellholme Cl. LE4: Leic 2D **20**
Bell La. LE5: Leic 2F **4** (1D **28**)
  LE8: Bur O 3H **49**
  LE19: Nar 4E **43**
Bell St. LE17: Lut 4H **63**
  LE18: Wig 6F **37**
Bell Vw. LE19: Nar 3E **43**
Belmont St. LE2: Leic 2H **35**
Belper Cl. LE2: Oad 6A **38**
  LE18: Wig 3G **45**
Belper St. LE4: Leic 4D **20**
Belton Cl. LE2: Leic 4B **36**
Belton St. LE3: Brau 1E **35**
Belton Wlk. LE2: Leic 4B **36**
Belvoir Cl. LE2: Oad 5C **38**
Belvoir Dr. LE2: Leic 3G **35**
  LE7: Sys 5G **7**
Belvoir Dr. E. LE2: Leic 3H **35**
Belvoir St. LE1: Leic 5D **5** (2B **28**)
Beman Cl. LE4: Leic 6C **14**
Bembridge Cl. LE3: Leic 5H **19**
Bembridge Rd. LE3: Leic 5G **19**
Bencroft Cl. LE7: Anst 5F **11**
Bendbow Ri. LE3: Leic 4B **26**
Benford Gdns. LE9: B Ast 3B **60**
Benjamin Russell Ct. LE2: Leic 7A **5**
Bennett Ri. LE9: Hun 3A **42**
Bennetts Hill LE17: D Bas 5F **61**
Bennett's La. LE7: Coss 1B **6**
Bennett Wlk. LE3: Leic 3D **26**
Bennett Way LE18: Wig 2G **45**
Bennion Rd. LE4: Beau L 6A **12**
  LE7: Bush 3G **31**
Benscliffe Gdns. LE2: Leic 6H **35**
Benskins Oval LE4: Beau L 4C **12**
Benskin Wlk. LE4: Leic 3F **19**
Benskyn Cl. LE8: Count 1D **54**
Benson St. LE5: Leic 2G **29**
Bens Way LE5: Leic 2B **30**
Bentburn Ho. LE5: Leic 6E **19**
Bentinghouse Gdns. LE2: Leic 5H **35**
Bentinghouse Rd. LE2: Leic 5H **35**
Bentley Rd. LE4: Birs 3G **13**
Beresford Dr. LE2: Leic 1F **37**
Berford Cl. LE9: B Ast 2B **60**
Berkeley Cl. LE2: Oad 4D **38**
Berkley St. LE1: Leic 1A **4** (6A **20**)
Berkshire Rd. LE2: Leic 2H **35**
Berners St. LE2: Leic 1D **28**
Berridge Dr. LE2: Oad 5B **38**
Berridge La. LE4: Leic 2D **20**
Berridge St. LE1: Leic 4C **4** (2B **28**)
Berridge Wlk. LE4: Leic 2D **20**
Berrington Cl. LE5: Leic 5G **21**
Berry Cl. LE16: G Bow 1F **65**
Berry's La. LE5: Ham 5C **16**
Bessingham Cl. LE5: Ham 3C **22**
Best Cl. LE18: Wig 2F **45**
Bestwood Cl. LE3: Leic 4F **19**
Beth-El LE18: Wig 3A **46**
Bevan Rd. LE4: Leic 3C **12**
Beverley Av. LE4: Leic 4D **20**
Beverley Cl. LE4: Thurm 4C **14**
Beverley Dr. LE9: B Ast 6A **52**
Bevington Cl. LE6: Ratby 4B **16**

Bewcastle Gro. LE4: Leic 6D **12**
Bewcastle Ho. LE4: Leic 6D **12**
Bewicke Rd. LE3: Leic 5F **27**
Bexhill Ri. LE5: Leic 6E **23**
Biam Way LE3: Brau 1E **35**
Biddle Rd. LE3: Leic 6F **19**
  LE19: Litt 4E **43**
Biddulph Av. LE2: Leic 3E **29**
Biddulph St. LE2: Leic 3E **29**
Bideford Cl. LE18: Wig 4B **46**
Bideford Rd. LE5: Leic 4D **30**
Bidford Cl. LE3: Brau 5C **26**
Bidford Ct. LE3: Brau 5C **26**
Bidford Rd. LE3: Brau 5C **26**
Biggin Hill Rd. LE5: Leic 5B **30**
Biggs Cl. LE8: Whet 6A **44**
Bignal Dr. LE3: Leic E 4H **25**
Bilberry Cl. LE3: Brau 3E **35**
Bill Crane Way LE17: Lut 2G **63**
Billesdon Cl. LE3: Leic 2C **18**
Billington Cl. LE4: Leic 2A **20**
Billington Rd. LE8: Count 1D **54**
Bilsdale Rd. LE18: Wig 2D **46**
Bilton Way LE17: Lut 2H **63**
Bindleys La. LE8: G Gle 2D **48**
Bingley Ct. LE19: Litt 5E **43**
Bingley Rd. LE19: Litt 5E **43**
Bintree Cl. LE5: Ham 3B **22**
Birch Cl. LE4: Leic 4F **21**
  LE67: Mark 5C **8**
Birch Ct. LE2: G Par 6E **35**
Birchfield Av. LE67: Mark 3B **8**
Birchtree Av. LE4: Birs 2G **13**
Birchtree Gdns. LE16: Mkt H 2E **65**
Birchtree Rd. LE18: Wig 5F **37**
Birchwood Cl. LE3: Leic E 5F **25**
  LE7: Sys 6G **7**
Birdie Cl. LE8: Kib B 5B **62**
Birds Nest Av. LE3: Leic 5D **18**
Birkby Cl. LE5: Ham 2C **22**
Birkdale Av. LE2: Leic 6F **29**
Birkdale Rd. LE7: Anst 5F **11**
Birkenshaw Rd. LE3: Leic 4E **19**
Birkenshaw Wlk. LE5: Leic 2B **30**
Birsmore Av. LE4: Leic 1F **21**
BIRSTALL **4G 13**
Birstall (Park & Ride) **2G 13**
Birstall Mdw. LE4: Wan 1F **13**
Birstall Rd. LE4: Birs 5H **13**
Birstall St. LE1: Leic 6D **20**
Birstow Cres. LE4: Leic 6D **12**
Birtley Coppice LE16: Mkt H 2C **64**
Bishop Cl. LE16: Mkt H 6D **64**
Bishopdale Rd. LE4: Leic 2G **19**
Bishopston Wlk. LE4: Leic 2B **30**
Bishop St. LE1: Leic 4D **4** (2B **28**)
Bisley St. LE3: Leic 4H **27**
BITTESWELL **2F 63**
Bitteswell Rd. LE17: Lut 3F **63**
BLABY **3B 44**
Blaby By-Pass LE8: Bla 4A **44**
Blaby Ind. Est. LE8: Bla 2A **44**
Blaby Rd. LE18: Wig 2F **45**
  LE19: End .6H **33**
Blackberry La. LE7: Coss 1C **6**
Blackbird Av. LE4: Leic 5H **19**
Blackbird Rd. LE4: Leic 5H **19**
Blackett Av. LE3: Leic 5E **19**
BLACK FRIARS **1H 27**
Blackfriars Pl. *LE16: Mkt H* *3D* **64**
               (off Roman Way)
Blackfriars St. LE3: Leic 3A **4** (1A **28**)
Blackmore Dr. LE3: Leic 2E **27**
Blacksmith Pl. LE5: Ham 2C **22**
Blacksmiths La. LE8: Smee W 6H **59**
Blackthorn Cl. LE17: Lut 4E **63**
Blackthorn Dr. LE4: Beau L 5A **12**
  LE7: Sys 6D **6**
Blackthorn La. LE2: Oad 2B **38**
Blackthorn Rd. LE3: Glen 6H **17**
               (not continuous)
Blackwell Cl. LE18: Wig 2C **46**
Bladen Cl. LE8: Count 1D **54**

Blairmore Rd. LE3: Leic 1A **26**
Blaise Gro. LE4: Leic 4F **21**
Blake Ct. LE19: End 6G **33**
Blakenhall Cl. LE3: Nar 3B **42**
Blakenhall Rd. LE5: Leic 2A **30**
Blakeshay Cl. LE3: Leic 3D **18**
Blakesley Rd. LE18: Wig 6H **37**
Blakesley Wlk. LE4: Leic 3F **19**
Blake St. LE1: Leic 2C **4** (1B **28**)
Blake Wlk. LE1: Leic 2C **4** (1B **28**)
Bland Rd. LE3: Leic 5D **18**
Blankley Dr. LE2: Leic 6F **29**
Blanklyn Av. LE5: Leic 2F **29**
Blaydon Cl. LE2: Leic 5F **19**
Bleasby Cl. LE4: Leic 1A **22**
Blenheim Cl. LE18: Wig 3F **45**
Blenheim Cres. LE3: B Ast 6H **51**
Blenheim Rd. LE4: Birs 3H **13**
Blenheim Way LE4: Leic 1A **20**
  LE16: Mkt H 1D **64**
Blickling Wlk. LE5: Leic 5G **21**
Blissett Rd. LE3: Leic 6E **19**
Bloomfield Rd. LE2: Leic 3B **36**
Blossom Rd. LE3: Leic 3E **27**
Blossoms, The LE67: Mark 5C **8**
Blount Rd. LE4: Thurm 5D **14**
Bloxham Cl. LE3: Leic 6F **19**
Bloxoms Cl. LE3: Brau 3D **34**
Blue Banks Av. LE2: G Par 6E **35**
Bluebell Cl. LE2: Oad 4E **39**
  LE7: Quen .3H **7**
  LE9: K Mux 1E **25**
Bluebell Dr. LE2: Leic 5B **36**
  LE6: Groby .2G **17**
Blue Gates Rd. LE4: Beau L 6H **11**
Blue Pots Cl. LE3: Leic E 5F **25**
Blundell Rd. LE5: Leic 4A **30**
Blunt's La. LE18: Wig 1A **46**
Bob Trewick Ho. LE1: Leic 6E **5** (3C **28**)
Bodenham Cl. LE18: Wig 3A **46**
Bodicoat Cl. LE8: Whet 6H **43**
Bodkin Wlk. LE4: Leic 2F **19**
Bodmin Av. LE18: Wig 3A **46**
Bodnant Av. LE5: Leic 4G **29**
Bodycote Cl. LE9: B Ast 2B **60**
Bollington Rd. LE2: Oad 3C **38**
Bolsover St. LE5: Leic 1G **29**
Bolton Rd. LE3: Leic 2G **27**
Bolus Rd. LE3: Brau 5A **26**
Bonchurch St. LE3: Leic 6H **19**
Bondman Cl. LE4: Leic 6E **13**
Boneham's La. LE17: Lut 1H **63**
Bonner Cl. LE4: Leic 5D **38**
Bonners La. LE2: Leic 6B **5** (3A **28**)
Bonney Rd. LE3: Leic 4D **18**
Bonnington Rd. LE2: Leic 6D **28**
Bonsall St. LE5: Leic 3E **29**
Bonville Pl. LE3: Leic 6F **27**
Booth Cl. LE5: Leic 2B **30**
Bordeaux Cl. LE19: End 6G **33**
Border Dr. LE4: Leic 6D **12**
Borlace St. LE3: Leic 1H **27**
Borrowcup Cl. LE8: Count 1C **54**
Borrowdale Way LE5: Leic 4D **30**
Boston Rd. LE4: Beau L 1D **18**
Boswell St. LE19: Nar 2C **42**
Bosworth St. LE3: Leic 1H **27**
Botley Wlk. LE5: Leic 1A **30**
Boulder La. LE2: Leic 3B **36**
Boulter Cres. LE18: Wig 6F **37**
Boulton Cl. LE9: B Ast 3B **60**
Boulton Ct. LE2: Oad 5E **39**
Boundary Rd. LE2: Leic 6H **27**
  LE17: Lut 4H **63**
Bourne Mall LE4: Beau L 1E **19**
Bourton Cres. LE2: Oad 4C **38**
Bowden Cl. LE16: Mkt H 2F **65**
Bowden La. LE16: Mkt H 2D **64**
Bowden M. LE16: Mkt H 1C **64**
Bowden Ridge LE16: Mkt H 1F **65**
Bowhill Gro. LE5: Leic 1E **31**
Bowhill Way LE5: Leic 6E **23**
Bowling Grn. St. LE1: Leic 4D **4** (2B **28**)

Bowmans Way LE3: Glen 5H **17**
Bowman's La. LE3: Leic 1A **4** (6A **20**)
Boyers Wlk. LE3: Leic E 4F **25**
Boynton Rd. LE3: Leic 3E **27**
Brabazon Rd. LE2: Oad 3H **37**
Bracken Cl. LE3: Leic E 5F **25**
  LE5: Leic 3B **30**
Bracken Dale LE7: E Gos 2H **7**
Brackenfield Way LE4: Thurm 3E **15**
Bracken Hill LE6: New L 3A **10**
Brackenthwaite LE7: Anst 2F **21**
Bracken Wlk. LE67: Mark 2C **8**
               (not continuous)
Bracken Way LE67: Mark 2C **8**
Brackley Cl. LE4: Leic 4G **21**
Brackley Ct. LE8: Bla 3B **44**
Bradbourne Rd. LE5: Leic 2F **29**
Bradbury Cl. LE9: Cosb 3F **53**
Bradfield Cl. LE5: Leic 2G **29**
Bradgate Av. LE4: Thurm 4D **14**
Bradgate Cl. LE7: Thurn 2E **31**
Bradgate Country Pk. **1B 10**
Bradgate Country Pk. Vis. Cen. **2D 10**
Bradgate Dr. LE6: Ratby 4C **16**
  LE18: Wig .5D **36**
Bradgate Hill LE6: Groby 6F **9**
Bradgate House (ruins) **2C 10**
Bradgate Mall LE4: Beau L 1F **19**
Bradgate Rd. LE6: New L 3A **10**
  LE7: Anst 3A **10**
  LE67: Mark .2C **8**
Bradgate St. LE4: Leic 5H **19**
Brading Rd. LE3: Leic 5G **19**
Bradshaw Av. LE2: G Par 6G **35**
Bradshaw Ct. LE2: G Par 6G **35**
Bradstone Cl. LE9: B Ast 2D **60**
Bradston Rd. LE2: Leic 4A **36**
Braemar Cl. LE4: Leic 1E **21**
Braemar Dr. LE4: Leic 1E **21**
Brailsford Rd. LE3: Leic 2D **26**
  LE8: Wig 5D **36**
Bramall Ct. LE5: Leic 6G **21**
Bramall Rd. LE5: Leic 6G **21**
Bramble Cl. LE4: Thurm 5C **14**
Bramble Cl. LE3: Glen 6B **18**
  LE5: Ham 3D **22**
Bramble Way LE3: Brau 6E **27**
Brambling Rd. LE5: Leic 6F **21**
Brambling Way LE2: Oad 4A **38**
Bramcote Rd. LE3: Leic 1F **35**
  LE18: Wig .6E **37**
Bramham Cl. LE3: Leic 4F **19**
Bramley Cl. LE9: B Ast 6A **52**
  LE16: Mkt H 1E **65**
Bramley Orchard LE7: Bush 2G **31**
Bramley Rd. LE3: Leic 1G **27**
  LE4: Birs 4H **13**
Brampton Av. LE3: Leic 1F **27**
Brampton Valley Way
  LE16: Mkt H, G Ox 5E **65**
Brampton Way LE2: Oad 3H **37**
Brancaster Cl. LE4: Leic 3H **19**
Brandon Ct. LE8: Bla 2B **44**
Brandon St. LE4: Leic 5C **20**
Bransdale Rd. LE18: Wig 1D **46**
Branson Cl. *LE9: S Stan* *3C* **50**
               (off Church St.)
Branston Ho. LE18: Wig 5C **36**
Branting Hill LE6: Groby 3H **17**
Branting Hill Av. LE3: Glen 3H **17**
Branting Hill Gro. LE3: Glen 3H **17**
Bratmyr LE8: Flec 4B **58**
Braunstone Av. LE3: Leic 5D **26**
Braunstone Cl. LE3: Brau 6D **26**
BRAUNSTONE FRITH **1B 26**
Braunstone Frith Ind. Est. LE3: Leic . .2H **25**
Braunstone Ga. LE3: Leic 5A **5** (2H **27**)
Braunstone La. LE3: Brau 4A **26**
               (not continuous)
Braunstone La. E. LE3: Leic 1F **35**
Braunstone Leisure Cen. **2D 26**
Braunstone Recreation Cen. **3B 26**

Braunstone Town—Bushnell Cl.

BRAUNSTONE TOWN . . . . **.6C 26**
Braunstone Way LE3: Leic 4C **26**
Braybrooke Rd. LE4: Leic 4G **21**
LE16: L Bow, Mkt H 4F **65**
Braymish Cl. LE8: Kib H 5B **62**
Brazil St. LE2: Leic 4A **28**
Brecon Cl. LE18: Wig 1F **45**
Breedon Av. LE18: Wig 6E **37**
Breedon St. LE2: Leic 2E **29**
Brent Ct. LE3: Brau 2D **34**
Brent Knowle Gdns. LE5: Leic 2D **30**
Brentwood Rd. LE2: Leic 6C **28**
Bretby Rd. LE2: Leic 3A **36**
Breton Cl. LE18: Kilby 2E **57**
Brettell Rd. LE2: Leic 5H **35**
Bretton Cl. LE4: Leic 2A **20**
Bretton Wlk. LE4: Leic 2A **20**
Brewer Cl. LE4: Leic 6C **14**
Brex Ri. LE3: Leic 1B **26**
Brian Rd. LE4: Leic 4H **19**
Brians Cl. LE7: Sys 5G **7**
Brianway, The LE5: Leic 6H **21**
Briar Cl. LE2: Oad 5B **38**
Briarfield Dr. LE5: Leic 4E **23**
Briargate Dr. LE4: Birs 3E **13**
Briar Meads LE2: Oad 6A **38**
Briar Rd. LE5: Leic 6D **22**
Briar Wlk. LE2: Oad 5B **38**
Brickman Cl. LE3: Leic E 5E **25**
Bridevale Rd. LE2: Leic 4A **36**
Bridge Bus. Pk. LE4: Thurm 4B **14**
Bridge Cl. LE4: Thurm 3D **14**
Bridge Grn. LE4: Birs 2F **13**
Bridgemere Cl. LE2: Leic 5F **35**
Bridge Pk. Rd. LE4: Thurm 4B **14**
Bridge Rd. LE5: Leic 1F **29**
Bridgewater Dr. LE8: G Gle 2D **48**
Bridge Way LE8: Whet 5H **43**
Bridle, The LE2: G Par 5F **35**
Bridle Cl. LE9: Crof 2G **51**
Bridlespur Way LE4: Leic 6E **13**
Bridport Cl. LE18: Wig 2B **46**
Brierfield Rd. LE9: Cosb 3F **53**
Briers Cl. LE19: Nar 4D **42**
Brighton Av. LE7: Sys 5G **7**
LE18: Wig 4E **37**
Brighton Cl. LE18: Wig 4E **37**
Brighton Rd. LE5: Leic 5F **21**
Brightside Rd. LE5: Leic 3G **29**
Brightwell Dr. LE3: Leic E 3H **25**
Brindley Cl. LE9: S Stan 3B **50**
Brindley Ri. LE5: Leic 4E **23**
Bringhurst Grn. LE3: Leic 6C **18**
Bringhurst Rd. LE3: Leic 6B **18**
Brington Cl. LE18: Wig 1C **46**
Brinsmead Rd. LE2: Leic 2D **36**
Bristol Av. LE4: Leic 4H **19**
Britannia St. LE1: Leic 1E **4** (6C **20**)
Britannia Wlk. LE16: Mkt H 4E **65**
Britannia Way LE4: Thurm 2C **14**
Britannia Works LE4: Thurm 2C **14**
Britford Av. LE18: Wig 3A **46**
Briton St. LE3: Leic 3H **27**
Brixham Dr. LE2: Leic 4C **36**
LE18: Wig 4C **36**
Brixworth Ri. LE5: Leic 1E **31**
Broad Av. LE5: Leic 1H **29**
Broadbent Cl. LE8: Whet 4H **43**
Broadfield Way LE8: Count 1D **54**
Broadford Cl. LE4: Leic 1F **21**
Broadgate Cl. LE4: Birs 3G **13**
Broadhurst St. LE4: Leic 3D **20**
Broad Mdw. LE18: Wig 2C **46**
Broadmead Rd. LE8: Bla 5A **44**
Broadnook Cl. LE3: Leic 2C **18**
Broad St. LE7: Sys 6E **7**
LE19: End 6H **33**
Broadway LE7: Sys 6E **7**
Broadway, The LE2: Oad 6H **29**
LE16: Mkt H 2D **64**
Broadway Furlong LE7: Anst 4G **11**
Broadway Rd. LE5: Leic 5F **29**
Broadway Ter. LE16: Mkt H 2E **65**
Brockenhurst Dr. LE3: Brau 1C **34**
Brocklesby Way LE5: Leic 5E **23**
Brocks Hill Cl. LE2: Oad 5B **38**
Brocks Hill Country Pk. . . . . **.6H 37**
Brocks Hill Dr. LE2: Oad 4B **38**
Brocks Hill Vis. Cen. . . . . **.5H 37**
Broctone Cl. LE9: B Ast 2D **60**
Broctone Dr. LE9: B Ast 6A **52**
Brodick Wlk. LE5: Leic 5F **21**
Brompton Rd. LE5: Ham 2C **22**
(not continuous)
Bromwich Cl. LE3: Brau 5A **26**
Bronte Cl. LE3: Leic 3E **27**
Bronze Barrow Cl. LE18: Wig 2D **46**
Brook Bank LE5: Leic 6H **21**
Brook Ct. LE8: Count 1F **55**
Brookdale Rd. LE3: Leic 2B **26**
Brook Dr. LE6: Ratby 5C **16**
Brookes Av. LE9: Crof 2G **51**
Brookfield LE8: G Gle 3C **48**
Brookfield Av. LE7: Sys 6F **7**
Brookfield Bowling Club . . . . **.4F 29**
Brookfield Ri. LE2: Leic 3B **36**
Brookfield Rise Nature Garden . . . . . **.3C 36**
Brookfield Rd. LE16: Mkt H 3B **64**
Brookfield St. LE7: Sys 6F **7**
Brookfield Way LE8: Kib B 5B **62**
LE17: Lut 4E **63**
Brook Furlong Dr. *LE4: Birs 2F* ***13***
(off Hallam Flds. Rd.)
Brook Gdns. LE2: G Par 6F **35**
Brookhouse Av. LE2: Leic 6F **5** (3D **28**)
Brookhouse St. LE2: Leic 6F **5** (3D **28**)
Brookland Rd. LE2: Leic 6C **28**
Brooklands Cl. LE8: Whet 4H **43**
LE9: B Ast 1B **60**
Brooklands Gdns. LE16: Mkt H 3D **64**
Brooklands Rd. LE9: Cosb 1F **53**
Brook Rd. LE5: Leic 6D **22**
Brooksby Cl. LE2: Oad 3A **38**
Brooksby Dr. LE2: Oad 3A **38**
Brooksby St. LE2: Leic 6A **28**
Brookside LE5: Leic 4F **29**
LE7: Bark 3H **15**
(not continuous)
LE7: Sys .5E **7**
(not continuous)
LE8: Whet 5H **43**
Brookside Dr. LE2: Oad 4C **38**
Brookside Gdns. LE8: Flec 6B **58**
Brook St. LE4: Thurm 4B **14**
LE7: Sys .5E **7**
LE8: Whet 4H **43**
LE9: Hun 4H **41**
LE19: End 6H **33**
Broombriggs Rd. LE3: Leic 2C **18**
Broome La.
LE7: E Gos, Rat W . . . . .1G **7** & 1H **7**
Broomfield LE7: E Gos 2H **7**
Broomhills Rd. LE19: Nar 3B **42**
Broomleys LE8: Count 1D **54**
Broom Way LE19: Nar 2B **42**
Brougham St. LE1: Leic 2F **4** (1C **28**)
BROUGHTON ASTLEY . . . . **.2C 60**
Broughton Cl. LE7: Anst 4G **11**
Broughton Ct. LE2: Leic 4A **36**
Broughton La. LE8: Will W 1H **61**
LE9: B Ast 3A **60**
LE9: Cosb 1H **61**
LE17: Leire 3A **60**
Broughton Rd. LE2: Leic 4A **36**
LE9: Cosb 5D **52**
LE9: Crof .1G **51**
LE9: S Stan 3C **50**
LE17: D Bas 4D **60**
Broughtons Fld. LE18: Wig 3C **46**
Broughton Way LE9: B Ast 5H **51**
Browning St. LE3: Leic 3G **27**
LE19: Nar 2C **42**
Brown's Cl. LE9: Sap 5C **50**
Browns Way LE8: Whet 6H **43**
Broxburn Cl. LE4: Leic 1F **21**
Broxfield Cl. LE2: Oad 6A **38**
Bruce St. LE3: Leic 4H **27**
Bruce Way LE8: Whet 6G **43**
Bruin St. LE4: Leic 4C **20**
Bruins Wlk. LE2: Oad 4H **37**
Brunel Av. LE3: Leic 5E **19**
Brunswick St. LE1: Leic 2F **4** (1D **28**)
Bruxby St. LE7: Sys 6D **6**
Bryngarth Cres. LE5: Leic 6B **22**
Bryony Rd. LE5: Ham 3D **22**
Buchan Wlk. LE3: Leic 2E **27**
Buckfast Cl. LE5: Leic 4H **29**
LE18: Wig 2A **46**
Buckhaven Cl. LE4: Leic 1F **21**
Buckingham Cl. LE6: Groby 3E **17**
Buckingham Dr. LE2: Leic 4F **35**
Buckingham Rd. LE8: Count 1F **55**
Buckland Rd. LE5: Leic 5F **21**
Buckminster Rd. LE3: Leic 5G **19**
Bucksburn Wlk. LE4: Leic 1F **21**
Buckwell Rd. LE9: Sap 5B **50**
Buddon Cl. LE3: Leic 2C **18**
Bude Dr. LE3: Glen 4A **18**
Bude Rd. LE18: Wig 2B **46**
Buller Rd. LE4: Leic 4C **20**
Buller St. LE8: Kib B 5H **59**
Bull Head St. LE18: Wig 5F **37**
Bulwer Rd. LE2: Leic 6D **28**
(not continuous)
Bumblebee Cl. LE6: Ratby 4C **16**
Burchnall Rd. LE3: Brau 6A **26**
Burdet Cl. LE3: Brau 6C **26**
Burdett Way LE4: Leic 1H **19**
Burdock Cl. LE5: Ham 3D **22**
Burfield St. LE4: Leic 5D **20**
Burford Cl. LE16: Mkt H 5C **64**
Burgess Rd. LE2: Leic 3A **36**
Burgess St. LE1: Leic 1B **4** (1A **28**)
LE18: Wig 6F **37**
Burghley Cl. LE16: L Bow 3F **65**
Burgin Rd. LE7: Anst 6F **11**
Burleigh Av. LE18: Wig 5D **36**
Burley Cl. LE9: Cosb 2F **53**
Burley Homes LE4: Birs 6F **13**
Burleys Flyover LE1: Leic 1D **4** (6B **20**)
Burleys Way LE1: Leic 1C **4** (6B **20**)
Burlington Rd. LE2: Leic 6E **29**
Burnaby Av. LE5: Leic 1F **29**
Burnaston Rd. LE2: Leic 3A **36**
Burnell Rd. LE3: Leic 5F **27**
Burneston Way LE18: Wig 1C **46**
Burnet Cl. LE5: Ham 3C **22**
Burnham Cl. LE18: Wig 4B **46**
Burnham Ct. LE9: Cosb 3F **53**
Burnham Dr. LE4: Leic 3H **19**
LE8: Whet 5H **43**
Burnmill Rd. LE16: G Bow, Mkt H 2D **64**
Burnmoor St. LE2: Leic 8B **5** (5A **28**)
Burnside Rd. LE2: Leic 3C **36**
LE9: B Ast 2B **60**
Burns St. LE2: Leic 1C **36**
LE19: Nar 2D **42**
Burroughs Rd. LE6: Ratby 4A **16**
Burrough Way LE17: Lut 2G **63**
Burrow Cl. LE3: Leic 2C **18**
Burrows, The LE7: E Gos 2G **7**
LE19: Nar 3B **42**
Burrows Cl. LE19: Nar 4D **42**
Bursdon Cl. LE3: Leic 1B **26**
Bursdon Ct. LE3: Leic 1B **26**
Bursom Ind. Est. LE4: Beau L 5C **12**
Bursom Rd. LE4: Beau L 5B **12**
Burton Cl. LE2: Oad 5D **38**
LE17: Lut 5H **63**
BURTON OVERY . . . . **.2H 49**
Burton St. LE1: Leic 3F **4** (1C **28**)
Buscot Cl. LE4: Leic 5F **21**
BUSHBY . . . . **.3G 31**
Bushby Rd. LE5: Leic 6F **21**
Bushey Cl. LE19: Nar 3D **42**
Bush Lock Cl. LE18: Wig 3G **45**
Bushloe Ct. LE18: Wig 1A **46**
Bushloe End LE18: Wig 1A **46**
Bushnell Cl. LE9: B Ast 3C **60**

BUSM Business Pk.—Charnwood Cl.

BUSM Business Pk. LE4: Leic 4C 20
Butcombe Rd. LE4: Leic 4H 19
Bute Way LE8: Count 2F 55
Butler Cl. LE4: Leic 1G 21
LE6: Ratby 5D 16
Butler Gdns. LE16: Mkt H 5B 64
Butt Cl. LE18: Wig 2C 46
Butt Cl. La. LE1: Leic 2C 4 (1B 28)
Buttercup Cl. LE6: Groby 2G 17
LE19: Nar 2C 42
Buttermere St. LE2: Leic 8A 5 (4A 28)
Butterwick Dr. LE4: Leic 1G 19
Buxton Cl. LE8: Whet 4A 44
Buxton St. LE2: Leic 1E 29
Buzzard Cl. LE9: B Ast 6B 52
Byfield Dr. LE18: Wig 6G 37
Byford Rd. LE4: Leic 3A 20
Byford Way LE4: Leic 4A 20
Byre Cres. LE9: B Ast 2B 60
Byron Cl. LE8: Flec 6C 58
LE17: Lut 2G 63
LE19: End 1C 42
Byron Ct. LE8: Flec 6B 58
Byron St. LE1: Leic 2E 4 (1C 28)
Byway Rd. LE5: Leic 5G 29

C

Cademan Cl. LE2: Leic 2D 36
Cadle Cl. LE9: S Stan 2B 50
Cairngorm Cl. LE2: Leic 2B 36
Cairns Cl. LE3: Brau 2D 34
Cairnsford Rd. LE2: Leic 3D 36
Calais Hill LE1: Leic 5E 5 (2C 28)
Calais St. LE1: Leic 5E 5 (2C 28)
Caldecote Rd. LE3: Leic 6E 27
Caldecott Cl. LE18: Wig 1C 46
Calder Rd. LE4: Leic 2G 19
Caledine Rd. LE3: Leic 5E 19
Calgary Rd. LE1: Leic 1F 4 (6C 20)
Callan Cl. LE19: Nar 3C 42
Calver Cres. LE9: Sap 6C 50
Calver Hey Rd. LE4: Leic 2E 19
Calverton Av. LE18: Wig 5E 37
Calverton Cl. LE6: Ratby 5D 16
Camborne Cl. LE18: Wig 2A 46
Cambrian Cl. LE9: Cosb 3F 53
Cambridge Cl. LE7: Sys 6G 7
Cambridge Rd. LE8: Whet 6G 43
LE9: Cosb 2F 53
Cambridge St. LE3: Leic 3G 27
Camden Rd. LE3: Brau 6E 27
Camden St. LE1: Leic 2E 4 (1C 28)
Camellia Cl. LE19: Nar 2B 42
Camelot Way LE19: Nar 2C 42
Cameron Av. LE4: Leic 2D 20
Camfield Ri. LE2: Leic 5H 35
Campbell Av. LE4: Thurm 5C 14
Campbell St. LE1: Leic 5F 5 (2C 28)
Campion Cl. LE19: Nar 3C 42
Campion Wlk. LE4: Leic 2F 19
Camville Rd. LE3: Leic 3D 26
Canada Flds. LE17: Lut 3G 63
Canalside LE16: Mkt H 2C 64
Canal St. LE2: Leic 2G 35
LE4: Thurm 3B 14
LE18: Wig 3F 45
Cank St. LE1: Leic 4C 4 (2B 28)
Cannam Cl. LE8: Whet 6A 44
Canning Pl. LE1: Leic 1C 4 (6B 20)
Canning St. LE1: Leic 1C 4 (6B 20)
Cannock St. LE4: Leic 1A 22
Canon Cl. LE2: Oad 4B 38
Canons Cl. LE19: Nar 3D 42
Canonsleigh Rd. LE4: Leic 2A 20
Canonsleigh Wlk. LE4: Leic 2A 20
Canon St. LE4: Leic 4D 20
Canterbury Ter. LE3: Leic 4F 27
Cantrell Rd. LE3: Leic 4B 26
Canvey Cl. LE18: Wig 6H 37
Capers Cl. LE19: End 6G 33
Capesthorne Cl. LE5: Leic 5F 21
Captains La. LE67: Mark 3B 8
Cara Cl. LE2: Leic 1E 37
Carbery Cl. LE2: Oad 5D 38
Cardigan Dr. LE18: Wig 1F 45
Cardinal Cl. LE6: Ratby 5D 16
Cardinals Wlk. LE5: Leic 5C 22
Carey Cl. LE18: Wig 3B 46
Carey Gdns. LE9: K Mux 2D 24
Carey Hill Rd. LE9: S Stan 3B 50
Carey Rd. LE9: Hun 4H 41
Carey's Cl. LE1: Leic 4B 4 (2A 28)
Carfax Av. LE2: Oad 2H 37
Carisbrooke Av. LE2: Leic 2E 37
Carisbrooke Ct. LE2: Leic 2E 37
Carisbrooke Gdns. LE2: Leic 1E 37
Carisbrooke Lawn Tennis Club 2E 37
Carisbrooke Pk. LE2: Leic 2E 37
Carisbrooke Rd. LE2: Leic 1E 37
Carlisle St. LE3: Leic 2F 27
Carlson Gdns. LE17: Lut 4H 63
(not continuous)
Carlson Ter. LE17: Lut 4H 63
Carl St. LE2: Leic 3G 35
Carlton Av. LE19: Nar 3E 43
Carlton Ct. LE3: Glen 5A 18
Carlton Dr. LE18: Wig 6E 37
Carlton Gdns. LE8: G Gle 4D 48
Carlton La. LE8: Bur O 3H 49
Carlton Pk. LE19: Nar 2D 42
Carlton Rd. LE8: Kib H 3A 62
Carlton St. LE1: Leic 6C 5 (3B 28)
Carlyon Ct. LE9: K Mux 2E 25
Carmen Gro. LE6: Groby 2D 16
Carnation Cl. LE3: Leic E 5F 25
Carnation St. LE4: Leic 3B 20
Carnoustie Rd. LE3: Leic 2B 26
Caroline Ct. LE2: Leic 3A 36
Carpenters Cl. LE3: Glen 6H 17
Carpe Rd. LE4: Leic 4F 21
Carrington Rd. LE5: Ham 2C 22
Carrow Rd. LE3: Leic 2H 25
Carter Cl. LE19: End 6G 33
Carter St. LE4: Leic 5E 21
Carts La. LE1: Leic 3C 4 (1B 28)
Cartwright Dr. LE2: Oad 4H 37
Carty Rd. LE5: Ham 2C 22
Carvers Cnr. LE2: G Par 6F 35
Cashmore Vw. LE4: Leic 1H 19
Castell Dr. LE6: Groby 2F 17
Castle Cl. LE9: Sap 6B 50
Castle Flds. LE4: Beau L 6A 12
Castleford Rd. LE3: Brau 1C 34
Castlegate Av. LE4: Birs 3F 13
Castle Hill Country Pk. 5G 11
Castle Ri. LE6: Groby 3F 17
Castle Rd. LE9: K Mux 2D 24
Castle St. LE1: Leic 4B 4 (2A 28)
Castleton Rd. LE18: Wig 5E 37
Castle Vw. LE1: Leic 5B 5 (2A 28)
Caswell Cl. LE4: Leic 1H 19
Caters Cl. LE7: Anst 5F 11
Catesby St. LE3: Leic 2H 27
Catherine St. LE4: Leic 5D 20
Catherine St. Ind. Est.
LE4: Leic 3F 21
Cathkin Cl. LE3: Leic 2B 26
Caudle Cl. LE7: Crop 1H 11
Causeway La. LE1: Leic 2B 4 (1A 28)
LE7: Crop 1G 11
Cavendish M. LE2: Leic 1A 36
Cavendish Rd. LE2: Leic 6A 28
Caversham Rd. LE2: Leic 6G 35
Cawsand Rd. LE18: Wig 2A 46
Cawston Cl. LE5: Ham 3B 22
Caxton St. LE16: Mkt H 5E 65
Cecil Gdns. LE2: Leic 1E 29
Cecilia Rd. LE2: Leic 5D 28
Cecil Rd. LE2: Leic 1D 28
Cedar Av. LE4: Birs 4G 13
LE17: Lut 4F 63
LE18: Wig 1B 46
Cedar Cl. LE3: Glen 4C 18
LE8: Kib B 5H 59
Cedar Ct. LE2: Leic 8C 5
LE5: Leic 5A 22
LE6: Groby 3F 17
Cedar Cres. LE19: Nar 4D 42
Cedar Dr. LE7: Sys 1F 15
Cedar Rd. LE2: Leic 3E 29
LE8: Bla 5B 44
Cedars, The LE2: Leic 2D 36
LE7: Bush 3H 31
Cedars Ct. LE2: Leic 4E 29
Cedarwood Cl. LE4: Leic 4F 21
Celandine Cl. LE2: Oad 5E 39
Celandine Rd. LE5: Ham 3C 22
Celt St. LE3: Leic 3H 27
Cemetery Rd. LE8: Whet 4H 43
Central Av. LE2: Leic 5E 29
LE7: Sys 5F 7
LE17: Lut 3G 63
LE18: Wig 1H 45
Central Cl. LE8: Whet 3H 43
Central Pk. LE17: Lut 2H 63
Central Rd. LE3: Leic 6H 19
Central St. LE8: Count 1F 55
Centre Ct. LE19: Brau 2B 34
Centurion Ct. LE6: Ratby 6D 16
Centurion Ct. Office Pk.
LE19: Brau 1B 34
Centurion Way LE19: Brau 6A 26
Century Ct. LE5: Leic 1C 30
Chadderton Cl. LE2: Leic 2C 36
Chadwell Rd. LE3: Leic 6C 18
Chadwick Wlk. LE4: Leic 2H 19
Chaffinch Cl. LE4: Beau L 5B 12
Chainama Cl. LE3: Leic 1A 26
Chale Rd. LE4: Leic 3B 20
Chalgrove Wlk. LE5: Leic 1A 30
Chalvington Cl. LE5: Leic 4C 30
Chamberlains Fld.
LE4: Birs 2F 13
Chambers Cl. LE67: Mark 2D 8
Champion Cl. LE5: Leic 2B 30
Chancel Rd. LE4: Leic 3D 12
Chancery St. LE1: Leic 5C 5 (2B 28)
Chandler Way LE9: B Ast 2D 60
Chandos St. LE2: Leic 3E 29
Chantry Cl. LE9: Hun 4H 41
Chapel Cl. LE7: Sys 5F 7
LE7: Thurc 1B 12
LE17: D Bas 5F 61
LE18: Kilby 2D 56
Chapel Ct. LE5: Leic 5B 30
LE19: Nar 4E 43
(off Leicester Rd.)
Chapel Grn. LE3: Leic E 4H 25
Chapel Hill LE6: Groby 2E 17
Chapel La. LE2: Leic 1D 36
LE6: Ratby 5C 16
LE9: Cosb 3F 53
LE18: Wig 1B 46
Chapel St. LE2: Oad 4A 38
LE7: Sys 5E 7
LE8: Bla 2B 44
LE17: Lut 4G 63
LE19: End 6G 33
Chaplin Ct. LE3: Brau 4B 26
Chappell Cl. LE4: Thurm 4C 14
Charlecote Av. LE3: Brau 6D 26
Charles Dr. LE7: Anst 5G 11
Charles Mall *LE1: Leic 3D 4*
(off Haymarket Cen.)
Charles St. LE1: Leic 2D 4 (1B 28)
LE16: Mkt H 3C 64
Charles Way LE2: Oad 4C 38
LE8: Whet 6A 44
Charlock Rd. LE5: Ham 3D 22
Charlotte Ct. LE8: Bla 3A 44
Charlton Cl. LE8: Whet 5A 44
Charnor Rd. LE3: Leic 6C 18
Charnwood LE6: Ratby 4B 16
Charnwood Av. LE4: Thurm 3D 14
LE8: Whet 3H 43
Charnwood Cl. LE3: Leic E 3G 25
LE4: Thurm 3D 14

76 A-Z Leicester

Charnwood Dr. LE3: Leic E 4G **25**
  LE7: Thurn 2F **31**
  LE67: Mark 3D **8**
Charnwood Ind. Units LE2: Leic 1D **28**
Charnwood Mnr. LE19: Nar 3E **43**
Charnwood Rd. LE7: Anst 4F **11**
Charnwood St. LE5: Leic 1E **29**
Charnwood Wlk. LE5: Leic 6E **21**
Charter St. LE1: Leic 1D **4** (6B **20**)
Chartley Rd. LE3: Leic 4G **27**
Chartwell Dr. LE18: Wig 6C **36**
Chartwell Ind. Est. LE18: Wig 6C **36**
Chartwell Point LE18: Wig 6D **36**
Chase, The LE3: Brau 2D **34**
  LE7: E Gos 1H **7**
  LE8: G Gle 2E **49**
  LE67: Mark 3C **8**
Chater Cl. LE5: Leic 6D **22**
Chater Ho. LE16: Mkt H 3F **65**
Chatham St. LE1: Leic 5D **5** (2B **28**)
Chatsworth Av. LE18: Wig 2G **45**
Chatsworth Dr. LE7: Sys 6D **6**
  LE16: L Bow 3F **65**
Chatsworth St. LE2: Leic 2E **29**
Chatteris Av. LE5: Leic 4D **30**
Chaucer St. LE2: Leic 4E **29**
  LE19: Nar 2C **42**
Cheapside LE1: Leic 3C **4** (1B **28**)
Checketts Cl. LE4: Leic 3D **20**
Checketts Rd. LE4: Leic 2C **20**
Checkland Rd. LE4: Thurm 3C **14**
Cheddar Rd. LE18: Wig 6G **37**
Cheer Cl. LE8: Whet 1H **53**
Chellaston Rd. LE8: Wig 5E **37**
Chelsea Cl. LE2: G Par 2D **44**
Cheltenham Rd. LE4: Leic 3G **19**
Cheney Ct. LE9: Hun 4H **41**
Cheney End LE9: Hun 4H **41**
Cheney Rd. LE4: Leic 1A **22**
Chepstow Rd. LE2: Leic 4E **29**
Cheriton Rd. LE2: Leic 4H **35**
Cherrybrook Cl. LE4: Beau L 4B **12**
Cherry Dr. LE7: Sys 1F **15**
Cherry Gro. LE8: G Gle 2E **49**
Cherry Hills Rd. LE3: Leic 1A **26**
Cherryleas Dr. LE3: Leic 3G **27**
Cherry Rd. LE8: Bla 4B **44**
Cherry St. LE18: Wig 1H **45**
Cherry Tree Av. LE9: Leic E 4E **25**
Cherrytree Av. LE17: Lut 5E **63**
Cherry Tree Cl. LE8: Count 1E **55**
Cherrytree Cl. LE7: Anst 6F **11**
Cherry Tree Cl. LE9: Leic E 4E **25**
Cherry Tree Gro. LE19: End 6G **33**
Cheshire Cl. LE17: Lut 6F **63**
Cheshire Dr. LE18: Wig 6B **36**
Cheshire Gdns. LE2: Leic 2H **35**
Cheshire Rd. LE2: Leic 2H **35**
Chester Cl. LE1: Leic 1F **4** (6D **20**)
  LE8: Bla 4C **44**
Chesterfield Rd. LE5: Leic 3F **29**
Chester Rd. LE8: Bla 4C **44**
Chesterton Ct. LE19: End 1C **42**
Chesterton Wlk. LE3: Leic 2E **27**
  (off Blackmore Dr.)
Chestnut Av. LE2: Oad 4H **37**
  LE5: Leic 4C **22**
  LE17: Lut 4E **63**
Chestnut Cl. LE7: Quen 4H **7**
  LE7: Sys 1F **15**
  LE9: B Ast 2C **60**
  LE19: Litt 5D **42**
Chestnut Dr. LE2: Oad 5G **39**
  LE7: Bush 3G **31**
Chestnut Grange LE9: B Ast 2B **60**
Chestnut Rd. LE3: Glen 5A **18**
Chestnuts, The LE8: Count 1E **55**
Chestnut Wlk. LE6: Groby 3F **17**
  LE67: Mark 5C **8**
Chettle Rd. LE3: Leic 6E **19**
Chevin Av. LE3: Leic 2B **26**
Cheviot Rd. LE2: Leic 3B **36**
Chilcombe Cl. LE4: Leic 2A **20**

Chilcombe Wlk. LE4: Leic 2A **20**
Chiltern Av. LE9: Cosb 3F **53**
Chiltern Cl. LE16: Mkt H 1E **65**
Chiltern Grn. LE2: Leic 3C **36**
Chislehurst Av. LE3: Brau 1C **34**
Chiswick Rd. LE2: Leic 6B **28**
Chitterman Way LE67: Mark 3C **8**
Chorley Wood Rd. LE5: Leic 3D **30**
Choyce Cl. LE7: Anst 6G **11**
Chrisett Cl. LE5: Leic 1B **30**
Christopher Cl. LE8: Count 2E **56**
Christopher Dr. LE4: Leic 1H **21**
Christow St. LE1: Leic 1F **4** (6C **20**)
Churchbell Way LE4: Beau L, Leic ..4B **12**
  (not continuous)
Church Cl. LE7: Sys 5F **7**
  LE8: Kib B 4A **62**
  LE9: B Ast 1B **60**
  LE17: D Bas 5F **61**
  LE17: Lut 4G **63**
Church Dr. LE67: Mark 3B **8**
Church Gate LE1: Leic 2C **4** (1B **28**)
  LE17: Lut 5G **63**
Church Hill LE4: Birs 5H **13**
  LE7: Scra 5F **23**
Church Hill Rd. LE4: Thurm 4C **14**
Churchill Cl. LE2: Oad 4A **38**
  LE17: Lut 5E **63**
Churchill Dr. LE3: Leic E 3H **25**
Churchill St. LE2: Leic 3D **28**
Churchill Way LE8: Flec 6C **58**
Church La. LE2: Leic 2D **36**
  LE2: S'ton 6E **31**
  LE4: Thurm 4C **14**
  LE6: Ratby 5C **16**
  LE7: Anst 5F **11**
  LE7: Thurn 3F **31**
  LE8: Flec 5B **58**
  LE8: Whet 3H **43**
  LE17: D Bas 6F **61**
  LE19: Nar 3E **43**
Church Nook LE18: Wig 6F **37**
Church Ponds Cl. LE6: Ratby 5D **16**
Church Rd. LE2: Leic 3G **35**
  LE3: Glen 4H **17**
  LE4: Leic 2C **20**
  LE5: Leic 5B **30**
  LE7: Wan 1A **14**
  LE8: G Gle 3C **48**
  LE8: Kib B 5A **62**
  LE9: K Mux 2D **24**
Church Sq. LE16: Mkt H 3D **64**
Church St. LE1: Leic 4E **4** (2C **28**)
  LE2: Oad 4A **38**
  LE4: Thurm 5B **14**
  LE8: Bla 3B **44**
  LE8: Count 2F **55**
  LE9: S Stan 3C **50**
  LE9: Sap 6B **50**
  LE9: Thurl 6A **32**
  LE16: Mkt H 3D **64**
  LE17: Lut 5G **63**
Church Vw. LE19: Nar 3E **43**
Church Wlk. LE4: Leic 2C **20**
  LE8: Bla 3B **44**
  LE9: Sap 6B **50**
  LE16: L Bow 4F **65**
Churchward Av. LE4: Leic 1G **19**
Cinema De Lux
  Leicester 3B **4** (1A **28**)
Circle, The LE5: Leic 2H **29**
City, The LE8: Kib H 3A **62**
Clarefield Rd. LE3: Leic 2F **27**
Clare Gro. LE3: Brau 5B **26**
Claremont Dr. LE16: L Bow 3F **65**
Claremont St. LE4: Leic 2C **20**
Clarence Rd. LE19: End 1F **43**
Clarence St. LE1: Leic 2D **4** (1B **28**)
  LE16: Mkt H 3E **65**
CLARENDON PARK 6D **28**
Clarendon Pk. Rd. LE2: Leic 6C **28**
Clarendon St. LE2: Leic 7B **5** (3A **28**)

Clarke Cres. LE8: Count 6C **44**
Clarke Gro. LE4: Birs 5G **13**
Clarkes Rd. LE18: Wig 1H **45**
Clarke St. LE4: Leic 2D **20**
  LE16: Mkt H 3C **64**
Clark Gdns. LE8: Bla 3A **44**
Clarks Cl. LE19: End 6C **34**
Claybrook Av. LE3: Brau 1E **35**
Claydon Rd. LE5: Leic 5G **21**
Claymill Rd. LE4: Leic 1H **21**
Clayton Dr. LE4: Thurm 5D **14**
Clematis Cl. LE4: Beau L 6A **12**
Clement Av. LE4: Leic 2C **20**
Clevedon Cres. LE4: Leic 5G **21**
Cleveland Rd. LE18: Wig 5F **37**
Cleveleys Av. LE3: Brau 1E **35**
Clickers Way LE9: Elm, Earl S 1A **40**
Cliffe Ho. M. LE8: Whet 3H **43**
Cliffe La. LE67: Mark, S Bar 2A **8**
  (not continuous)
Cliffe Rd. LE4: Birs 5F **13**
Clifford St. LE3: Leic 2H **27**
  LE18: Wig 1F **45**
Cliffwood Av. LE4: Birs 4F **13**
Clifton Dr. LE18: Wig 3G **45**
Clifton Rd. LE2: Leic 1A **36**
Clint Hill Dr. LE9: S Stan 2C **50**
Clipper Rd. LE4: Leic 2H **21**
Clipstone Cl. LE18: Wig 1C **46**
Clipstone Gdns. LE18: Wig 1C **46**
Clipstone Ho. LE2: Leic 2D **28**
Clipston St. LE16: Mkt H 5E **65**
Clock Tower
  Leicester 3D **4** (1B **28**)
Clock Twr. Mall LE1: Leic 3D **4**
  (off Haymarket Cen.)
Close, The LE6: Ratby 4C **16**
  LE7: Anst 4F **11**
  LE8: Bla 2B **44**
  LE19: End 1C **42**
Clovelly Rd. LE3: Glen 4B **18**
  LE5: Leic 3H **29**
Clover Cl. LE19: Nar 3C **42**
Cloverdale Rd. LE5: Ham 2C **22**
Clover Way LE7: Sys 1E **15**
Clumber Dr. LE7: Sys 4F **7**
Clumber Rd. LE5: Leic 2G **29**
Clyde St. LE1: Leic 2F **4** (1C **28**)
Coalbourn Cl. LE4: Leic 1A **20**
Coales Av. LE8: Whet 6A **44**
Coales Gdns. LE16: Mkt H 1C **64**
Coatbridge Av. LE4: Leic 1F **21**
Coates Av. LE3: Leic 6E **19**
Cobbett Rd. LE3: Brau 5B **26**
Cobden St. LE1: Leic 5D **20**
Cobden St. Ind. Est. LE4: Leic 5E **21**
Cobwells Cl. LE8: Flec 6C **58**
Cokayne Rd. LE3: Leic 1B **26**
Colbert Dr. LE3: Brau 2E **35**
Colbrook Wlk. LE5: Leic 4G **29**
Colby Dr. LE4: Thurm 6D **14**
Colby Rd. LE4: Thurm 6D **14**
Colchester Rd. LE5: Leic 1B **30**
Colebrook Cl. LE5: Leic 4G **29**
Coleford Rd. LE4: Leic 6E **15**
Coleman Cl. LE5: Leic 6H **21**
Coleman Ct. LE5: Leic 6H **21**
Coleman Rd. LE5: Leic 6H **21**
  LE8: Flec 5A **58**
Coleridge Dr. LE19: End 6G **33**
Coles Cl. LE4: Leic 6B **14**
Colindale Av. LE4: Birs 3G **13**
Colin Grundy Dr. LE5: Leic 4B **22**
Collaton Rd. LE18: Wig 1A **46**
College Av. LE2: Leic 3D **28**
College Hall LE2: Leic 1D **36**
College Ho. LE8: Whet 3H **43**
College Rd. LE7: Sys 1F **15**
  LE8: Whet 3H **43**
College St. LE2: Leic 5F **5** (3D **28**)
Collett Rd. LE4: Leic 1G **19**
Collingham Rd. LE3: Leic 5G **27**
Collin Pl. LE4: Leic 3E **21**

Collins Cl. LE3: Brau	.5B 26
Colne Cl. LE2: Oad	.4D 38
Colsterdale Cl. LE4: Leic	.6D 12
Coltbeck Av. LE19: Nar	.3C 42
Colthurst Way LE5: Leic	.1E 31
Colton Sq. LE1: Leic	.4E 4 (2C 28)
Colton St. LE1: Leic	.4E 4 (2C 28)
Coltsfoot Rd. LE5: Ham	.3C 22
Coltsfoot Way LE9: B Ast	.3C 60
Columbia Cl. LE19: End	.6G 33
Columbine Cl. LE3: Brau	.5C 26
Columbine Rd. LE5: Ham	.2B 22
Colwell Rd. LE3: Leic	.5H 19
Combe Cl. LE3: Leic	.5G 19
Comet Cl. LE3: Leic	.6F 19
Commercial Sq. LE2: Leic	.5B 28
Common, The LE5: Leic	.4A 30
Commons, The LE16: Mkt H	.3D 64
Compass Point Bus. Pk.	
LE16: Mkt H	.6E 65
Compass Rd. LE5: Leic	.6C 22
Compton Dr. LE9: Hun	.3H 41
Compton Rd. LE3: Leic	.5G 27
Comrie Ct. LE5: Leic	.6E 23
Conaglen Rd. LE2: Leic	.3F 35
Condor Cl. LE9: B Ast	.6B 52
Conduit St. LE2: Leic	.5F 5 (2C 28)
Cone La. LE2: Leic	.5E 29
Conery, The LE4: Leic	.3C 20
Conery La. LE19: End	.5G 33
Coneygrey LE8: Flec	.4A 58
Conifer Cl. LE3: Leic	.3E 29
LE17: Lut	.4F 63
Conifers Mobile Pk. LE6: Ratby	.6D 16
Coninsby Cl. LE3: Leic	.6F 27
Coniston Av. LE2: Leic	.8A 5 (4A 28)
Coniston Way LE9: Crof	.1H 51
Connaught Rd. LE16: Mkt H	.2E 65
Connaught St. LE2: Leic	.3D 28
Connery Leys Rd. LE4: Birs	.2F 13
Constable Av. LE4: Leic	.5D 20
Constance Rd. LE5: Leic	.2F 29
Constitution Hill LE1: Leic	.4F 4 (2C 28)
Conway Rd. LE2: Leic	.4F 29
Cooden Av. LE3: Leic	.3F 27
Cooke Cl. LE3: Brau	.5B 26
LE4: Thurm	.4D 14
Cooke's Dr. LE9: B Ast	.1A 60
Cooks La. LE9: Sap	.6B 50
LE18: Wig	.3C 46
Cookson Rd. LE4: Leic	.6E 15
Cooks Wlk. LE3: Glen	.5A 18
Coombe Pl. LE2: Oad	.5B 38
Coombe Ri. LE2: Oad	.5C 38
Co-operation St. LE19: End	.6H 33
Cooper Cl. LE2: Leic	.3G 35
LE9: Hun	.3A 42
Cooper Gdns. LE2: Oad	.5D 38
Cooper La. LE6: Ratby	.5D 16
Cooper's La. LE17: D Bas	.5F 61
Cooper's Nook LE7: E Gos	.2H 7
Cooper St. LE4: Leic	.4C 20
Copdale Rd. LE5: Leic	.2G 29
Copeland Av. LE3: Leic	.4E 19
Copeland Rd. LE4: Birs	.5F 13
Copgrove Cl. LE5: Ham	.1D 22
Copinger Rd. LE2: Leic	.2B 36
Coplow Av. LE5: Leic	.5G 29
Coplow Cres. LE7: Sys	.1E 15
Coppice, The LE2: Oad	.1H 37
LE4: Thurm	.4E 15
LE8: Count	.1E 55
LE19: Nar	.3C 42
LE67: Mark	.3C 8
Coppice Ct. LE4: Thurm	.4E 15
Copse, The LE2: Oad	.5G 39
LE7: Bush	.3H 31
Copse Cl. LE2: Leic	.6G 35
LE2: Oad	.2C 38
LE3: Leic E	.6F 25
Copthall Ho. LE18: Wig	.6B 36
Copthorne Cl. LE3: Leic	.1B 26
Copt Oak Ct. LE19: Nar	.3C 42

Copt Oak Rd. LE19: Nar	.2B 42
Corah Cl. LE7: Scra	.5G 23
Corah St. LE3: Leic	.5A 5 (2A 28)
Coral St. LE4: Leic	.4C 20
Corbet Cl. LE4: Leic	.2F 19
Cordelia Cl. LE5: Leic	.5G 21
Cordery Rd. LE5: Leic	.3B 30
Cordonnier Cl. LE9: B Ast	.3C 60
Corfield Ri. LE3: Leic	.4C 26
Coriander Rd. LE2: Leic	.7A 5 (3H 27)
Cork La. LE2: G Par	.1A 44
Cork St. LE5: Leic	.2E 29
Cornfield Cl. LE19: Litt	.4E 43
Cornwallis Av. LE4: Leic	.3F 19
Cornwall Rd. LE4: Leic	.4H 19
LE18: Wig	.1F 45
Cornwall St. LE19: End	.6H 33
Coronation Av. LE9: B Ast	.1A 60
LE18: Wig	.1H 45
Coronet Cl. LE7: Anst	.5G 11
Corporation Rd. LE4: Leic	.3B 20
Corshaw Wlk. LE5: Leic	.5F 21
Cort Cres. LE3: Leic	.3C 26
COSBY	.3F 53
Cosby La. LE9: Cosb	.1H 61
Cosby Rd. LE8: Count	.2B 54
LE9: B Ast	.1B 60
LE19: Litt	.5E 43
COSSINGTON	.1B 6
Cossington La. LE7: Coss	.2D 6
Cossington Rd. LE12: Sileby	.1A 6
Cossington St. LE4: Leic	.4D 20
Cossington Street Sports Cen.	.4D 20
Cotley Rd. LE4: Leic	.6C 12
Cotman Wlk. LE4: Leic	.5D 20
Cotswold Av. LE9: Cosb	.2G 53
Cotswold Grn. LE4: Leic	.6C 12
Cottage Cl. LE6: Ratby	.4C 16
Cottage Farm Cl. LE3: Brau	.3D 34
Cottage La. LE9: B Ast	.1C 60
LE67: Ulv	.1A 8
Cottage La. Ind. Est. LE9: B Ast	.1C 60
Cottage Rd. LE18: Wig	.2C 46
Cottage Row LE3: Brau	.1F 35
Cottagers Cl. LE2: Leic	.4A 36
Cottesbrooke Cl. LE18: Wig	.1B 46
Cottesmore Av. LE2: Oad	.5D 38
Cottesmore Rd. LE5: Leic	.6F 21
Cotton Cl. LE4: Leic	.6B 14
LE9: B Ast	.2C 60
Coulson Cl. LE8: Whet	.5A 44
Coulter Cl. LE7: Scra	.5F 23
Council St. LE17: Lut	.4G 63
COUNTESTHORPE	.2E 55
Countesthorpe Rd. LE8: Bla	.5F 45
LE8: Whet	.3G 53
LE9: Cosb	.3F 53
LE18: Wig	.2F 45
Counting Ho. Rd. LE2: Leic	.5B 28
Countryman M. LE16: G Bow	.1F 65
Countryman's Way LE7: E Gos	.1H 7
Countryman Way LE67: Mark	.3C 8
County Court	
Leicester	.6E 5 (3C 28)
Court Cl. LE9: K Mux	.2E 25
Courtenay Rd. LE3: Leic	.4G 19
Court Rd. LE2: G Par	.1B 44
LE7: Thurn	.3F 31
Courtyard Workshops LE16: Mkt H	.5D 64
Coventry Rd. LE9: Sap, B Ast, Crof	.6E 51
LE16: Mkt H	.4C 64
LE17: Lut	.5E 63
LE19: Nar	.6B 42
Coventry St. LE3: Leic	.2H 27
Coverack Wlk. LE5: Leic	.3H 29
Coverdale Rd. LE18: Wig	.2D 46
Coverside Rd. LE8: G Gle	.2D 48
Covert, The LE7: E Gos	.1H 7
Covert Cl. LE2: Oad	.3C 38
LE7: Sys	.6C 6
Covert La. LE7: Scra	.6F 23

Covett Way LE3: Leic	.2C 26
Cowdall Rd. LE3: Leic	.4C 26
Cow La. LE6: Ratby	.3A 16
Cowley Way LE5: Leic	.6E 23
Cowslip Cl. LE19: Nar	.3B 42
Coxwold Cl. LE5: Ham	.1C 22
Crabtree Cnr. LE2: Leic	.4C 36
Cradock Rd. LE2: Leic	.5D 28
Cradock St. LE1: Leic	.1D 28
Crafton St. E. LE1: Leic	.2F 4 (1C 28)
Crafton St. W. LE1: Leic	.2E 4 (1C 28)
Craftsmans Way LE7: E Gos	.2H 7
Craig Gdns. LE2: Leic	.1B 26
Craighall Rd. LE2: Leic	.1D 36
Craighill Wlk. LE2: Leic	.1D 36
Cranberry Cl. LE3: Brau	.5B 26
Cranborne Gdns. LE2: Oad	.1B 38
Cranbourne St. LE4: Leic	.5C 20
Cranbrook Rd. LE7: Thurn	.1F 31
Crane Ley Rd. LE6: Groby	.2E 17
Cranesbill Rd. LE5: Ham	.4C 22
Crane St. LE1: Leic	.1C 4 (6B 20)
Cranfield Rd. LE2: Leic	.3H 35
Cranmer Cl. LE8: Bla	.5A 44
Cranmer Dr. LE7: Sys	.6D 6
Cranmer St. LE3: Leic	.3H 27
Cransley Cl. LE5: Ham	.2C 22
Cranstone Cres. LE3: Glen	.6A 18
Crantock Cl. LE5: Leic	.4D 30
Cranwell Cl. LE5: Leic	.5B 30
Craven St. LE1: Leic	.1B 4 (6A 20)
Crawford Cl. LE3: Leic	.1F 27
Crawford Ho. LE18: Wig	.6C 36
Crawleyfield LE7: Anst	.1D 18
Crayburn Ho. LE3: Leic	.5E 19
Crayford Way LE5: Leic	.4D 22
Craythorne Way LE18: Wig	.1D 46
Creaton Ct. LE18: Wig	.1C 46
Creaton Rd. LE18: Wig	.1C 46
Crediton Cl. LE18: Wig	.3B 46
Crescent, The LE1: Leic	.6D 5 (3B 28)
LE8: Bla	.4B 44
LE8: G Gle	.3D 48
	(off Church Rd.)
LE16: Mkt H	.2E 65
LE18: Wig	.5E 37
Crescent Cl. LE16: Mkt H	.2E 65
Crescent Rd. LE17: Lut	.3G 63
Crescent St. LE1: Leic	.6D 5 (3B 28)
Cressida Ct. LE3: Brau	.5C 26
Cressida Pl. LE3: Leic	.5C 26
Cresswell Cl. LE4: Thurm	.5E 15
Crest Ri. LE2: Leic	.3H 21
Crestway, The LE8: Whet	.3H 43
Crete Av. LE18: Wig	.1E 45
Crick's Retreat LE8: G Gle	.2B 48
Crief Cl. LE5: Leic	.6E 23
Critchlow Rd. LE9: Hun	.3H 41
CROFT	.1G 51
Croft, The LE9: K Mux	.2E 25
Croft Av. LE2: Leic	.3G 35
Croft Dr. LE18: Wig	.4D 36
Crofters Cl. LE3: Glen	.5G 17
Crofters Dr. LE5: Leic	.6A 22
Croft Hill Rd. LE9: Hun	.5G 41
Croft La. LE9: Thurl	.3E 41
Croft Pasture Nature Reserve	.1F 51
Croft Rd. LE4: Beau L	.4C 12
LE9: Cosb	.6B 42
LE9: Thurl	.2E 41
Crofts, The LE67: Mark	.2B 8
Croft Way LE9: B Ast	.1C 60
Croftway LE67: Mark	.3B 8
Cromarty Cl. LE4: Leic	.2F 21
Cromer St. LE2: Leic	.4E 29
Cromford Av. LE18: Wig	.2G 45
Cromford Rd. LE9: Cosb	.1F 53
Cromford St. LE2: Leic	.1E 29
Cromford Way LE9: B Ast	.1D 60
Cromwell Cres. LE16: Mkt H	.5C 64
Cromwell Ho. LE2: Leic	.1B 36
Cromwell Rd. LE8: G Gle	.3D 48
CROPSTON	.1G 11

Cropston Cl. LE3: Leic 1B 26
Cropston Rd. LE7: Anst, Crop 1G 11
Cropthorne Av. LE5: Leic 2H 29
Crosby Rd. LE16: Mkt H 5E 65
Cross, The LE19: End 6H 33
Cross Farm Ct. LE9: S Stan 3C 50
Cross Hedge Cl. LE4: Leic 1G 19
Cross Keys Grn. LE5: Leic 6E 23
Crossleys LE8: Flec 6B 58
Crossley St. LE3: Glen 5A 18
Cross Rd. LE2: Leic 5E 29
Cross St. LE2: Oad 2A 38
  LE4: Leic 4C 20
  LE7: Sys .6F 7
  LE8: Bla 3B 44
  LE16: Mkt H 4E 65
  LE18: Wig 1B 46
  LE19: End 6H 33
Cross Wlk. LE5: Leic 1A 30
Crossway, The LE2: Leic 3B 36
  LE3: Brau 1E 35
Crossways, The LE4: Birs 4G 13
Crossways Ho's. LE8: Bla 3B 44
Crowan Dr. LE18: Wig 3A 46
Crowfoot Way LE9: B Ast 3B 60
Crowhurst Dr. LE3: Brau 1C 34
Crow La. LE3: Leic 4H 27
Crown Cl. LE8: G Gle 4D 48
Crown Court
  Leicester 6E 5 (3C 28)
CROWN HILLS 1A 30
Crown Hills Av. LE5: Leic 2G 29
Crown Hills Ri. LE5: Leic 2G 29
Croyde Cl. LE5: Leic 3H 29
Croyland Grn. LE5: Leic 1E 31
Cufflin Cl. LE6: Ratby 5D 16
Cuffling Cl. LE3: Leic 1B 26
Cuffling Dr. LE3: Leic 1B 26
Culham Av. LE5: Leic 5F 21
Culver Rd. LE3: Leic 5G 19
Culworth Dr. LE18: Wig 1C 46
Cumberland Rd. LE18: Wig 6A 36
Cumberland St. LE1: Leic . . .2A 4 (1A 28)
Cumberwell Dr. LE19: End 2F 43
Cunningham Dr. LE17: Lut 5E 63
Curlew Cl. LE7: Sys 5D 6
Curlew Wlk. LE5: Leic 6E 21
Curteys Cl. LE3: Leic 6F 27
Curtis Cl. LE8: Whet 4A 44
Curve (Performing Arts Cen.)
  . . . . .3E 4 (1C 28)
Curzon Av. LE4: Birs 5G 13
  LE18: Wig 2G 45
Curzon Cl. LE7: Quen 4H 7
Curzon Rd. LE2: Leic 2A 36
Curzon St. LE1: Leic 6D 20
Cutchel, The LE17: Lut 5G 63
  (off Church Gate)
Cutters Cl. LE19: Nar 4D 42
Cuttings, The LE7: Thurn 1F 31
Cygnet Cl. LE7: Sys 5D 6
Cyprus Rd. LE2: Leic 3A 36
Cyril St. LE3: Brau 1E 35

D

Dabey Cl. LE67: Mark 3B 8
Dairy Way LE8: Kib H 4H 59
Daisy Cl. LE6: Groby 2G 17
Dakyn Rd. LE5: Leic 1D 30
Dalby Av. LE4: Birs 3H 13
  LE7: Bush 2G 31
Dalby Dr. LE6: Groby 2F 17
Dalby Rd. LE7: Anst 4F 11
Dale Acre LE8: Count 1F 55
Dale Av. LE18: Wig 5C 36
Dale Cl. LE4: Birs 2G 13
  LE7: Anst 4E 11
Dales, The LE8: Count 1C 54
Dale St. LE2: Leic 2E 29
Dalkeith Rd. LE4: Leic 1F 21
Dalley Cl. LE7: Sys 1F 15

Dallison Cl. LE16: Mkt H 6D 64
Dalton Rd. LE5: Ham 2D 22
Danbury Dr. LE4: Leic 3H 19
Danbury Gdns. LE5: Leic 5H 21
Danbury Pl. LE5: Leic 5H 21
Dandees Cl. LE67: Mark 2C 8
Danehill LE6: Ratby 4C 16
DANE HILLS 1F 27
Danehurst Av. LE3: Leic 1F 27
Daneshill Rd. LE3: Leic 2G 27
Danes Mdw. Rd. LE4: Wan 2F 13
Dane St. LE3: Leic 2H 27
Dannett St. LE3: Leic 1H 27
Dannett Wlk. LE3: Leic 2H 27
Danvers Rd. LE3: Leic 4G 27
Darby Way LE19: Nar 4C 42
Darenth Dr. LE4: Leic 2E 19
Darien Way LE3: Brau 5A 26
Darker St. LE1: Leic 2C 4 (1B 28)
Darley Av. LE18: Wig 2G 45
Darley Rd. LE8: Bla 4A 44
Darley St. LE2: Leic 2E 29
Darlington Rd. LE3: Leic 5E 19
Darnall Rd. LE2: Leic 8A 5 (4H 27)
Dart Cl. LE2: Oad 4C 38
Dartford Rd. LE2: Leic 6H 27
Darwen Cl. LE3: Leic 5F 19
Darwin Cl. LE3: Brau 6A 26
  LE9: B Ast 2B 60
Dashwood Rd. LE2: Leic 4E 29
Davenport Av. LE2: Oad 4H 37
Davenport Rd. LE5: Leic 2B 30
  LE18: Wig 2A 46
Davett Cl. LE5: Leic 1B 30
David Av. LE4: Leic 6E 13
David Lloyd Leisure
  Leicester, Carlton Pk. 2D 42
  Leicester, Lubbesthorpe Way 1C 34
Davies Cl. LE16: Mkt H 1C 64
Davison Cl. LE5: Leic 1A 30
Dawlish Cl. LE5: Leic 2D 30
Daybell Cl. LE8: Whet 2H 43
Day St. LE4: Leic 2C 20
Deacon Cl. LE16: Mkt H 1C 64
  LE17: Bitt 2E 63
Deacon Rd. LE4: Leic 3D 12
Deacon St. LE2: Leic 7B 5 (3A 28)
Deancourt Rd. LE2: Leic 3D 36
Deanery Cres. LE4: Leic 3D 12
Dean Rd. LE4: Leic 4E 21
Deansburn Ho. LE3: Leic 5D 18
Debdale La. LE8: Smee W 6A 62
Deene Cl. LE16: L Bow 3F 65
Deepdale LE5: Leic 1H 29
Delaware Rd. LE5: Leic 3E 31
De Lisle Cl. LE16: Mkt H 4C 64
Dell, The LE5: Leic 4B 30
De Montfort Ct. LE7: Anst 5F 11
De Montfort Hall 8F 5 (4D 28)
De Montfort M. LE1: Leic 6C 5 (3B 28)
De Montfort M. LE1: Leic 6F 5 (3C 28)
De Montfort Pl. LE1: Leic 6F 5 (3C 28)
De Montfort Sq. LE1: Leic 7E 5 (3C 28)
  (not continuous)
De Montfort St. LE1: Leic 8E 5 (4C 28)
De Montfort University
  Bede Island Rd. 6A 5 (3A 28)
  Charles Frears Campus 5E 29
  Leicester City Campus . .6B 5 (3A 28)
Dempsey Cl. LE17: Lut 2G 63
Denacre Av. LE18: Wig 2G 45
Denbigh Cl. LE17: Lut 5G 63
  (off High St.)
Denbigh Pl. LE17: Lut 3G 63
Denbydale LE18: Wig 2D 46
Denegate Av. LE4: Birs 3F 13
Denham Cl. LE3: Leic 1A 26
Denis Cl. LE3: Leic 1F 27
Deniston Av. LE9: B Ast 6H 51
Denman La. LE9: Hun 3H 41
Denmark Rd. LE2: Leic 1A 36
Denmead Av. LE18: Wig 6E 37
Dennis David Cl. LE17: Lut 2G 63

Denton St. LE3: Leic 2F 27
Denton Wlk. LE18: Wig 1C 46
Derby Cl. LE9: B Ast 2C 60
Derry Wlk. LE4: Leic 1A 20
Dersingham Rd. LE4: Leic 3H 19
Derwent St. LE2: Leic 2E 29
Derwent Wlk. LE2: Oad 4C 38
Desford La. LE6: Ratby 6B 16
  LE9: K Mux, New U 1A 24
Desford Rd. LE9: Des, Thurl 1B 32
  LE9: K Mux, Des 1D 24
  LE9: Thurl 5A 32
  LE19: End, Thurl 3D 32
  LE19: Nar 3D 42
Devana Rd. LE2: Leic 4E 29
Devenports Hill LE7: Bush 2H 31
De Verdon Rd. LE17: Lut 5E 63
Devitt Way LE9: B Ast 3B 60
Devonia Rd. LE2: Oad 5D 38
Devonshire Av. LE18: Wig 2G 45
Devonshire Cl. LE2: Oad 5B 38
Devonshire Rd. LE4: Leic 4A 20
Devonshire Wlk. LE2: Oad 6C 38
Devon Way LE5: Leic 2H 29
Dicken, The LE8: Whet 4H 43
Dickens Ct. LE3: Leic 2E 27
Dickinson Way LE4: Thurm 4D 14
Didsbury St. LE3: Leic 3C 26
Digby Cl. LE3: Leic 4F 27
Digby Hall LE2: Leic 2H 37
Dillon Grn. LE3: Leic 4D 18
Dillon Ri. LE3: Leic 5D 18
Dillon Rd. LE3: Leic 5D 18
Dillon Way LE3: Leic 4D 18
Dimmingsdale Cl. LE7: Anst 4G 11
Dingley Av. LE4: Leic 4E 21
Dingley Link LE18: Wig 6H 37
Dingley Rd. LE16: G Bow 1G 65
Dingley Ter. LE16: Mkt H 3E 65
Discovery Rd. LE4: Leic 4B 20
Diseworth St. LE2: Leic 2E 29
Disney Cl. LE9: S Stan 3B 50
Disraeli Cl. LE8: Kib B 5H 59
Disraeli St. LE2: Leic 2G 35
Ditchling Av. LE3: Leic 1E 27
Dixon Dr. LE2: Leic 4E 29
Dobney Av. LE7: Quen 3G 7
Doddridge Rd. LE16: Mkt H 2D 64
Dog and Gun La. LE8: Whet 6H 43
Dogwood Cl. LE2: Oad 3A 38
Dolphin Sq. LE1: Leic 4D 4
Dominion Rd. LE3: Glen, Leic 5A 18
Dominus Way LE19: Brau 1B 34
Donald Cl. LE4: Leic 1H 21
Donaldson Rd. LE4: Leic 5C 20
Donata Ho. LE17: Lut 4G 63
Doncaster Rd. LE4: Leic 4D 20
Donnett Cl. LE5: Leic 1B 30
Donnington St. LE2: Leic 2E 29
Dorchester Cl. LE8: Bla 5C 44
  LE18: Wig 3B 46
Dorchester Rd. LE2: Leic 2E 27
Dore Rd. LE5: Leic 3E 29
Dorfold Wlk. LE4: Leic 4F 21
Dorothy Av. LE2: G Par 6F 35
  LE4: Thurm 5B 14
Dorothy Rd. LE5: Leic 2F 29
Dorset Av. LE3: Glen 4A 18
  LE18: Wig 6A 36
Dorset St. LE4: Leic 5C 20
Double Rail Cl. LE18: Wig 2G 45
Doudney Cl. LE9: S Stan 4B 50
Douglas Bader Dr. LE17: Lut 2G 63
Douglas Ct. LE2: Leic 8B 5
Douglass Dr. LE16: Mkt H 1E 65
Dovecote Cl. LE9: Sap 6B 50
Dovecote Rd. LE9: Crof 6G 41
Dovedale Av. LE8: Bla 4B 44
Dovedale Ct. LE2: Leic 6G 29
Dovedale Rd. LE2: Leic 6G 29
  LE4: Thurm 4C 14
Dover Ho. LE1: Leic 5E 5 (2C 28)
Dove Ri. LE2: Oad 3C 38

Dover St.—Enderby Rd.

Dover St. LE1: Leic 5E 5 (2C 28)
LE8: Kib B 5H 59
Downham Av. LE4: Leic 3A 20
Downing Dr. LE5: Leic 4C 30
Down St. LE4: Leic 4D 20
Drage Cl. LE17: Lut 2H 63
Draper St. LE2: Leic 4E 29
Drayton Rd. LE3: Leic 6C 18
Dribdale LE8: Flec 6C 58
Drinkstone Rd. LE5: Leic 2G 29
Drive, The LE4: Birs 5G 13
LE7: Scra 5F 23
LE8: Count 2B 54
LE8: Kib B 5B 62
Driveway, The LE7: Bush 2G 31
Dronfield St. LE5: Leic 2E 29
Drovers Way LE19: Nar 4D 42
Drumcliff Rd. LE5: Leic 1E 31
Drummond Rd. LE4: Leic 2B 20
LE19: End 6G 33
Drury La. LE2: Oad 3H 37
Dryden St. LE1: Leic 2E 4 (6C 20)
Dudleston Cl. LE5: Leic 2A 30
Dudley Av. LE5: Leic 1C 30
Dudley Cl. LE5: Leic 1C 30
Dudley Whenham Cl. LE7: Sys 5E 7
Duffield Av. LE18: Wig 5D 36
Duffield St. LE2: Leic 2E 29
Dukes Cl. LE4: Thurm 4D 14
LE18: Wig 6D 36
Dukes Dr. LE2: Leic 5E 29
Dukes Dr. Flats LE2: Leic 5E 29
Duke St. LE1: Leic 6D 5 (3B 28)
Dulverton Cl. LE18: Wig 3B 46
Dulverton Rd. LE3: Leic 3G 27
Dumbleton Av. LE3: Leic 6G 27
Dunbar Rd. LE4: Leic 3G 21
Dunblane Av. LE4: Leic 1F 21
Duncan Av. LE9: Hun 3H 41
Duncan Rd. LE2: Leic 2H 35
Duncombe Rd. LE3: Leic 4E 19
Dundee Rd. LE8: Bla 5B 44
Dundonald Rd. LE4: Leic 4C 20
Dunholme Rd. LE4: Leic 4G 21
Dunire Cl. LE4: Leic 2G 19
Dunkirk St. LE1: Leic 6E 5 (2C 28)
Dunley Way LE17: Lut 3G 63
Dunlin Rd. LE5: Leic 6E 21
Dunmore Rd. LE16: L Bow 5F 65
Dunnock Ct. LE3: Leic 5C 18
Dunslade Cl. LE16: L Bow 4G 65
Dunslade Gro. LE16: L Bow 4G 65
Dunslade Rd. LE16: L Bow 4F 65
Duns La. LE3: Leic 5A 5 (2A 28)
Dunstall Av. LE3: Brau 5B 26
Dunster St. LE3: Leic 2F 27
Dunsville Wlk. LE4: Leic 2F 21
DUNTON BASSETT 5F 61
Dunton La. LE17: Leire 6B 60
Dunton Rd. LE9: B Ast 3D 60
LE17: Leire 6B 60
Dunton St. LE3: Leic 6H 19
LE18: Wig 2F 45
Dupont Cl. LE3: Glen 6B 18
Dupont Gdns. LE3: Glen 6B 18
Durban Rd. LE4: Beau L 4C 12
Durham Dr. LE18: Wig 5C 36
Durnford Rd. LE18: Wig 3A 46
Durston Cl. LE5: Leic 3D 30
Duxbury Rd. LE5: Leic 6G 21
Dwyer Cl. LE7: Sys 1D 14
Dysart Way LE1: Leic 6C 20
Dyson Cl. LE17: Lut 3G 63

E

Eagle Cl. LE9: B Ast 6A 52
Eaglesfield End LE17: Leire 6B 60
Ealing Rd. LE2: Leic 6B 28
Eamont Cl. LE2: Leic 6H 35
Eamont Grn. LE2: Leic 6H 35
Earl Howe St. LE2: Leic 3D 28
Earl Howe Ter. LE3: Leic 2H 27
Earl Russell St. LE2: Leic 3G 35
Earls Cl. LE4: Thurm 4D 14
Earls Cl. Ind. Est. LE4: Thurm 4D 14
Earl Shilton Rd.
LE9: Thurl . . . . .2A 40 & 6A 32
Earl Smith Cl. LE8: Whet 4A 44
Earl St. LE1: Leic 2E 4 (1C 28)
Earl's Way LE4: Thurm 4D 14
Earlswood Rd. LE5: Leic 4D 30
Earnshaw Rd. LE9: S Stan 2C 50
East Av. LE2: Leic 5E 29
LE7: Sys 5G 7
LE8: Whet 3H 43
E. Bond St. LE1: Leic 2C 4 (1B 28)
Eastcourt Rd. LE2: Leic 3E 37
Eastern Blvd. LE2: Leic 8A 5 (4A 28)
EAST FARNDON 6A 64
Eastfield Ct. LE3: Leic 2E 27
Eastfield Rd. LE3: Leic 2F 27
LE4: Thurm 3D 14
East Gates LE1: Leic 3C 4 (1B 28)
EAST GOSCOTE 2H 7
E. Goscote Ind. Est.
LE7: E Gos 2G 7
Eastleigh Rd. LE3: Leic 4G 27
East Link LE19: Brau 2C 34
Eastmere Rd. LE18: Wig 6H 37
East Pk. Rd. LE5: Leic 3E 29
East Rd. LE4: Birs 6G 13
East St. LE1: Leic 5E 5 (2C 28)
LE2: Oad .3A 38
LE16: Mkt H 3C 64
East Wlk. LE6: Ratby 4C 16
Eastway Rd. LE18: Wig 5F 37
Eastwood Rd. LE2: Leic 4H 35
Ebchester Cl. LE2: Leic 6G 35
Ebchester Rd. LE2: Leic 6G 35
Ecob's Way LE18: Wig 3B 46
EcoHouse 2D 26
Edale Cl. LE3: Leic 4C 26
Eddystone Rd. LE5: Leic 6E 23
Eden Cl. LE2: Oad 3C 38
Eden Gdns. LE4: Beau L 4C 12
Edenhall Cl. LE2: Oad 5D 38
LE4: Leic .2F 21
Edenhurst Av. LE3: Brau 2D 34
Eden Rd. LE2: Oad 3C 38
Edensor St. LE4: Leic 2E 21
Eden Way LE2: Leic 1D 44
Edgbaston Cl. LE4: Beau L 4D 12
Edgecote Ct. LE5: Leic 5G 21
Edgefield Cl. LE5: Ham 2B 22
Edgehill Cl. LE8: G Gle 3D 48
Edgehill Rd. LE4: Leic 3G 21
Edgeley Cl. LE3: Leic 4E 19
Edgeley Rd. LE8: Count 1E 55
Edinburgh Cl. LE16: Mkt H 2E 65
Edith Av. LE3: Brau 2E 35
Edith Murphy Cl. LE4: Birs 5F 13
Edmonton Rd. LE1: Leic 1F 4 (6C 20)
Edna Bowley Ct. *LE16: Mkt H 4E 65*
(off Springfield St.)
Edward Av. LE3: Brau 1D 34
Edward Cl. LE2: Oad 4C 38
Edward Dr. LE2: G Par 2E 45
Edward Rd. LE2: Leic 5D 28
LE8: Flec .6B 58
LE16: Mkt H 2C 64
Edward St. LE5: Leic 6E 21
LE7: Anst .5G 11
Egerton Av. LE4: Leic 3A 20
Egginton St. LE5: Leic 3E 29
Eglantine Cl. LE2: Oad 2A 38
Eider Cl. LE8: Whet 1H 53
Eileen Av. LE4: Leic 3A 20
Elder Cl. LE3: Leic 2D 18
Eldon St. LE1: Leic 2E 4 (1C 28)
Elfin Gro. LE17: D Bas 5G 61
Elgin Av. LE3: Leic 5D 18
Elisha Cl. LE9: S Stan 3C 50
Elizabethan Way LE17: Lut 3H 63
Elizabeth Cl. LE8: Flec 6E 59
Elizabeth Ct. LE3: Glen 4H 17
LE9: S Stan 3B 50
LE18: Wig 1A 46
Elizabeth Cres. LE18: Wig 5D 36
Elizabeth Dr. LE2: Oad 5C 38
LE4: Thurm 3C 14
Elizabeth Gdns. LE8: Whet 4H 43
Elizabeth Ho. LE2: Leic 5F 5
LE3: Leic .6E 19
Elizabeth Pk. Sports & Community Cen.
. . . . .3C 14
Elizabeth Rd. LE8: Flec 6E 59
Elizabeth St. LE5: Leic 2G 29
Elland Rd. LE3: Leic 2H 25
Ellesmere Pl. LE3: Leic 5F 27
Ellesmere Rd. LE3: Leic 5F 27
Elliot Cl. LE2: Oad 5D 38
LE8: Kib B 5A 62
LE8: Whet 1A 54
Elliott Dr. LE3: Leic E 4H 25
LE4: Thurm 5E 15
Elliott Rd. LE4: Leic 1H 19
Elliotts End LE7: Scra 5G 23
Elliotts Yd. LE8: Count 2F 55
Ellis Av. LE4: Leic 4C 20
Ellis Cl. LE3: Glen 5H 17
Ellis Dr. LE9: Leic E 4F 25
Ellis Flds. LE2: Oad 6E 39
Ellison Cl. LE9: S Stan 2B 50
LE18: Wig 3F 45
Ellis St. LE7: Anst 5F 11
Ellwood Cl. LE5: Leic 3B 30
Elm Av. LE17: Lut 4F 63
Elm Cl. LE6: Groby 3F 17
Elm Ct. LE2: Leic 8B 5
Elmcroft Av. LE5: Leic 6B 22
Elmdale St. LE4: Leic 3C 20
Elm Dr. LE16: Mkt H 4B 64
Elmfield Av. LE2: Leic 4E 29
LE4: Birs .4F 13
Elmfield Gdns. LE2: Leic 4E 29
Elmhirst Rd. LE17: Lut 5F 63
Elmhurst Cl. LE19: Nar 4C 42
Elms, The LE8: Bla 4B 44
LE8: Count 1E 55
LE67: Mark 1B 8
Elms Cl. LE2: Oad 5B 38
Elms Ct. LE2: Leic 1E 37
LE7: Anst .5G 11
Elms La. LE8: Bur O 2H 49
Elmsleigh Av. LE2: Leic 6F 29
Elms Rd. LE2: Leic 6E 29
Elms Rd. Ho's. LE2: Leic 1F 37
Elmsthorpe Ri. LE3: Leic 4E 27
Elm Tree Av. LE3: Glen 5G 17
Elmtree Cl. LE5: Ham 3C 22
Elm Tree Ct. LE2: Leic 1F 37
Elm Tree Gdns. LE2: Leic 1F 37
Elm Tree Rd. LE9: Cosb 3E 53
Elmwood Row LE2: Leic 5C 36
Elsadene Av. LE4: Leic 2D 20
Elsadene Ct. LE2: Leic 6F 29
Elsadene Wlk. LE4: Leic 1C 20
Elsalene Cl. LE6: Groby 6G 9
Elsalene Dr. LE6: Groby 6G 9
Elsham Cl. LE3: Leic 2B 26
Elston Flds. LE2: Leic 3B 36
Elstree Av. LE5: Leic 5E 23
Elsworthy Wlk. LE3: Leic 1B 26
Elwells Av. LE17: D Bas 5F 61
Elwin Av. LE18: Wig 5F 37
Emberton Cl. LE18: Wig 6H 37
Emburn Ho. LE3: Leic 5D 18
Emerson Cl. LE4: Leic 2E 19
Emperor Way LE8: Whet 1H 53
Empingham Dr. LE7: Sys 6G 7
Empire Rd. LE3: Leic 6H 19
ENDERBY 6H 33
Enderby (Park & Ride) 5C 34
Enderby La. LE19: End, Leic E 1F 33
Enderby Leisure Cen. 1D 42
Enderby Rd. LE8: Bla, Whet 2G 43
LE9: Thurl 6A 32

80 A-Z Leicester

Enderby Rd. Ind. Est. LE8: Whet 2H 43
Englefield Rd. LE5: Leic 2D 30
Englewood Cl. LE4: Leic 4H 19
Ennerdale Cl. LE2: Oad 5D 38
Ensbury Gdns. LE5: Leic 4B 30
Enterprise Ho. LE9: K Mux 1D 24
Epping Way LE2: Leic 6G 35
Epsom Rd. LE4: Leic 3D 20
Equity Rd. LE3: Leic 3H 27
    LE19: End 6G 33
Erdyngton Rd. LE3: Leic 3D 26
Erith Rd. LE2: Leic 6B 36
Ernee Cl. LE3: Glen 6B 18
Erringtons Cl. LE2: Oad 1A 48
Erskine St. LE1: Leic 2E 4 (1C 28)
Ervington Ct. LE19: Brau 3B 34
Ervin's Lock Rd. LE18: Wig 3G 45
Eskdale Cl. LE2: Oad 5D 38
Eskdale Rd. LE4: Leic 2H 19
Essex Gdns. LE16: Mkt H 5C 64
Essex Rd. LE4: Leic 4G 21
    LE18: Wig 6B 36
Estelle Ho. LE4: Thurm 5C 14
Estima Cl. LE2: Leic 1E 37
Estley Rd. LE9: B Ast 6A 52
Estoril Av. LE18: Wig 5G 37
Ethel Rd. LE5: Leic 3G 29
Eton Cl. LE2: Leic 1D 36
Eunice Av. LE9: Hun 4H 41
Euro Bus. Pk. LE16: L Bow 2G 65
Euston St. LE2: Leic 6B 28
Evelyn Dr. LE3: Leic 5G 27
Evelyn Rd. LE3: Brau 5C 26
Everard Way LE19: End 4D 34
Everest Ct. LE1: Leic 1F 4 (6D 20)
Everett Cl. LE4: Thurm 5E 15
Everson Cl. LE9: B Ast 2B 60
Every St. LE1: Leic 4D 4 (2B 28)
Evesham Rd. LE3: Leic 5G 27
EVINGTON 5B 30
EVINGTON CENTRE 2A 30
Evington Cl. LE5: Leic 3G 29
Evington Cl. LE5: Leic 4A 30
Evington Dr. LE5: Leic 4F 29
Evington Footpath LE2: Leic 3D 28
Evington La. LE5: Leic 4F 29
    (not continuous)
Evington M. LE5: Leic 4B 30
Evington Parks Rd. LE2: Leic 4F 29
Evington Pl. LE2: Leic 3E 29
Evington Pool 4C 30
Evington Rd. LE2: Leic 3D 28
    LE5: Leic 2D 29
Evington St. LE2: Leic 2D 28
Evington Valley Gdns. LE5: Leic 3F 29
Evington Valley Rd. LE5: Leic 4F 29
Excalibur Cl. LE3: Leic E 5G 25
Exchange, The LE2: Leic 5A 36
Exeter Rd. LE18: Wig 6D 36
Exmoor Av. LE4: Leic 5H 19
Exmoor Cl. LE18: Wig 2B 46
Exploration Dr. LE4: Leic 4A 20
Exton Cl. LE7: Sys 1G 15
Exton Rd. LE5: Leic 6G 21
Eyebrook Cl. LE5: Ham 2C 22
Eynsford Cl. LE2: Leic 1G 37
EYRES MONSELL 6H 35

Facers La. LE7: Scra 5F 23
Factory La. LE16: Mkt H 3D 64
Fairbourne Rd. LE3: Brau 6E 27
Fairburn Ho. LE3: Leic 5D 18
Faircharm Trad. Est. LE3: Leic 5H 27
Fairefield Cres. LE3: Glen 3B 18
Faire Rd. LE3: Glen 4B 18
Fairestone Av. LE3: Glen 5A 18
Fairfax Cl. LE4: Leic 3G 21
Fairfax Ct. LE8: G Gle 3D 48
Fairfax Rd. LE4: Leic 3G 21
    LE16: Mkt H 4D 64

Fairfield Rd. LE2: Oad 3B 38
    LE16: Mkt H 2C 64
Fairfield St. LE5: Leic 2E 29
    LE18: Wig 1F 45
Fairford Av. LE5: Leic 4B 30
Fairhaven Rd. LE7: Anst 3G 11
Fairholme Rd. LE2: Leic 3D 36
Fair Isle Way LE8: Count 2F 55
Fairstone Hill LE2: Oad 5B 38
Fairview Av. LE8: Whet 4H 43
Fairway LE8: Kib B 5B 62
    LE16: Mkt H 2C 64
Fairway, The LE2: Leic 3A 36
    LE2: Oad 6H 29
    LE8: Bla 4A 44
    LE9: K Mux 3F 25
Falcon Cl. LE3: Leic E 5E 25
    LE9: B Ast 6A 52
Falconer Cres. LE3: Leic 5C 18
Falcon Rd. LE7: Anst 6E 11
Faldo Cl. LE4: Leic 6C 14
Fallow Cl. LE8: Whet 6H 43
Fallow Cl. LE3: B Ast 2B 60
Fallowfield Rd. LE5: Leic 3D 30
Falmouth Dr. LE18: Wig 2A 46
Falmouth Rd. LE5: Leic 3H 29
Faraday Cl. LE9: B Ast 3B 60
Faringdon Av. LE17: Lut 4H 63
Farleigh Av. LE18: Wig 5F 37
Farleigh Cl. LE9: B Ast 6A 52
Farley Rd. LE2: Leic 1F 37
Farley Way LE9: K Mux 1F 25
Farm Cl. LE4: Birs 4H 13
    LE19: Litt 4E 43
Farm Cl., The LE2: Leic 4B 36
Farmers Cl. LE3: Glen 5G 17
Farmway LE3: Brau 2C 34
Farndale LE18: Wig 1D 46
Farndale Cl. LE2: Leic 8B 5 (4A 28)
Farndale Vw. LE16: Mkt H 4A 64
Farndon Ct. LE16: Mkt H 4C 64
Farndon Dr. LE9: S Stan 3A 50
Farndon Rd. LE16: Mkt H 5B 64
Farnham St. LE5: Leic 1E 29
Farnworth Cl. LE4: Leic 2F 21
Far Pastures Rd. LE4: Birs 2F 13
Farrier La. LE4: Leic 2F 19
Farrier's Way LE7: E Gos 2H 7
Farringdon St. LE5: Leic 6E 21
Farringdon Wlk. LE5: Leic 6E 21
    (off Farringdon St.)
Farr Wood Cl. LE6: Groby 2E 17
Farthingdale Cl. LE9: Cosb 2G 53
Fastnet Rd. LE5: Leic 6E 23
Faversham Cl. LE3: Leic 1A 26
Fayrhurst Rd. LE2: Leic 3A 36
Featherby Dr. LE2: G Par 6E 35
Featherstone Dr. LE2: Leic 1C 44
Feature Rd. LE4: Thurm 2C 14
Federation St. LE19: End 6G 33
FEILDING PALMER HOSPITAL 4H 63
Feilding Way LE17: Lut 3G 63
Feldspar Cl. LE19: End 4G 33
Fell Cl. LE8: Flec 6F 59
Felley Way LE3: Leic 5G 19
Felstead Rd. LE4: Leic 1H 19
Fencote Rd. LE5: Ham 1C 22
Fenners Cl. LE4: Beau L 4C 12
Fenton Cl. LE2: Oad 6A 38
Fenwick Rd. LE2: Oad 5E 39
Fermain Cl. LE5: Leic 2D 30
Fern Bank LE5: Leic 1E 29
Fern Cl. LE7: Thurn 2E 31
Fern Cres. LE6: Groby 1D 16
Ferndale Dr. LE6: Ratby 5D 16
Ferndale Rd.
    LE2: Leic 3D 36
    LE4: Thurm 5C 14
Ferndown Cl. LE3: Leic 1A 26
Fernfield Cl. LE16: L Bow 2G 65
Fernhurst Rd. LE3: Brau 1D 34
Fernie Cl. LE2: Oad 5C 38
Fernie Dene LE8: G Gle 2E 49

Fernie Rd. LE5: Leic 6F 21
    LE16: Mkt H 3E 65
Fernlea LE19: Nar 2B 42
Fern Ley Cl. LE16: L Bow 4G 65
Fernleys Cl. LE4: Leic 2F 19
Fern Ri. LE5: Leic 4C 22
Ferrars Ct. LE3: Brau 6B 26
Ferrers Ri. LE6: Groby 2E 17
Ferrers Rd. LE17: Lut 5E 63
Ferrers St. LE2: Leic 4B 36
Ferrous Cl. LE4: Leic 5E 21
Festival Av. LE4: Thurm 5B 14
Field Cl. LE3: Leic E 4H 25
    LE19: Litt 4E 43
Field Ct. Rd. LE6: Groby 2F 17
Fieldfare Wlk. LE5: Leic 6E 21
Fieldgate Cres. LE4: Birs 3E 13
Field Ga. Gdns. LE3: Glen 3A 18
FIELD HEAD 3D 8
Fieldhead Cl. LE16: Mkt H 3B 64
Fieldhead Rd. LE67: Mark 1A 8
Fieldhouse Rd. LE4: Leic 2D 20
Fieldhurst Av. LE3: Brau 1C 34
Fielding La. LE6: Ratby 5D 16
Fielding Rd. LE4: Birs 4F 13
Field Leys Way LE4: Wan 2F 13
Fields Ct. LE18: Wig 2G 45
Field Vw. LE4: Thurm 4E 15
    LE7: Sys 6C 6
Fieldway, The LE9: B Ast 2B 60
Fieldway Cres. LE8: G Gle 2D 48
Filbert St. LE2: Leic 8A 5 (4A 28)
Filbert St. E. LE2: Leic 8C 5 (4B 28)
Filbert Village LE2: Leic 8A 5 (4A 28)
Filbert Way LE2: Leic 8A 5 (4A 28)
Finch Cl. LE3: Leic 2C 26
Finch Way LE19: Nar 4C 42
Fineshade Av. LE3: Leic 5G 19
Finsbury Rd. LE4: Leic 4E 21
Finson Cl. LE18: Wig 6F 37
Fiona Dr. LE7: Thurn 2F 31
Firestone Cl. LE3: Leic 1A 26
Firfield Av. LE4: Birs 4G 13
Firs, The LE7: Sys 1E 15
    LE16: Mkt H 3B 64
    LE18: Wig 5G 37
Fir Tree Av. LE8: Count 1E 55
    LE17: Lut 4F 63
Fir Tree Cl. LE18: Wig 4E 37
Fir Tree La. LE6: Groby 1E 17
Fir Tree Wlk. LE16: Mkt H 2D 64
Firtree Wlk. LE6: Groby 2E 17
Fisher Cl. LE7: Coss 1B 6
    LE9: S Stan 3A 50
Fishley Cl. LE3: Glen 6H 17
Fishponds Cl. LE3: Glen 5H 17
Fishpools LE3: Brau 2C 34
Fitness First (for Women) Health Club
    Leicester 3E 4
Fitness First Health Club
    Leicester Central 5A 28
Fitzroy St. LE3: Leic 2H 27
Fitzwilliam Cl. LE2: Oad 5D 38
Flamborough Rd. LE5: Leic 6D 22
Flamingo Dr. LE8: Whet 1H 53
Flatholme Rd. LE5: Leic 5E 23
Flatten Way LE7: Sys 5E 7
Flaxfield Cl. LE6: Groby 2F 17
Flaxland Cl. LE16: L Bow 3G 65
Flax Rd. LE4: Leic 3D 20
FLECKNEY 6B 58
Fleckney Ind. Est. LE8: Flec 6C 58
Fleckney Rd. LE8: Kib B 5F 59
    LE8: Sad 6F 59
    LE18: Kilby 3E 57
Fleckney Sports & Leisure Cen. 4B 58
Fleet, The LE9: S Stan 1C 50
Fleet St. LE1: Leic 2E 4 (1C 28)
Fleetwood Cl. LE16: Mkt H 5C 64
Fleetwood Ct. LE2: Leic 6C 28
Fleetwood Gdns. LE16: Mkt H 5C 64
Fleetwood Rd. LE2: Leic 6C 28
Fletcher Mall LE4: Beau L 1E 19

Fletcher Rd. LE9: S Stan	.2C 50
Fletchers Cl. LE19: Nar	.4D 42
Fletcher's Way LE7: E Gos	.2H 7
Fletton Cl. LE4: Leic	.2A 22
Flora St. LE3: Leic	.2H 27
Florence Av. LE18: Wig	.2G 45
Florence Rd. LE5: Leic	.1E 29
Florence St. LE2: Leic	.2A 36
Florence Wragg Way	
LE2: Oad	.5D 38
Floyd Cl. LE4: Leic	.6C 14
Fludes Ct. LE2: Oad	.4C 38
Fludes La. LE2: Oad	.4C 38
Folley Rd. LE8: Kib B	.5G 59
Folville Ri. LE3: Leic	.5E 27
Fontwell Dr. LE2: Leic	.4F 35
Forbes Cl. LE3: Glen	.6A 18
Ford, The LE2: G Par	.3C 44
LE8: Bla	.3C 44
Ford Cl. LE2: Leic	.6G 35
Ford Ri. LE2: Leic	.6G 35
Fordview Cl. LE8: G Gle	.2C 48
Forest Av. LE4: Thurm	.3B 14
Forest Cl. LE6: Groby	.2D 16
Forest Ct. LE2: Leic	.8B 5
Forest Dr. LE9: K Mux	.3E 25
Foresters Cl. LE3: Glen	.5H 17
Foresters Row LE7: E Gos	.2H 7
Forest Ga. LE7: Anst	.5F 11
Forest Ho. La. LE3: Leic E	.6E 25
Forest Ri. LE2: Oad	.3C 38
LE6: Groby	.2D 16
LE7: Thurn	.2F 31
LE9: Leic E	.4F 25
Forest Rd. LE5: Leic	.5E 21
LE9: Hun	.3H 41
LE19: End, Nar	.4F 33
LE67: Mark	.2A 8
Forest Vw. LE6: Groby	.2D 16
Forge Cl. LE3: Glen	.5G 17
LE8: Flec	.5B 58
Forge Cnr. LE8: Bla	.3B 44
Forge Ct. LE7: Sys	.5F 7
Forrester Cl. LE9: Cosb	.2G 53
Forryan Cl. LE9: Cosb	.3F 53
Forryans Cl. LE18: Wig	.3C 46
Forsythia Cl. LE17: Lut	.4E 63
Fosse Cl. LE3: Brau	.3D 34
LE19: End	.1F 43
Fosse La. LE3: Leic	.6G 19
Fosse Pk. Av. LE19: Brau	.4D 34
Fosse Pk. Shop. Cen.	
LE19: Brau	.4D 34
Fosse Pk. Sth. LE19: End	.4D 34
Fosse Plaza LE19: End	.4D 34
Fosse Rd. Central	
LE3: Leic	.2G 27
Fosse Rd. Nth. LE3: Leic	.1G 27
Fosse Rd. Sth. LE3: Leic	.5F 27
Fosse Way LE7: Rat W, Sys	.1D 14
FOSTON	.3A 56
Foston Ga. LE18: Wig	.3C 46
Foston La. LE8: Fost	.2A 56
LE8: Peat M, Fost	.6H 55
Foston Rd. LE8: Count, Fost	.1F 55
Fothergill Cl. LE16: L Bow	.3G 65
Foulds La. LE8: Bla	.2A 44
Foundry La. LE1: Leic	.6C 20
LE7: Sys	.6D 6
Foundry Sq. LE1: Leic	.1E 4 (6B 20)
Fountains Av. LE2: Leic	.6H 35
Fount Ct. LE16: Mkt H	.5E 65
Fowler Cl. LE4: Leic	.1G 19
Foxbank Ind. Est. LE9: S Stan	.2B 50
Fox Cl. LE8: Flec	.6F 59
Fox Covert LE8: Whet	.6H 43
Fox Covert LE7: Thurc	.2C 12
Foxcroft Cl. LE3: Leic	.1G 35
Fox End LE9: Thurl	.6A 32
Foxfield Cl. LE17: Lut	.5H 63
Foxglove Cl. LE7: E Gos	.1H 7
LE9: B Ast	.3C 60
LE19: Nar	.3C 42

Foxglove Dr. LE6: Groby	.2G 17
Foxglove Rd. LE5: Ham	.3C 22
Foxhill Dr. LE2: G Par	.6E 35
Foxholes Rd. LE3: Leic	.3B 26
Fox Hollow LE2: Oad	.5D 38
LE7: Crop	.1H 11
LE7: E Gos	.1H 7
Foxhunter Dr. LE2: Oad	.3H 37
Foxhunter Gdns. LE19: End	.1F 43
Foxhunter Rdbt. LE19: End	.1F 43
Fox La. LE1: Leic	.3D 4 (1B 28)
LE9: K Mux	.2D 24
Foxon St. LE3: Leic	.5A 5 (2H 27)
Foxon Way LE3: Brau	.6B 26
Fox Pond La. LE2: Oad	.2A 48
Fox St. LE1: Leic	.4F 4 (2C 28)
Foxton Lock Cl. LE18: Wig	.3G 45
Foxton Rd. LE5: Ham	.2C 22
Framework Knitters Cotts.	
LE2: Oad	.3A 38
Framland Ho. LE2: Leic	.2D 28
Frampton Av. LE3: Leic	.2F 27
Frances Way LE19: End	.4B 34
Franche Rd. LE3: Leic	.1G 27
Francis Av. LE3: Brau	.2D 34
Francis Ct. LE2: Leic	.3G 35
Francis St. LE2: Leic	.6F 29
Francis Wlk. LE2: Leic	.5G 29
Franklin Way LE8: Whet	.6H 43
Franklyn Rd. LE2: Leic	.3F 35
Frankson Av. LE3: Brau	.6E 27
Fraser Cl. LE1: Leic	.1F 4 (6C 20)
Frederick Rd. LE5: Leic	.1E 29
Frederick St. LE18: Wig	.6F 37
Fredscott Cl. LE5: Leic	.6E 23
Freeboard Rd. LE3: Brau	.2D 34
Freehold Rd. LE4: Birs	.6G 13
Freehold St. LE1: Leic	.6D 20
Free La. LE1: Leic	.3D 4 (1B 28)
Freeman Rd. Nth. LE5: Leic	.6H 21
Freemans Ct. LE6: Ratby	.5D 16
Freemans Holt LE2: Leic	.2G 35
Freeman's Way LE7: E Gos	.1H 7
Freemantle Rd. LE2: Leic	.6G 29
Freemen's Comn. Ho's.	
LE2: Leic	.5C 28
Freemen's Comn. Rd.	
LE2: Leic	.5B 28
Freemen's Comn. Trad. Est.	
LE2: Leic	.5B 28
Freer Cl. LE8: Bla	.3B 44
LE18: Wig	.3C 46
Freeschool La. LE1: Leic	.3B 4 (1A 28)
French Rd. LE5: Leic	.6G 21
Frensham Cl. LE2: Oad	.5A 38
Freshwater Cl. LE18: Wig	.4B 46
Fretter Cl. LE9: B Ast	.3D 60
Frewen Dr. LE9: Sap	.5B 50
Frewin St. LE5: Leic	.6G 21
Friar La. LE1: Leic	.5B 5 (2A 28)
Friars C'way. LE1: Leic	.3A 4 (1A 28)
Friday St. LE1: Leic	.1B 4 (6A 20)
Friendship Ho. LE4: Leic	.5D 20
Frinton Av. LE5: Leic	.3D 30
Frisby Rd. LE5: Leic	.5E 21
Fritchley Cl. LE9: Hun	.4A 42
Frith Cl. LE3: Glen	.5A 18
Froanes Cl. LE19: End	.5G 33
FROG ISLAND	.1A 4 (6A 20)
Frog Island LE3: Leic	.1A 4 (6A 20)
Frolesworth Rd. LE3: Leic	.1C 26
LE9: B Ast	.3A 60
LE17: Leire	.6A 60
Frolesworth Way	
LE3: Leic	.1C 26
Frome Av. LE2: Oad	.3D 38
Front St. LE4: Birs	.4H 13
Fulbeck Av. LE5: Leic	.3D 30
Fulford Rd. LE3: Leic	.2A 26
Fullhurst Av. LE3: Leic	.4F 27
Fulmar Rd. LE7: Anst	.5F 11
Furlong Cl. LE7: Sys	.6G 7
Furlongs, The LE16: L Bow	.3G 65

Furnival Cl. LE8: Flec	.5A 58
Furrows Cl. LE19: Litt	.4E 43

G

Gables Hall, The LE2: Leic	.1H 37
Gaddesby Av. LE3: Leic	.4G 27
Gainsborough Rd. LE2: Leic	.1C 36
LE8: Kib H	.4A 62
Galahad Cl. LE3: Leic E	.5G 25
Galaxy Wlk. LE2: Leic	.2E 29
Galby St. LE5: Leic	.6F 21
Gale Cl. LE17: Lut	.2G 63
Gallards Hill LE3: Leic	.4B 26
(not continuous)	
Galleywood Dr. LE4: Leic	.3H 19
Gallimore Cl. LE3: Glen	.4C 18
Gallowtree Ga. LE1: Leic	.3D 4 (1B 28)
Galsworthy Cl. LE3: Leic	.2E 27
Galway Rd. LE4: Leic	.6E 13
Gamble Cl. LE7: Sys	.6G 7
Gamekeepers Ct. LE5: Ham	.2C 22
Gamel Rd. LE5: Leic	.2B 30
Gamel Wlk. LE5: Leic	.2B 30
Ganton Rd. LE3: Leic	.1A 26
Garden Cl. LE2: Oad	.4A 38
LE3: Leic E	.5A 26
Gardenfield Rd. LE4: Leic	.1H 21
Garden St. LE1: Leic	.1D 4 (6B 20)
LE4: Thurm	.4C 14
LE18: Wig	.2F 45
Gardiner St. LE16: Mkt H	.3B 64
Garendon Rd. LE3: Leic	.1D 28
Garendon Way LE6: Groby	.3E 17
Garfield Cl. LE16: L Bow	.4E 65
Garfield Pk. LE8: G Gle	.1D 48
Garfield St. LE4: Leic	.5C 20
Garfit Rd. LE9: K Mux	.2E 25
Garland Cres. LE4: Leic	.5F 19
Garnett Cres. LE2: Leic	.5G 35
Garratt Sq. LE8: Whet	.4H 43
Garrick Wlk. LE1: Leic	.3D 4
Garsdale LE18: Wig	.1D 46
Garsington Wlk. LE5: Leic	.1A 30
Garth Av. LE4: Leic	.1A 20
Gartree Rd. LE2: Leic	.6G 29
(not continuous)	
Gaskell Wlk. LE3: Leic	.2E 27
Gas La. LE18: Wig	.2F 45
Gas St. LE1: Leic	.1D 4 (6B 20)
Gate Cotts. LE8: Peat M	.6H 55
Gateway, The LE2: Leic	.6B 5 (3A 28)
Gateway Ho. LE19: End	.4C 34
Gateway St. LE2: Leic	.6B 5 (3A 28)
Gaulby La. LE2: S'ton	.1D 38
Gaul St. LE3: Leic	.3H 27
Gavin Cl. LE3: Brau	.5A 26
Gayhurst Cl. LE3: Brau	.2D 34
LE18: Wig	.1C 46
Gayton Av. LE4: Leic	.4E 21
Gayton Hgts. LE19: End	.5G 33
Geary Cl. LE6: Ratby	.5E 17
LE19: Nar	.4D 42
GEC Ind. Est. LE8: Whet	.5G 43
Gedding Rd. LE5: Leic	.2G 29
Geddington Cl. LE18: Wig	.1C 46
Gedge Way LE2: Leic	.3A 36
Gees Lock Cl. LE2: Leic	.5F 35
Gelert Av. LE5: Leic	.1D 30
Georgeham Cl. LE18: Wig	.2B 46
George Hill Cl. LE9: S Stan	.2B 50
George Marriott Cl. LE9: S Stan	.4A 50
George St. LE1: Leic	.1E 4 (6C 20)
LE7: Anst	.5F 11
LE17: Lut	.4G 63
LE19: End	.6G 33
George Toon Ct. LE7: Sys	.5E 7
Gerrard Gdns. LE16: Mkt H	.6C 64
Gervas Rd. LE5: Leic	.6C 22
Geveze Way LE9: B Ast	.3C 60
Gibbon's Cl. LE4: Leic	.5C 20
Gibson Cl. LE18: Wig	.6F 37

Gibson Way LE17: Lut 5E 63
Gifford Cl. LE5: Leic 4B 30
Gilbert Cl. LE4: Leic 1G 21
   LE16: L Bow 4G 65
Gilbert Murray Hall LE2: Oad 1A 38
Gillam Butts LE8: Count 2E 55
Gillbank Dr. LE6: Ratby 5C 16
Gilliver St. LE2: Leic 1D 36
Gillman Rd. LE3: Leic 5E 19
Gilmorton Av. LE2: Leic 5E 35
Gilmorton Cl. LE2: Leic 5F 35
Gilmorton La. LE17: Ash M, D Bas . . .6G 61
Gilmorton Rd. LE17: Ash M 6H 61
   LE17: Lut 4H 63
Gilmour Cl. LE4: Beau L 6B 12
Gilroes Crematorium LE3: Leic 3E 19
Gilson Cres. LE9: S Stan 2C 50
Gilstead Cl. LE7: Thurn 3F 31
Gimson Av. LE9: Cosb 2F 53
Gimson Cl. LE5: Leic 4A 22
Gimson Rd. LE3: Leic 1F 27
Gipsy La. LE4: Leic 3E 21
   LE5: Leic 4H 21
Gipsy Rd. LE4: Leic 3D 20
Gisbourne Ct. LE5: Leic 5A 30
Glade, The LE3: Brau 2D 34
Gladstone M. LE9: B Ast 6A 52
   (off Estley Rd.)
Gladstone St. LE1: Leic 2E 4 (1C 28)
   LE7: Anst 5G 11
   LE8: Flec 6B 58
   LE8: Kib B 5H 59
   LE16: Mkt H .4E 65
   LE17: Lut 4H 63
   LE18: Wig 6F 37
Glaisdale Cl. LE4: Leic 2G 19
Glaisdale Rd. LE18: Wig 2C 46
Glamorgan Av. LE18: Wig 1F 45
Glazebrook Rd. LE3: Leic 4D 18
Glazebrook Sq. LE3: Leic 5E 19
Glean Cl. LE9: B Ast 3B 60
Glebe Cl. LE2: Leic 2G 37
   LE3: Glen 5H 17
   LE18: Wig 6F 37
Glebe Dr. LE8: Count 2D 54
Glebe Gdns. LE2: Leic 1H 37
Glebe Ho. LE8: Bla 3C 44
Glebeland LE8: Kib H 4H 59
Glebelands, The LE8: G Gle 3C 48
Glebelands Rd. LE4: Leic 3D 12
Glebe Rd. LE2: Leic 2G 37
   LE6: Groby 2E 17
   LE9: B Ast 1A 60
   LE16: L Bow .4F 65
Glebe St. LE2: Leic 5F 5 (3C 28)
Glebe Way LE7: Sys 5C 6
Glenbarr Av. LE4: Leic 5H 19
Glenborne Rd. LE2: Leic 5C 36
Glencoe Av. LE4: Leic 1E 21
Glencroft LE2: G Par 2D 44
Glendale Av. LE3: Glen 3A 18
Glendon St. LE4: Leic 4D 20
Glendower Cl. LE5: Leic 1B 30
Gleneagles Av. LE4: Leic 1E 21
Gleneagles Wlk. LE4: Leic 1E 21
GLENFIELD 4H 17
Glenfield Cres. LE3: Leic 5A 18
GLENFIELD HOSPITAL 3D 18
Glenfield La. LE9: K Mux 1E 25
Glenfield Rd. LE3: Leic 6C 18
Glenfield Rd. E. LE3: Leic 2G 27
Glenfrith Cl. LE3: Leic 2D 18
Glenfrith Way LE3: Leic 4D 18
Glengarry Cl. LE3: Leic 6E 19
Glengarry Ct. LE3: Leic 6D 18
Glengarry Way LE3: Leic 5D 18
Glengate LE18: Wig 1F 45
Glen Gorse Rdbt. LE2: Oad 1A 48
Glenhills Blvd. LE2: Leic 4G 35
   (not continuous)
Glenhills Way LE2: Leic 4G 35
Glenmore Rd. LE4: Leic 2F 21

Glen Pk. Av. LE3: Glen 3H 17
GLEN PARVA 6E 35
Glen Ri. LE2: G Par 5F 35
   LE2: Oad 1A 48
Glen Rd. LE2: Oad 4C 38
   LE8: New H .5G 47
Glenrothes Cl. LE3: Leic 2A 26
Glen St. LE4: Leic 3D 20
Glenville Av. LE2: G Par 1B 44
   LE3: Glen 3A 18
Glen Way LE2: Oad 5C 38
Glenwood Cl. LE2: Leic 6F 29
Glossop St. LE5: Leic 3E 29
Gloucester Av. LE7: Sys 5G 7
Gloucester Cres. LE18: Wig 6A 36
Glover Ct. LE2: Leic 3G 35
Glovers Wlk. LE4: Leic 1G 19
Goals Soccer Cen.
   Leicester 3H 29
Goddard Cl. LE7: Bush 2G 31
Goddard Ct. LE16: Mkt H 2D 64
Goddards Cl. LE2: Oad 4H 37
   LE4: Leic 3F 19
   LE18: Kilby .2E 57
Goddards Slang LE2: Oad 4H 37
Godfrey Cl. LE4: Beau L 5A 12
Godstow Wlk. LE5: Leic 1A 30
Godwin Av. LE18: Wig 1C 46
Godwin Cl. LE18: Wig 1B 46
Goldfinch Cl. LE3: Leic 5C 18
Goldhill Cl. LE2: Leic 4C 36
Goldhill Gdns. LE2: Leic 2F 37
Goldhill Rd. LE2: Leic 2F 37
Goldsmith Rd. LE3: Leic 3E 27
Golf Course La. LE3: Leic 2A 28
Goode's Av. LE7: Sys 1F 15
Goode's La. LE7: Sys 6E 7
Goodheart Way LE3: Brau, Leic E 5A 26
Gooding Av. LE3: Leic 3D 26
   (not continuous)
Gooding Cl. LE3: Leic 4F 27
GOODWOOD 2B 30
Goodwood Bowling Club 6A 22
Goodwood Cl. LE16: L Bow 3G 65
Goodwood Cres. LE5: Leic 2B 30
Goodwood Rd. LE5: Leic 1B 30
Gopsall St. LE2: Leic 3D 28
Gordon Av. LE2: Leic 3D 28
Gordon Ho. LE2: Leic 2D 28
Gores La. LE16: L Bow 3F 65
Gorham Ri. LE9: B Ast 6H 51
Gorseburn Ho. LE3: Leic 5D 18
Gorse Hill LE7: Anst 6G 11
   (not continuous)
Gorse Hill City Farm 4F 19
Gorse Hill Ind. Est. LE4: Beau L 1E 19
Gorse La. LE2: Oad 6D 38
   LE7: Sys 6D 6
Gorsty Cl. LE4: Leic 2F 19
Goscote Dr. LE17: Lut 4G 63
Goscote Hall Rd. LE4: Birs 5F 13
Goscote Ho. LE2: Leic 2D 28
Goshawk Cl. LE9: B Ast 6A 52
Gosling Ct. LE2: Leic 4A 36
Gosling St. LE2: Leic 6B 5 (3A 28)
Gotham St. LE2: Leic 3D 28
Gough Rd. LE5: Leic 1G 29
Goward St. LE16: Mkt H 3D 64
Gower St. LE1: Leic 1D 4 (6C 20)
Grace Cl. LE2: Leic 1A 36
Grace Gdns. LE2: Leic 2A 36
Graceland Mobile Home Pk.
   LE16: Mkt H 4B 64
Grace Road .2A 36
Grace Rd. LE2: Leic 1A 36
   LE9: Sap 5C 50
Grafton Dr. LE18: Wig 1D 46
Grafton Pl. LE1: Leic 1C 4 (6B 20)
Graham St. LE5: Leic 1D 28
Grampian Cl. LE2: Leic 2B 36
Granary Cl. LE3: Glen 6H 17
   LE8: Kib B 6A 62
Granary M. LE1: Leic 2C 4

Granby Av. LE5: Leic 1F 29
Granby Bldgs. LE1: Leic 4D 4
Granby Pl. LE1: Leic 4D 4 (2B 28)
Granby Rd. LE2: Leic 2H 35
Granby St. LE1: Leic 4D 4 (2B 28)
Grange, The LE2: Leic 6C 5
   LE19: Nar 4D 42
Grange Av. LE3: Leic E 4H 25
Grange Bus. Pk. LE8: Whet 2H 43
Grange Cl. LE2: Leic 6G 35
   LE3: Glen 5H 17
   LE6: Ratby 5D 16
   LE8: G Gle 2D 48
Grange Ct. LE2: Leic 8B 5
Grange Dr. LE2: G Par 6F 35
   LE8: Whet 3H 43
Grange La. LE2: Leic 6B 5 (3B 28)
   LE7: Thurn 3F 31
Grange Pk. LE7: Thurn 3E 31
   LE19: End 6A 34
Grange Rd. LE9: B Ast 1A 60
   LE18: Wig 4E 37
Grangeway Rd. LE18: Wig 5F 37
Granite Cl. LE19: End 5G 33
Granite Way LE7: Sys 1C 14
Grantham Av. LE9: B Ast 5H 51
Grantham Rd. LE5: Leic 5C 22
Grant Way LE2: Leic 5A 36
Granville Av. LE2: Oad 3H 37
Granville Cres. LE18: Wig 4D 36
Granville Rd. LE1: Leic 4D 28
   LE18: Wig 4D 36
Granville St. LE16: Mkt H 4D 64
Grape St. LE1: Leic 2B 4 (1A 28)
Grasmere Rd. LE18: Wig 6H 37
Grasmere St. LE2: Leic 6A 5 (3A 28)
Grass Acres LE3: Brau 2C 34
Grassington Cl. LE4: Leic 1G 19
Grassington Dr. LE18: Wig 2C 46
Grassy La. LE67: Mark 3A 8
Gravel, The LE8: Bur O 3H 49
Gravel Pit Rd. LE4: Birs 2F 13
Gravel St. LE1: Leic 2C 4 (1B 28)
Graylyn Ct. LE4: Thurm 5C 14
Grays Ct. LE19: End 6G 33
Grayswood Dr. LE4: Beau L 4A 12
Gt. Arler Rd. LE2: Leic 1C 36
GREAT BOWDEN 1F 65
Gt. Bowden Rd. LE16: Mkt H 3F 65
Great Central Railway
   Leicester North Station 6F 13
Gt. Central St. LE1: Leic 2A 4 (1A 28)
GREAT GLEN 3D 48
Gt. Glen By-Pass LE2: Oad 1A 48
   LE8: Bur O, G Gle 4C 48
Great Mdw. Rd. LE4: Leic 3F 19
GREAT STRETTON 4H 39
Grebe Way LE8: Whet 6H 43
Green, The LE7: Anst 5E 11
   LE7: Sys 5F 7
   LE8: Bla 3C 44
   LE8: Kib B 5H 59
   LE9: Crof 6G 41
   LE9: Hun 4H 41
   LE17: Bitt 2F 63
   LE17: Leire .6A 60
   LE67: Mark 2B 8
Greenacre Dr. LE5: Leic 2B 30
Greenacres Dr. LE17: Lut 4E 63
Greenbank Dr. LE2: Oad 4B 38
Greenbank Rd. LE5: Leic 4D 22
Greencoat Ct. LE3: Leic 6C 18
Greencoat Rd. LE3: Leic 6C 18
Greencroft LE9: S Stan 4B 50
Greendale Rd. LE2: G Par 6F 35
Green Farm Ct. LE7: Anst 5E 11
Greenfields LE8: Whet 4H 43
Greengate La. LE4: Leic 4D 12
Greenhill Cl. LE19: Nar 4C 42
Greenhill Rd. LE2: Leic 6C 28
Greenhithe Rd. LE2: Leic 6H 27
Greenhithe Wlk. LE2: Leic 6A 28
Greenland Av. LE5: Leic 5A 22

Greenland Dr. LE5: Leic 5A 22
Green La. LE8: Count 1F 55
  LE16: Mkt H 5D 64
Green La. Cl. LE5: Leic 1H 29
Green La. Rd. LE5: Leic 6F 21
Greenlawn Wlk. LE4: Leic 5H 19
Green Rd. LE9: B Ast 6A 52
Greens Health & Fitness Cen.
  Leicester 4A 20
Greenside Pl. LE2: Leic 4B 36
Green Wlk. LE3: Leic 2C 26
Greenway LE8: Kib B 5B 62
Greenway, The LE4: Leic 3C 20
Greenwich Cl. LE3: Leic 4F 19
  LE19: Nar .3D 42
Greenwood Cl. LE4: Thurm 5E 15
Greenwood Rd. LE5: Leic 1H 29
Greetham Way LE7: Sys 6G 7
Gregory Cl. LE4: Thurm 4E 15
Gregorys Cl. LE3: Brau 6B 26
Gregson Cl. LE4: Leic 6B 14
Grendon Cl. LE18: Wig 6G 37
Grenfell Rd. LE2: Leic 1G 37
Grenfell Wlk. LE2: Leic 1G 37
Grenville Gdns. LE16: Mkt H 5C 64
Gresley Cl. LE4: Leic 1G 19
  LE7: Thurn 1F 31
Gretna Way LE5: Leic 6E 23
Grey Cl. LE6: Groby 2F 17
Grey Cres. LE6: New L 2H 9
Grey Friars LE1: Leic 4C 4 (2B 28)
Greylag Cl. LE8: Whet 1H 53
Greylands Paddock LE6: Groby 2F 17
Greys Dr. LE6: Groby 3E 17
Greystoke Cl. LE4: Leic 2A 20
Greystoke Wlk. LE4: Leic 2A 20
Greystone Av. LE5: Leic 1B 30
Griffin Cl. LE4: Thurm 6E 15
Grimston Cl. LE4: Leic 1A 22
Grisedale Cl. LE2: Leic 8B 5 (4A 28)
Grittar Cl. LE18: Wig 6G 37
Grizedale Gro. LE19: Nar 2B 42
GROBY 2F 17
Groby By-Pass LE6: Groby 1F 17
Groby La. LE6: New L 4H 9
Groby Rd. LE3: Glen 2H 17
  LE3: Leic .4C 18
  LE6: Ratby, Groby 4C 16
    (not continuous)
  LE7: Anst .1A 18
Groby Rd. Gdns. LE3: Leic 4D 18
Groby Trad. Est. LE6: Groby 1E 17
Grocot Rd. LE5: Leic 4A 30
Grosvenor Cl. LE2: G Par 2D 44
Grosvenor Cres. LE2: Oad 2H 37
Grosvenor Ga. LE5: Leic 4H 21
Grosvenor Ho. LE1: Leic 5C 5 (2A 28)
Grosvenor St. LE1: Leic 1E 4 (6C 20)
Grovebury Rd. LE4: Leic 2A 20
Grovebury Wlk. LE4: Leic 2B 20
Grove Ct. LE19: End 4B 34
Grove Farm Triangle LE19: End 4C 34
Grove Pk. LE19: End 4C 34
Grove Rd. LE5: Leic 1E 29
  LE8: Bla, Whet 5H 43
Grove Way LE19: End 5D 34
Guestwick Grn. LE5: Ham 3C 22
Guild Cl. LE7: Crop 1H 11
Guildhall La. LE1: Leic 4B 4 (2A 28)
Guildhall Mus. 4B 4
Guilford Dr. LE18: Wig 4D 36
Guilford Rd. LE2: Leic 1F 37
Guilford St. LE2: Leic 3E 29
Guinevere Way LE3: Leic E 5G 25
Gullet La. LE9: K Mux 3B 24
Gumley Sq. LE19: End 6H 33
Gunthorpe Rd. LE3: Leic 3B 26
Gurnall Rd. LE4: Beau L 1E 19
Gurney Cres. LE19: Litt 5E 43
Guru Nanak Sikh Mus. 3A 4 (1A 28)
Guthlaxton Av. LE2: Oad 2D 28
  LE17: Lut .4G 63
Guthlaxton Gap LE9: Crof 1A 52

Guthlaxton St. LE2: Leic 2D 28
Guthlaxton Way LE18: Wig 3C 46
Guthridge Cres. LE3: Leic 4F 27
Gwencole Av. LE3: Brau 1E 35
Gwencole Cres. LE3: Brau 2E 35
Gwendolen Rd. LE5: Leic 2F 29
    (not continuous)
Gwendolen Rd. Gdns. LE5: Leic 2G 29
Gwendolin Av. LE4: Birs 4H 13
Gwendoline Dr. LE8: Count 2D 54
Gynsill Cl. LE7: Anst 6G 11
Gynsill La. LE7: Anst 2B 18
Gynsills Hall LE3: Glen 2B 18
Gypsum Cl. LE4: Leic 2H 21

H

Hackett Rd. LE3: Leic 5D 18
Haddenham Rd. LE3: Leic 5G 27
Haddon Cl. LE7: Sys 6D 6
Haddon St. LE2: Leic 2E 29
Hadrian Cl. LE7: Sys 1C 14
Hadrian Rd. LE4: Leic 6D 12
  LE4: Thurm 4C 14
Hagley Cl. LE4: Leic 4F 21
  LE16: L Bow 3G 65
Haig Pl. LE3: Leic 5E 27
Halcroft Ri. LE18: Wig 2B 46
Half Croft, The LE7: Sys 5E 7
Half Moon Cres. LE2: Oad 2C 38
Halford Cl. LE8: G Gle 3D 48
  LE8: Whet .5H 43
Halford Ho. LE8: G Gle 2D 48
Halford Rd. LE8: Kib B 5H 59
Halford St. LE1: Leic 4D 4 (2B 28)
  LE7: Sys 6E 7
Halfpenny Cl. LE4: Birs 2G 13
Halifax Dr. LE4: Leic 2A 20
Halkin St. LE4: Leic 4D 20
Hallam Av. LE4: Birs 4F 13
Hallam Cl. LE19: Litt 5E 43
Hallam Cres. E. LE3: Leic 5D 26
Hallam Flds. Rd. LE4: Birs, Wan 2F 13
Hallam Wlk. LE4: Birs 2F 13
Hallaton Dr. LE7: Sys 6G 7
Hallaton Rd. LE5: Leic 5H 21
Hallaton St. LE2: Leic 2A 36
Hallbrook Rd. LE9: B Ast 3B 60
Hall Cl. LE2: G Par 6F 35
  LE7: Coss 1B 6
  LE8: Kib H .4H 59
Hallcroft Av. LE8: Count 2E 55
Hallcroft Gdns. LE8: Count 2E 55
Hall Dr. LE2: Oad 3B 38
Halley Cl. LE4: Beau L 5A 12
Hall Farm Cres. LE9: B Ast 2C 60
Hall Farm Rd. LE7: Thurc 1B 12
Hall Gdns. LE8: G Gle 3D 48
Hallgate Dr. LE3: Leic 2D 18
Hall La. LE2: Leic 2G 35
Hall Rd. LE7: Scra 5F 23
Halls Ct. LE9: S Stan 3C 50
Hall Wlk. LE19: End 5H 33
Halsbury St. LE2: Leic 4F 29
Halstead St. LE5: Leic 1F 29
Halter Slade LE18: Wig 2C 46
Hambledon Grn. LE4: Leic 6D 12
Hamble Rd. LE2: Oad 3C 38
Hambleton Cl. LE3: Leic E 4F 25
Hamelin Rd. LE3: Leic 3D 26
Hamilford Cl. LE7: Scra 4E 23
HAMILTON 2C 22
Hamilton Bus. Pk. LE5: Ham 1B 22
Hamilton Circ. LE5: Ham 2D 22
Hamilton La. LE7: Bark T, Scra 3E 23
Hamilton St. LE2: Leic 3D 28
Hamilton Way LE5: Leic 3B 22
Hammercliffe Rd. LE5: Leic 5E 21
Hammond Way LE16: Mkt H 2D 64
Hampden Rd. LE4: Leic 3G 21
Hampshire Rd. LE2: Leic 2H 35

Hampstead Cl. LE19: Nar 3D 42
Hampton Cl. LE2: G Par 2D 44
  LE18: Wig .1C 46
Hanbury Rd. LE5: Leic 3D 30
Hand Av. LE3: Leic 3C 26
    (not continuous)
Hand Cl. LE3: Leic 3C 26
Handley St. LE2: Leic 2A 36
Hannah Pde. LE4: Birs 4G 13
Hannam Ct. LE1: Leic 2D 4 (1B 28)
Hanover Cl. LE5: Leic 4B 22
Hansen Ct. LE18: Wig 1G 45
Hanworth Cl. LE5: Ham 3C 22
Haramead Bus. Cen. LE1: Leic 6D 20
Haramead Rd. LE1: Leic 6D 20
Harborough Leisure Cen. 6E 65
Harborough Mus. 3D 64
Harborough Rd. LE2: Oad 3A 38
  LE8: Kib B, Kib H 4B 62
  LE16: Bray .6H 65
  LE16: Din 1H 65
  LE16: E Farn 6A 64
  LE16: G Ox .6E 65
  LE16: Lub 3A 64
  LE16: Mkt H 1B 64
Harborough Theatre 3D 64
Harcourt Cl. LE7: Sys 5E 7
Harcourt Est. LE8: Kib H 4A 62
Harcourt Rd. LE8: Kib B 5H 59
  LE18: Wig .2C 46
Harcourt St. LE16: Mkt H 3C 64
Harcourt Way LE19: Brau 3B 34
Hardie Cres. LE3: Brau 5B 26
Harding St. LE1: Leic 1A 4 (6A 20)
Hardwick Ct. LE3: Leic 4G 27
Hardwick Cres. LE7: Sys 6D 6
Hardwicke Rd. LE19: Nar 3B 42
Hardwick Rd. LE5: Leic 3E 31
Hardy's Av. LE4: Leic 1E 21
Harebell Cl. LE5: Ham 2B 22
Harecroft Cres. LE9: Sap 5C 50
Harefield Av. LE3: Leic 1F 35
Harene Cres. LE9: Leic E 4E 25
Harewood St. LE5: Leic 6F 21
Harland Cl. LE9: Cosb 2F 53
Harlaxton St. LE3: Leic 5F 27
Harlaxton Wlk. LE3: Leic 5G 27
Harlequin Way LE8: Whet 1H 53
Harleston Cl. LE5: Leic 6E 23
Harold's La. LE19: End 5H 33
Harold St. LE2: Leic 1A 36
Harrier Cl. LE9: B Ast 6A 52
Harrington Rd. LE18: Wig 6G 37
Harrington St. LE4: Leic 5E 21
Harringworth Rd. LE5: Leic 3B 30
Harris Cl. LE9: B Ast 2B 60
Harris Grn. LE3: Brau 4A 26
Harrison Cl. LE3: Glen 5A 18
  LE6: Ratby .5D 16
  LE8: Whet 6A 44
  LE16: Mkt H 6C 64
  LE18: Wig .2H 45
Harrison Rd. LE4: Leic 5D 20
Harrison's Row LE7: Sys 5F 7
Harrison St. LE4: Thurm 3C 14
Harris Rd. LE4: Leic 2F 19
Harrod Dr. LE16: Mkt H 2F 65
Harrogate Rd. LE4: Leic 4E 21
Harrogate Way LE18: Wig 1C 46
Harrop Cl. LE8: Bla 3A 44
Harrow Cl. LE3: Leic E 6F 25
Harrowden Cl. LE5: Leic 1A 30
Harrowden Ri. LE5: Leic 1A 30
Harrowgate Dr. LE4: Birs 2E 13
Harrow Pl. LE2: Leic 1D 36
Harrow Rd. LE3: Leic 3G 27
Hart Cl. LE8: Whet 6H 43
Hartfield Rd. LE5: Leic 5D 22
Hartington Rd. LE2: Leic 1E 37
Hartland Dr. LE16: L Bow 3F 65
Hartopp Cl. LE7: Bush 2G 31
Hartopp Rd. LE2: Leic 5D 28
Hart Rd. LE5: Leic 1E 29

Hartshorn Cl.—Hinckley Rd.

Hartshorn Cl. LE4: Thurm 5D 14
Harvard Cl. LE2: Oad 3B 38
Harvest Cl. LE4: Leic 2F 19
LE19: Litt 5F 43
Harvester Cl. LE3: Leic E 6F 25
Harvesters Cnr. LE7: E Gos 2H 7
Harvest Way LE9: B Ast 3B 60
Harvey Cl. LE8: Bla 2B 44
Harveys Ct. LE9: Sap 6B 50
Harvey Wlk. LE1: Leic 4B 4 (2A 28)
Harwin Rd. LE5: Leic 3B 30
Haskell Cl. LE3: Brau 5B 26
Hassal Rd. LE3: Leic 5C 18
Hastings, The LE3: Brau 6B 26
Hastings Cl. LE8: Flec 6F 59
Hastings Mdw. Cl. LE9: K Mux 2C 24
Hastings Rd. LE5: Leic 5F 21
LE9: K Mux 3E 25
Hastings Wlk. LE3: Brau 6C 26
Hathaway Av. LE3: Brau 6D 26
Hatherleigh Rd. LE5: Leic 4H 29
Hat Rd. LE3: Brau 2C 34
Hattern Av. LE4: Leic 1H 19
Havelock Gdns. LE4: Thurm 3C 14
Havelock St. LE2: Leic 7B 5 (3A 28)
Haven Cl. LE3: Leic E 5F 25
Havencrest Dr. LE5: Leic 6B 22
Haven Wlk. LE5: Leic 1E 31
Hawarden Av. LE5: Leic 6H 21
Hawk Cl. LE9: B Ast 6A 52
Hawker Rd. LE2: Oad 5D 38
Hawkesbury Rd. LE2: Leic 2A 36
Hawkes Hill LE2: Leic 4B 36
Hawthorn Av. LE4: Birs 3H 13
Hawthorn Cl. LE9: Leic E 5E 25
Hawthorn Ct. LE2: Leic 8B 5
Hawthorn Dr. LE8: Bla 5B 44
Hawthorne Cl. LE2: Oad 6G 39
Hawthorne Ct. LE5: Leic 5A 30
Hawthorne Dr. LE5: Leic 4A 30
Hawthorne St. LE3: Leic 6F 19
Hawthorn Gro. LE2: Oad 2B 38
Hawthorn Ri. LE6: Groby 2F 17
Hawthorns, The LE2: Leic 6F 29
LE8: Count 1E 55
LE17: Lut 4F 63
LE67: Mark 3C 8
Haybarn Cl. LE19: Litt 5F 43
Hayden Av. LE2: Oad 5D 38
Hayden Cl. LE4: Leic 2A 20
Hayden Wlk. LE2: Oad 5D 38
Hayes Rd. LE18: Wig 6G 37
Hayfield Cl. LE3: Glen 5H 17
Hayling Cres. LE5: Leic 5A 22
Haymarket LE1: Leic 3D 4 (1B 28)
Haymarket Cen. LE1: Leic 3D 4 (1B 28)
Haymes Cl. LE8: Kib H 3H 59
Haynes Rd. LE5: Leic 6G 21
Haywood Cl. LE5: Leic 3B 30
Hazeland Ct. LE17: Lut 4G 63
Hazelbank Cl. LE4: Leic 3H 19
Hazelbank Rd. LE8: Count 1F 55
Hazel Cl. LE4: Birs 3H 13
LE8: G Gle 2D 48
LE19: Litt 5E 43
Hazeldene Rd. LE5: Ham 3D 22
Hazel Dr. LE3: Brau 3D 34
LE17: Lut 4F 63
Hazelhead Rd. LE7: Anst 5F 11
Hazelnut Cl. LE5: Leic 3B 30
Hazel St. LE2: Leic 8C 5 (4B 28)
Hazelwood Rd. LE5: Leic 4F 29
LE18: Wig 3G 45
Hazlemere Cl. LE8: Bla 4B 44
Heacham Dr. LE4: Leic 2F 19
Headingley Cl. LE4: Beau L 4C 12
Headland Rd. LE5: Leic 4A 30
Headlands, The LE16: Mkt H 2E 65
Headley Rd. LE3: Brau 2D 34
Healey Cl. LE4: Leic 1H 19
Healey St. LE18: Wig 2F 45
Heanor St. LE1: Leic 1B 4 (6A 20)
Heards Cl. LE18: Wig 3C 46
Heard Wlk. LE4: Leic 2F 19
Hearth St. LE16: Mkt H 3C 64
Heath Av. LE7: Sys 6D 6
LE19: End 1G 43
Heathbrook Dr. LE6: Ratby 5D 16
Heathcott Rd. LE2: Leic 2A 36
Heatherbrook Rd. LE4: Beau L 5A 12
Heather Rd. LE2: Leic 1C 36
Heather Way LE8: Count 2F 55
Heathfield Rd. LE18: Wig 4F 37
Heathgate Cl. LE4: Birs 3F 13
Heathley Cl. LE3: Leic E 5F 25
Heathley Pk. Dr. LE3: Leic 4E 19
Heawood Way LE3: Brau 6B 26
Heays Cl. LE3: Leic 5C 18
Hebden Cl. LE2: Leic 1C 44
Heddington Cl. LE2: Leic 4C 36
Heddington Way LE2: Leic 4C 36
Hedgerow La. LE9: K Mux 2D 24
Hedgerow Rd. LE3: Leic 3E 27
Hefford Gdns. LE4: Leic 1H 19
Heighton Cres. LE19: Litt 5E 43
Heights, The LE16: L Bow 4G 65
Helena Cres. LE4: Leic 1A 20
Helmdon Rd. LE2: Leic 4H 27
Helmsley Rd. LE2: Leic 3B 36
Helston Cl. LE18: Wig 2A 46
Hemington Rd. LE5: Leic 4D 30
Hemlock Cl. LE19: Nar 2B 42
Hendon Grange LE2: Leic 1G 37
Henley Cres. LE3: Brau 6D 26
Henley Rd. LE3: Leic 1G 27
Henray Av. LE2: Leic 1C 44
Henry Cl. LE3: Leic E 5F 25
Henshaw St. LE2: Leic 6C 5 (3B 28)
Hensman Cl. LE8: Flec 6F 59
Henson Cl. LE4: Birs 5F 13
Henton Rd. LE3: Leic 2G 27
Herbert Av. LE4: Leic 3D 20
Herbert Cl. LE8: Whet 4H 43
Herdsmans Cl. LE19: Litt 4E 43
Hereford Rd. LE2: Leic 2H 35
Hereward Dr. LE7: Thurn 2F 31
Heritage Way LE5: Ham 2D 22
Herle Av. LE3: Leic 5D 26
Herle Wlk. LE3: Leic 5D 26
Hermitage Cl. LE2: Oad 4A 38
Hermitage Ct. LE2: Oad 4A 38
Hermitage Rd. LE4: Birs 6G 13
Heron Cl. LE8: G Gle 2D 48
Herongate Rd. LE5: Leic 4H 21
Heron Rd. LE5: Leic 6E 21
Heron's Way LE7: E Gos 1H 7
Heron Way LE7: Sys 5D 6
LE19: End 1F 43
Herrick Cl. LE19: End 6G 33
Herrick Dr. LE7: Thurn 2F 31
Herrick Rd. LE2: Leic 1C 36
Herricks Av. LE4: Leic 6D 14
Herrick Way LE18: Wig 3C 46
Herschell St. LE2: Leic 4E 29
Herthull Rd. LE5: Leic 1C 30
Hesilrige Wlk. LE5: Leic 5B 22
Hesketh Av. LE2: Leic 6G 35
Hesketh Cl. LE2: Leic 6G 35
Hewes Cl. LE2: G Par 6E 35
Hewett Cl. LE8: G Gle 3C 48
Hewitt Dr. LE9: K Mux 3F 25
Hextall Rd. LE5: Leic 4A 30
Hexter Cl. LE8: Whet 1H 53
Heybridge Rd. LE5: Leic 5H 21
Heybrook Av. LE8: Bla 4A 44
Heycock Cl. LE8: Flec 6F 59
Heyford Rd. LE3: Leic 3B 26
Heygate St. LE16: Mkt H 2D 64
Heythrop Cl. LE2: Oad 5D 38
Heyworth Rd. LE3: Leic 6G 27
Hidcote Rd. LE2: Oad 5A 38
Higgs Cl. LE5: Leic 2A 30
Highbrow LE8: G Gle 2E 49
Highbury Rd. LE4: Leic 5E 21
Highcliffe Rd. LE5: Ham 2A 22
Highcroft Av. LE2: Oad 4B 38
Highcroft Rd. LE2: Oad 6D 38
Highcross LE1: Leic 3B 4 (1A 28)
Highcross La. LE1: Leic 3B 4 (1A 28)
Highcross St. LE1: Leic 2A 4 (1A 28)
(not continuous)
LE16: Mkt H 3B 64
Higher Grn. LE8: G Gle 3D 48
Highfield Cres. LE18: Wig 5F 37
Highfield Dr. LE18: Wig 5F 37
Highfield Rd. LE6: Groby 2E 17
HIGHFIELDS 2E 29
Highfields Adventure Playground 1E 29
Highfields Farm Ent. Cen.
LE9: S Stan 1B 50
Highfield St. LE2: Leic 3D 28
LE7: Anst 5G 11
LE8: Flec 5A 58
LE9: S Stan 2B 50
LE16: Mkt H 3C 64
Highgate LE2: Leic 4C 36
Highgate Av. LE4: Birs 3E 13
Highgate Dr. LE2: Leic 4D 36
Highgrove Cres. LE2: Leic 4F 35
Highland Av. LE9: Leic E 5E 25
High Leys Dr. LE2: Oad 5A 38
Highmeres Rd. LE4: Leic 2H 21
High St. LE1: Leic 3B 4 (1A 28)
LE2: Oad 3A 38
LE5: Leic 5B 30
LE7: Sys 5E 7
LE8: Flec 5B 58
LE8: G Gle 3C 48
LE8: Kib B 5H 59
LE8: Whet 3H 43
LE16: Mkt H 3D 64
LE17: Lut 5G 63
LE19: End 6H 33
High Vw. Cl. LE4: Leic 2H 21
Highway Rd. LE4: Thurm 3D 14
LE5: Leic 5G 29
Hilary Cres. LE6: Groby 2D 16
Hilcot Grn. LE3: Brau 5A 26
(not continuous)
Hilders Rd. LE3: Leic 1E 27
Hildyard Rd. LE4: Leic 4C 20
Hillary Pl. LE3: Leic 5E 27
Hillberry Cl. LE19: Nar 3C 42
Hill Ct. LE7: Thurn 3F 31
Hillcrest Av. LE8: Kib B 4H 59
LE16: Mkt H 2C 64
Hillcrest Rd. LE2: Leic 4D 36
Hillcroft Cl. LE4: Thurm 3D 14
Hillcroft Rd. LE5: Leic 2G 29
Hill Dr. LE17: Lut 5G 63
Hill Fld. LE2: Oad 5E 39
Hill Gdns. LE16: Mkt H 3B 64
Hill Hole Quarry Local Nature Reserve 2B 8
Hillier Rd. LE5: Ham 2C 22
Hill La. LE8: Count, Whet 2A 54
LE67: Mark 2A 8
Hill La. Cl. LE67: Mark 1B 8
Hill Ri. LE4: Birs 3G 13
LE4: Leic 6D 14
Hillrise Av. LE3: Brau 1E 35
Hillsborough Cl. LE2: G Par 1C 44
Hillsborough Cres.
LE2: G Par 1C 44
Hillsborough Rd. LE2: G Par, Leic 1C 44
Hillside LE67: Mark 2B 8
Hillside Av. LE18: Wig 2B 46
Hillside Rd. LE16: Mkt H 2E 65
Hillside Tennis Club 6A 22
Hill St. LE1: Leic 2E 4 (1C 28)
LE9: Crof 1G 51
Hill Top Av. LE8: G Gle 2E 49
Hill Top Cl. LE16: Mkt H 3B 64
Hilltop Rd. LE5: Ham 2B 22
Hill Vw. LE19: End 6C 34
Hill Vw. Dr. LE9: Cosb 2F 53
Hill Way LE2: Oad 5C 38
Hinckley Rd. LE3: Leic, Leic E 4G 25
LE9: Des 2A 32

A-Z Leicester 85

Hinckley Rd. LE9: S Stan 4A 50
LE9: Sap 5A 50
Hincks Av. LE7: Scra 5F 23
Hind Cl. LE8: Whet 5A 44
Hind M., The LE17: Lut 5G 63
Hindoostan Av. LE18: Wig 1E 45
Hipwell Cres. LE4: Leic 2A 20
HMP Leicester LE1: Leic 7D **5** (3B **28**)
HMYOI Glen Parva
LE2: G Par 1E 45
Hoball Cl. LE3: Leic 5C 18
Hobart St. LE2: Leic 2D 28
Hobby Cl. LE9: B Ast 6B 52
Hobill Cl. LE3: Leic E 5H 25
LE9: Hun 3A 42
Hobrook Rd. LE8: Flec 6F 59
Hobson Rd. LE4: Leic 2B 20
Hoby St. LE3: Leic 1H 27
Hockley Farm Rd.
LE3: Leic 3A 26
Hodgson Cl. LE3: Leic 4E 19
Hodson Cl. LE8: Whet 5H 43
Hoffler Cl. LE8: Count 1C 54
Hogarth Rd. LE4: Leic 2C 12
Hoke Ct. LE17: Leire 6A 60
Holbeck Dr. LE9: B Ast 1C 60
Holbrook LE2: Oad 5E 39
Holbrook Rd. LE2: Leic 2G 37
Holdenby Cl. LE16: L Bow 3G 65
Holden Cl. LE8: Whet 6A 44
Holden St. LE4: Leic 3C 20
Holderness Rd. LE4: Leic 6D 12
Holgate Cl. LE7: Anst 4G 11
Holkham Av. LE4: Leic 4F 21
Holland Rd. LE2: Leic 1D 28
Holland Way LE19: Nar 3D 42
Holliers Way LE9: Crof 1G 51
Hollies Cl. LE9: Thurl 6A 32
Hollies Way LE7: Thurn 3F 31
Hollington Rd. LE5: Leic 3F 29
Hollins Rd. LE3: Leic 3C 26
Hollinwell Cl. LE3: Leic 2A 26
Hollow, The LE5: Leic 5B 30
Hollow Rd. LE7: Anst 4F 11
Hollowtree Rd. LE5: Ham 3C 22
Hollybank Cl. LE5: Ham 3C 22
Hollybank Cl. LE2: Leic 4D 28
Hollybrook Cl. LE4: Thurm 5E 15
Hollybush Cl. LE5: Leic 6D 22
LE7: Sys 5D **6**
Holly Cl. LE16: Mkt H 2D 64
Holly Ct. LE2: Oad 2A 38
Holly Dr. LE17: Lut 4F 63
Holly Gro. LE8: Bla 3B 44
Hollytree Av. LE4: Birs 3G 13
Hollywood Bowl
Leicester **6C 26**
Holman Row LE5: Leic 1A 30
Holmdale Rd. LE7: Sys 6E **7**
Holmden Av. LE18: Wig 1H 45
Holme Dr. LE2: Oad 2B 38
Holmes Cl. LE6: Groby 2E 17
Holmewood Dr. LE9: K Mux 3F 25
Holmfield Av. LE2: Leic 5F 29
Holmfield Av. E. LE3: Brau 4A 26
Holmfield Av. W. LE3: Leic E 4A 26
Holmfield Cl. LE17: Lut 4E 63
Holmfield Rd. LE2: Leic 5E 29
Holmleigh Gdns. LE7: Thurn 3F 31
Holmwood Ct. LE3: Leic 4C 18
Holmwood Dr. LE3: Leic 4C 18
Holt Cl. LE9: S Stan 3B 50
Holt Cres. LE9: Thurl 6A 32
Holt Dr. LE9: K Mux 3F 25
Holt La. LE9: Cosb 1H 61
LE17: Ash M 4H 61
Holt Rd. LE4: Birs 5G 13
Holts Cl. LE2: Leic 5F 35
Holy Bones LE1: Leic 3A **4** (1A **28**)
Holyoake St. LE19: End 1D 42
Holyrood Dr. LE8: Count 1D 54
Holywell Rd. LE2: Leic 3G 35
Home Av. LE3: Brau 6A 26

Home Cl. LE8: Bla 3B 44
LE8: Kib B 5A 62
Home Farm Cl. LE4: Leic 2G 19
LE7: Anst 5F 11
Home Farm Ct. LE4: Leic 2G 19
Home Farm Sq. LE4: Leic 2G 19
Home Farm Wlk. LE4: Leic 2G 19
Homemead Av. LE4: Leic 3H 19
Homer Dr. LE19: Nar 3C 42
Homestead Cl. LE7: Coss 1B **6**
Homestead Dr. LE18: Wig 2B 46
Homestead Ho. LE9: Sap 6B 50
Homestone Gdns. LE5: Leic 1E 31
Homestone Ri. LE5: Leic 1E 31
Homeway Rd. LE5: Leic 4G 29
Homewelland Ho. LE16: Mkt H 2C **64**
(off Poplars Ct.)
Honeybourne Cl. LE2: Oad 4A 38
Honeycomb Cl. LE19: Nar 3C 42
Honeysuckle Cl. LE17: Lut 4E 63
Honeysuckle Rd. LE5: Ham 3C 22
Honeywell Cl. LE2: Oad 4A 38
Honiton Cl. LE18: Wig 2A 46
Hoods Cl. LE4: Leic 5D 12
Hooks Cl. LE7: Anst 5F 11
Hopefield Rd. LE3: Leic 5G 27
Hoppner Cl. LE4: Leic 2D 12
Hopton Flds. LE16: Mkt H 6C 64
Hopwood Cl. LE4: Leic 2F 19
Hopyard Cl. LE2: Leic 5F 35
Hornbeam Cl. LE2: Oad 2A 38
LE19: Nar 3C 42
Hornby Rd. LE5: Ham 2C 22
Horndean Av. LE18: Wig 6E 37
Horsefair Cl. LE16: Mkt H 2C 64
Horsefair St. LE1: Leic 4C **4** (2B **28**)
Horseshoe Cl. LE9: Cosb 1F 53
Horseshoe La. LE16: G Bow 1G 65
Horsewell La. LE18: Wig 3B 46
HORSTON HILL **4G 29**
Horston Rd. LE5: Leic 4G 29
Horton Ct. LE8: Bla 3A 44
Horton's Cl. LE2: G Par 6F 35
Horwood Cl. LE18: Wig 5G 37
Hoskins Cl. LE18: Wig 3C 46
Hospital Cl. LE5: Leic 3H 29
Hospital La. LE8: Bla 4C 44
Hotel St. LE1: Leic 4C **4** (2B **28**)
Hotoft Rd. LE5: Leic 5B 22
Houghton La. LE7: Hou H 6F 31
Houghton St. LE5: Leic 6F 21
Houlditch Rd. LE2: Leic 1D 36
Housman Wlk. LE4: Leic 5D 20
Howard Rd. LE2: G Par 1B 44
LE2: Leic 6C 28
Howards Ct. LE9: K Mux 1E 25
Howard Way LE16: Mkt H 5C 64
Howden Rd. LE2: Leic 5G 35
Howdon Rd. LE2: Oad 6B 38
Howe Cl. LE9: S Stan 4A 50
Howe La. LE5: Ham 1C 22
Hoylake Cl. LE5: Leic 5G 29
Hubbard Cl. LE8: Whet 6A 44
Hudson Cl. LE3: Leic 5E 19
Huggett Cl. LE4: Leic 1G 21
Hughenden Dr. LE2: Leic 6A 28
Humber Cl. LE5: Leic 4B 22
HUMBERSTONE **5B 22**
Humber Stone, The **2A 22**
Humberstone Dr. LE5: Leic 5B 22
Humberstone Dr. LE5: Leic 6H 21
HUMBERSTONE GARDEN CITY **4C 22**
Humberstone Ga. LE1: Leic . . .3D **4** (1B **28**)
Humberstone La.
LE4: Thurm, Leic 5B 14
Humberstone Mall LE1: Leic 3D **4**
(off Haymarket Cen.)
Humberstone Pk. Cl. LE5: Leic 1A 30
Humberstone Rd. LE1: Leic . . .3E **4** (1C **28**)
LE5: Leic 2F **4** (1D **28**)
Humble La. LE7: Coss 1B **6**
Humes Cl. LE8: Whet 1H 53
Humphreys Cl. LE4: Leic 4A 20

Humphreys Way LE4: Leic 4A 20
Humphries Cl. LE5: Leic 2A 30
HUNCOTE **3H 41**
Huncote Rd. LE9: Crof 5F 41
LE9: Hun 4A 42
LE9: S Stan 2B 50
LE19: Hun, Nar 4A 42
Hungarton Blvd. LE5: Leic 5B 22
Hungarton Dr. LE7: Sys 6G **7**
Hunter Rd. LE4: Leic 4C 20
Hunters Dr. LE17: Lut 5F 63
Hunter's Row LE9: Cosb 1F 53
Hunters Way LE2: Oad 5D 38
LE3: Leic E 5F 25
Huntingdon Gdns.
LE16: Mkt H 5C 64
Huntingdon Rd. LE4: Leic 3G 21
Huntings, The LE9: K Mux 2C 24
Huntsman Cl. LE67: Mark 3C **8**
Huntsman's Dale LE7: E Gos 1H **7**
Huntsmans Way LE4: Leic 2F 21
Hurds Cl. LE7: Anst 5F 11
Hurlingham Rd. LE16: Mkt H 5D 64
Hursley Cl. LE2: Oad 4C 38
Hurst Ri. LE5: Leic 2A 30
Hutchinson St. LE2: Leic 2D 28
Hutchinson Wlk. LE2: Leic 4F **4** (2D **28**)
Hyde Cl. LE2: Oad 6C 38
LE3: Leic 3F 19
LE19: Nar 3D 42
Hydra Wlk. LE2: Leic 2D 28
Hylion Rd. LE2: Leic 3C 36

I

Ibbetson Av. LE3: Glen 6A 18
Ibsley Way LE2: Leic 6H 35
Ickworth Cl. LE5: Leic 5G 21
Iffley Cl. LE5: Leic 1A 30
Iffley Ct. LE5: Leic 1A 30
Iliffe Av. LE2: Oad 4H 37
Iliffe Rd. LE4: Leic 4G 21
Illingworth Rd. LE5: Leic 1A 30
Ilmington Cl. LE3: Glen 4A 18
Imperial Av. LE3: Leic 4F 27
Imperial Rd. LE2: Kib B 5H 59
Impey Cl. LE3: Brau 6A 26
Infirmary Cl. LE1: Leic 7C **5** (3B **28**)
Infirmary Rd. LE1: Leic 7C **5** (3B **28**)
Infirmary Sq. LE1: Leic 6C **5** (3B **28**)
Ingarsby Dr. LE5: Leic 4C 30
Ingleby Rd. LE18: Wig 6E 37
Ingle Dr. LE6: Ratby 5C 16
Inglenook Pk. Mobile Home Pk.
LE4: Thurm 2D 14
Ingle St. LE3: Leic 6F 19
Ingold Av. LE4: Leic 2H 19
Ingrams Way LE18: Wig 3C 46
Invergarry Cl. LE4: Leic 1F 21
Iona Cl. LE4: Leic 2F 19
Iona Rd. LE7: Sys 5D **6**
Iona Way LE8: Count 2F 55
Ipswich Cl. LE4: Beau L 5A 12
Irene Pollard Ho.
LE4: Leic 2D 20
Ireton Av. LE4: Leic 3H 21
Ireton Rd. LE4: Leic 4G 21
LE16: Mkt H 5C 64
Iris Av. LE2: G Par 6F 35
LE4: Birs 3H 13
Irlam St. LE18: Wig 3F 45
Ironworks Rd. LE4: Leic 5E 21
Isabel La. LE8: Kib B 5A 62
Isis Cl. LE2: Oad 3D 38
Islington St. LE2: Leic 5B 28
Isobella Cl. LE3: Brau 6A 26
Ivanhoe Cl. LE3: Glen 6A 18
Ivanhoe Rd. LE18: Wig 1F 45
Ivanhoe St. LE3: Leic 1G 27
Ivatt Cl. LE7: Thurn 2G 31
Ivychurch Cres. LE5: Leic 4D 22
Ivydale Cl. LE4: Thurm 5D 14

Ivydale Rd. LE4: Thurm 5D 14
Ivy Rd. LE3: Leic 4G 27

J

Jack Hardy Cl. LE7: Sys 5G 7
Jacklin Dr. LE4: Leic 6B 14
Jackson Cl. LE2: Oad 4D 38
LE16: Mkt H 6D 64
Jackson St. LE4: Leic 3D 20
Jacob Cl. LE19: End 6G 33
Jacqueline Rd. LE67: Mark 3D 8
Jacques Cl. LE19: End 6G 33
James Bond Cvn. Pk.
LE17: Lut 6F 63
James Gavin Way LE2: Oad 5E 39
James St. LE7: Anst 4F 11
LE8: Bla .3A 44
LE9: S Stan 2B 50
Jamesway LE9: Cosb 1F 53
Janes Way LE67: Mark 3C 8
Jarrett Cl. LE19: End 6G 33
Jarrom Ct. LE2: Leic 7B 5 (3A 28)
Jarrom St. LE2: Leic 8A 5 (4A 28)
Jarvis St. LE3: Leic 3A 4 (1A 28)
Jasmine Cl. LE5: Ham 2B 22
LE17: Lut 4E 63
Jasmine Ct. LE18: Wig 1F 45
LE19: Nar 2B 42
Jean Dr. LE4: Leic 4H 19
Jellicoe Rd. LE5: Leic 1G 29
Jennett Cl. LE5: Leic 1C 30
Jeremy Cl. LE4: Leic 3D 20
Jermyn St. LE4: Leic 3D 20
Jersey Rd. LE4: Leic 6D 12
Jerwood Way LE16: L Bow 4E 65
Jessons Cl. LE4: Leic 2F 21
Jessop Cl. LE3: Leic 5E 19
Jetty, The LE1: Leic 4C 4
Jewry Wall .4A 4
Jewry Wall Mus. 4A 4 (2A 28)
Jewsbury Way LE3: Brau 5A 26
John Bold Av. LE9: S Stan 2C 50
John Minto Ho. LE4: Leic 5D 20
Johnnie Johnson Dr. LE17: Lut 2G 63
John Sandford Sports Cen. . . .5A 5 (2A 28)
Johnscliffe Cl. LE6: New L 2H 9
Johns Ct. LE8: Bla 3B 44
Johnson Cl. LE8: Whet 4A 44
LE9: B Ast 2C 60
Johnson Ri. LE9: S Stan 4C 50
Johnson Rd. LE4: Birs 4F 13
Johnson St. LE1: Leic 1A 4 (6A 20)
John St. LE19: End 1D 42
Jonathan Cl. LE6: Groby 2G 17
Jongleurs 4D 4
Jordan Av. LE18: Wig 2G 45
Jordan Cl. LE3: Glen 5A 18
LE16: L Bow 3F 65
Jordan Ct. LE6: Ratby 5D 16
Joseph Cl. LE7: Crop 1G 11
Journeymans Grn. LE6: Ratby 5D 16
Jowett Cl. LE3: Leic 4E 19
Joyce Rd. LE3: Leic 5F 19
Jubilee Cl. LE7: Sys 4F 7
Jubilee Cres. LE19: Nar 4E 43
Jubilee Dr. LE3: Glen 6A 18
Jubilee Gdns. LE4: Leic 5F 21
LE16: Mkt H 2E 65
Jubilee Ho. LE9: K Mux 2D 24
Jubilee Rd. LE1: Leic 1D 4 (6B 20)
LE9: B Ast 1A 60
Judith Dr. LE5: Leic 3B 30
LE8: Count 1F 55
Julian Rd. LE2: Leic 1C 44
Junction 21 App. LE19: End 3B 34
Junction Rd. LE1: Leic 1E 4 (6C 20)
LE18: Wig 6F 37
June Av. LE4: Leic 6D 14
Junior St. LE1: Leic 2B 4 (1A 28)
Juniper Cl. LE3: Leic E 5F 25
LE17: Lut 3F 63

Juno Cl. LE3: Glen 6A 18
Jupiter Cl. LE2: Leic 1D 28

K

Kamloops Cres. LE1: Leic 1E 4 (6C 20)
Karting Nation Broughton Astley 4G 51
Kashmir Rd. LE1: Leic 6D 20
Kate St. LE3: Leic 2H 27
Kay Rd. LE3: Leic 5D 18
Keats Cl. LE19: End 6G 33
Keats Wlk. LE4: Leic 5D 20
Keays Way LE7: Scra 5F 23
Keble Dr. LE7: Sys 6F 7
Keble Rd. LE2: Leic 6C 28
Kedleston Av. LE4: Birs 6G 13
Kedleston Rd. LE5: Leic 4F 29
Keenan Cl. LE2: Leic 4F 35
Keep, The LE9: K Mux 2D 24
Keepers' Cft. LE7: E Gos 2H 7
Keepers Wlk. LE4: Leic 2F 19
Kegworth Av. LE5: Leic 2H 29
Keightley Rd. LE3: Leic 4C 18
Keightley Wlk. LE3: Leic 4D 18
(off Keightley Rd.)
LE4: Thurm 5D 14
Kelbrook Cl. LE4: Leic 1G 19
Kelmarsh Av. LE18: Wig 1B 46
Kelso Grn. LE2: Leic 6H 35
Kelvon Cl. LE3: Glen 4B 18
Kemble Gallery LE1: Leic 3D 4
(off Haymarket Cen.)
Kemble Sq. LE1: Leic 3D 4
Kemp Rd. LE3: Leic 4C 18
Kempson Rd. LE2: Leic 1A 44
Kendal Cl. LE2: Leic 8B 5 (4A 28)
Kendall's Av. LE9: Crof 1G 51
Kendal Rd. LE4: Leic 2F 21
Kendrick Dr. LE2: Oad 4B 38
Kenilworth Cl. LE9: B Ast 5A 52
Kenilworth Dr. LE2: Oad 4H 37
Kenilworth Rd. LE18: Wig 6B 36
Ken Mackenzie Cl. LE17: Lut 2G 63
Kennedy Way LE3: Leic E 5H 25
Kenneth Gamble Ct. LE18: Wig 5D 36
Kenneth Holmes Hall LE1: Leic 6E 5
Kenny Cl. LE8: Whet 5A 44
Kensington Cl. LE2: G Par 2D 44
LE2: Oad 6C 38
Kensington Dr. LE18: Wig 4F 37
Kensington St. LE4: Leic 4C 20
Kent Cres. LE18: Wig 6B 36
Kenton Av. LE18: Wig 2A 46
Kent Dr. LE2: Oad 4C 38
Kent St. LE2: Leic 1D 28
LE5: Leic 1D 28
Kenwood Rd. LE2: Leic 2E 37
Kepston Cl. LE2: Leic 5H 35
Kepwick Rd. LE5: Ham 1D 22
Kerrial Gdns. LE3: Leic 6C 18
Kerrial Rd. LE3: Leic 6C 18
Kerrysdale Av. LE4: Leic 3F 21
Kertley LE8: Flec 5B 58
Kestian Cl. LE16: Mkt H 1C 64
Kestrel Cl. LE3: Leic E 5E 25
LE5: Leic 6E 21
LE7: Sys 5D 6
LE8: Flec 6F 59
LE9: B Ast 6A 52
Kestrel La. LE5: Ham 3B 22
Keswick Cl. LE2: Leic 6G 35
LE4: Birs 3H 13
Keswick Rd. LE8: Bla 4A 44
Kettering Rd. LE16: L Bow, Mkt H 3E 65
Kevern Cl. LE18: Wig 2A 46
Kew Dr. LE2: Oad 6C 38
LE18: Wig 4D 36
Keyham Cl. LE5: Leic 4B 22
Keyham Ct. LE5: Leic 5A 22
Keyham La. LE5: Leic 4C 22
(not continuous)
LE7: Bee, Keyh 1H 23

Keyham La. E. LE7: Scra 3G 23
Keyham La. W. LE5: Leic 4D 22
Keythorpe St. LE2: Leic 1D 28
KIBWORTH BEAUCHAMP 5A 62
Kibworth Ct. LE8: Kib B 5A 62
KIBWORTH HARCOURT 4A 62
Kibworth Harcourt Windmill 4B 62
Kibworth Rd. LE8: Carl C, Kib H 1C 62
LE8: Flec 6C 58
LE8: Kib H 4C 62
LE8: Sad, Kib B 5E 59
LE8: Wist 1H 57
Kibworth Sports Cen. 6A 62
Kielder Cl. LE19: Nar 1B 42
Kilburn Av. LE2: Oad 3H 37
KILBY 2E 57
Kilby Av. LE4: Birs 6G 13
KILBY BRIDGE 5B 46
Kilby Dr. LE18: Wig 2C 46
Kilby Rd. LE8: Flec 4F 57
LE8: Wist 1F 57
Kildare St. LE1: Leic 3D 4 (1B 28)
Kildare Wlk. LE1: Leic 3D 4
Kilmelford Cl. LE4: Leic 1F 21
Kiln Av. LE4: Thurm 5D 14
Kiln Cl. LE9: B Ast 2C 60
Kilverstone Av. LE5: Leic 4D 30
Kilworth Dr. LE5: Leic 4G 29
Kimberley Rd. LE2: Leic 4E 29
Kimberley St. LE8: Kib B 5H 59
Kincaple Rd. LE4: Leic 1F 21
Kinchley Cl. LE3: Leic 2D 18
Kincraig Rd. LE4: Leic 1F 21
Kinder Cl. LE8: Whet 6A 44
Kingcup Cl. LE3: Leic E 5F 25
King Edward Av. LE19: Nar 4D 42
King Edward Rd. LE5: Leic 6H 21
Kingfisher Av. LE5: Leic 6E 21
Kingfisher Cl. LE3: Leic E 5E 25
LE7: Sys 5D 6
LE8: G Gle 2D 48
Kingfisher Ct. LE2: Leic 6B 5
Kingfisher Wlk. LE5: Leic 6E 21
King Richards Rd. LE3: Leic 2G 27
Kingsbridge Cl. LE19: Nar 3C 42
Kingsbridge Cres. LE4: Beau L 4B 12
Kingsbury Av. LE5: Leic 3C 30
Kingscliffe Cres. LE5: Leic 3D 30
Kings Ct. LE19: End 6H 33
Kings Dr. LE3: Leic E 5G 25
LE18: Wig 6F 37
Kingsfield Rd. LE9: Cosb 3E 53
Kingsgate Av. LE4: Birs 3F 13
King's Head Pl. LE16: Mkt H 3D 64
Kingsley Cl. LE19: Nar 2C 42
Kingsley Ind. Pk. LE8: Kib B 5B 62
Kingsley St. LE2: Leic 1C 36
Kings Lock Cl. LE2: Leic 5F 35
Kingsmead Cl. LE2: Leic 3E 37
Kingsmead Rd. LE2: Leic 2E 37
Kings Newton St. LE2: Leic 3E 29
King's Rd. LE16: Mkt H 3D 64
Kingsthorpe Cl. LE4: Leic 2B 20
Kingston Av. LE18: Wig 5D 36
Kingston Rd. LE2: Leic 4E 29
Kingston Way LE16: Mkt H 1C 64
King St. LE1: Leic 5D 5 (2B 28)
LE2: Oad 4B 38
LE7: Bark T 4H 15
LE8: Whet 4H 43
LE19: End 6H 33
Kings Wlk. LE3: Leic E 4G 25
Kings Way LE6: Groby 3F 17
LE17: Lut 5F 63
Kingsway LE3: Brau 6C 26
Kingsway Nth. LE3: Brau 5C 26
Kingsway Rd. LE5: Leic 5G 29
Kingswood Av. LE3: Leic 3F 27
Kingswood Ct. LE18: Wig 1A 46
King William Cl. LE19: End 6H 33
King William's Way LE7: Anst 4G 11
Kinley Rd. LE4: Leic 1A 20
Kinross Av. LE5: Leic 1E 31

Kinsdale Dr. LE5: Leic 6E 23
Kintyre Dr. LE4: Leic 1E 21
Kipling Dr. LE19: End 1C 42
Kipling Gro. LE4: Leic 3E 19
Kirby Cl. LE9: Sap 5B 50
KIRBY FIELDS 3F 25
Kirby La. LE9: Leic E 4F 25
KIRBY MUXLOE 2D 24
Kirby Muxloe Castle (remains) 1E 25
Kirby Rd. LE3: Glen 6F 17
    LE3: Leic 2G 27
Kirkdale Rd. LE18: Wig 1F 45
Kirke Wlk. LE3: Leic 1B 26
Kirkfield Rd. LE8: Count 1F 55
Kirkland Rd. LE3: Brau 1D 34
Kirk La. LE19: End 6H 33
Kirkscroft Wlk. LE4: Leic 2B 20
Kirkstead Wlk. LE4: Leic 2A 20
Kirkstone Cl. LE3: Glen 4B 18
Kirkwall Cres. LE5: Leic 6E 23
Kirloe Av. LE3: Leic E 4F 25
Kirminton Gdns. LE5: Leic 1C 30
Kirtley Way LE9: B Ast 1C 60
Kitchener Rd. LE5: Leic 6G 21
    LE7: Anst 4G 11
Kite Cl. LE9: B Ast 5A 52
KNIGHTON 2D 36
Knighton Chu. Rd. LE2: Leic 2E 37
Knighton Cl. LE9: B Ast 3C 60
Knighton Ct. LE2: Leic 5E 29
Knighton Dr. LE2: Leic 1E 37
KNIGHTON FIELDS 6C 28
Knighton Flds. Rd. E. LE2: Leic 1C 36
Knighton Flds. Rd. W. LE2: Leic 1B 36
Knighton Grange Rd. LE2: Leic 1G 37
Knighton Hall LE2: Leic 1E 37
Knighton Junc. La. LE2: Leic 6C 28
Knighton La. LE2: Leic 1A 36
Knighton La. E. LE2: Leic 1B 36
Knighton Lodge LE2: Leic 1E 37
Knighton Pk. Rd. LE2: Leic 5D 28
Knighton Ri. LE2: Leic 6G 29
Knighton Rd. LE2: Leic 1D 36
Knighton St. LE2: Leic 7C 5 (3B 28)
Knighton Tennis Club 2C 36
Knighton Way LE1: Leic 5C 28
Knightsbridge Rd. LE2: G Par 2D 44
Knights Cl. LE4: Thurm 4D 14
    LE9: S Stan 2B 50
Knight's End Rd. LE16: G Bow 1G 65
Knight's Rd. LE4: Beau L 5C 12
Knollgate Cl. LE4: Birs 3E 13
Knoll St. LE16: Mkt H 3B 64
Knossington Dr. LE7: Sys 6H 7
Knowle, The LE2: Leic 1E 37
Knowles Rd. LE3: Leic 6C 18
Krefeld Way LE4: Leic 2E 19

L

Labrador Cl. LE1: Leic 1F 4 (6C 20)
Laburnum Av. LE17: Lut 4F 63
Laburnum Rd. LE5: Leic 4C 22
Lacey Cl. LE17: Lut 2G 63
Ladbroke Gro. LE8: Count 1F 55
Lady Augusta Rd. LE4: Birs 2G 13
Lady Hay Rd. LE3: Leic 2C 18
Lady Jane Pk. LE6: New L 3A 10
Lady Jane Wlk. LE7: Scra 5F 23
Lady Leys LE9: Cosb 2E 53
Ladysmith Rd. LE9: K Mux 2D 24
    LE18: Wig 6A 36
Ladywood Ct. LE17: Lut 3G 63
Laithwaite Cl. LE4: Beau L 5B 12
Lakeside Bus. Pk. LE4: Thurm 5A 14
Lakeside Ct. LE7: Thurn 3F 31
Lakeview Chase LE5: Ham 2C 22
Lakin Dr. LE3: Brau 5A 26
Lambert Rd. LE3: Leic 5G 27
Lamborne Rd. LE2: Leic 4C 36
Lambourne Rd. LE4: Birs 3H 13
Lamen Rd. LE3: Leic 4C 18

Lamplighters LE8: Flec 6B 58
Lamport Cl. LE18: Wig 1D 46
Lancashire St. LE4: Leic 2D 20
Lancaster Cl. LE17: Lut 5G 63
Lancaster Ct. LE6: Groby 3E 17
Lancaster Pl. LE1: Leic 8E 5 (4C 28)
Lancaster Rd. LE1: Leic 7D 5 (3B 28)
    (not continuous)
Lancaster St. LE5: Leic 1F 29
Lancaster Wlk. LE1: Leic 7D 5 (3B 28)
Lancaster Way LE2: G Par 2E 45
Lancelot Cl. LE3: Leic E 5G 25
Lancing Av. LE3: Leic 1E 27
Landscape Dr. LE5: Leic 3C 30
Landseer Rd. LE2: Leic 6D 28
Lane Cl. LE3: Glen 5A 18
Lanesborough Dr. LE7: Thurc 1B 12
    (off Mill Rd.)
Lanesborough Rd. LE4: Leic 1D 20
Lanes Ct. LE18: Wig 1B 46
Lanes Hill Gro. LE9: S Stan 4C 50
Langdale LE8: Leic 5B 58
Langdale Rd. LE4: Thurm 4D 14
Langdale Wlk. LE16: Mkt H 5D 64
Langford Way LE4: Leic 4H 21
Langham Dr. LE19: Nar 3C 42
Langham Rd. LE4: Leic 2H 21
Langhill, The LE5: Leic 1H 29
Langholm Rd. LE5: Leic 1E 31
Langley Av. LE4: Leic 2B 20
Langley Cl. LE9: Hun 3A 42
Langley Gdns. LE4: Leic 2B 20
Langley Wlk. LE4: Leic 2A 20
Langton Ct. LE16: Mkt H 3D 64
Langton Rd. LE8: Kib H 3A 62
    LE18: Wig 2B 46
Lansdowne Gro. LE18: Wig 3F 45
Lansdowne Rd. LE2: Leic 1A 36
Lapwing Cl. LE4: Beau L 5B 12
Lapwing Ct. LE19: Nar 4C 42
Larch Dr. LE17: Lut 4F 63
Larch Gro. LE3: Brau 4A 26
Larch St. LE5: Leic 6E 21
Larchwood LE8: Count 1E 55
Larchwood Av. LE6: Groby 2F 17
Larchwood Cl. LE2: Leic 2C 36
Lark Cl. LE3: Leic E 5F 25
Larkspur Cl. LE5: Ham 2B 22
Larkswood LE8: Kib B 5B 62
Lastingham Cl. LE2: Leic 3C 36
Lathkill St. LE16: Mkt H 5E 65
Latimer Cl. LE8: Bla 5A 44
Latimer Ct. LE7: Anst 6F 11
Latimer Cres. LE16: L Bow 4E 65
Latimer Pl. LE4: Leic 5C 20
Latimer Rd. LE7: Crop 1H 11
Latimer St. LE3: Leic 3H 27
    LE7: Anst 6G 11
Launceston Ho. LE18: Wig 3A 46
Launceston Rd. LE18: Wig 2A 46
Launde Pk. LE16: L Bow 4F 65
Launde Rd. LE2: Oad 2C 38
    LE67: Mark 3D 8
Laundon Cl. LE6: Groby 3F 17
Laundon Way LE6: Groby 4E 17
    LE8: Whet 6A 44
Laundry La. LE4: Leic 3D 20
Laurel Cl. LE3: Glen 5C 18
    LE8: Count 1E 55
Laurel Dr. LE2: Oad 6D 38
Laurel Rd. LE2: Leic 3E 29
    LE8: Bla .3B 44
Laurels, The LE67: Mark 5C 8
Laureston Dr. LE2: Leic 5F 29
Lavender Cl. LE8: Bla 3A 44
    LE17: Lut 4E 63
Lavender Rd. LE3: Leic 4G 27
Lavershall Way LE19: Brau 3C 34
Laverstock Rd. LE18: Wig 3A 46
Lawford Rd. LE2: Leic 5H 35
Lawn Av. LE4: Birs 4H 13
Lawn Cl. LE4: Thurm 4D 14

Lawnhurst Way LE4: Birs 2F 13
Lawns, The LE2: Leic 5E 29
Lawnwood Rd. LE6: Groby 2D 16
Lawrence Cl. LE4: Leic 2C 12
Lawrence Wlk. LE3: Leic 2E 27
Law St. LE4: Leic 4C 20
Lawyers La. LE2: Oad 4A 38
Laxford Cl. LE4: Leic 3G 19
Laxton Cl. LE4: Birs 3H 13
    LE18: Wig 1D 46
Layton Rd. LE5: Leic 6G 21
Lea, The LE8: Kib B 5B 62
Lea Cl. LE4: Thurm 4B 14
    LE9: B Ast 2C 60
Lealand, The LE16: E Farn 6A 64
Leamington Dr. LE8: Bla 5B 44
Leas Cl. LE7: Thurn 1F 31
Ledbury Cl. LE2: Oad 5D 38
Ledbury Rd. LE4: Leic 6D 12
Ledwell Dr. LE3: Glen 4A 18
Lee Circ. LE1: Leic 2E 4 (1C 28)
Lee Cl. LE9: S Stan 2C 50
Lee Ri. LE6: Ratby 5D 16
Leeson St. LE2: Leic 2A 36
Lee St. LE1: Leic 2D 4 (1B 28)
Legion Way LE19: Brau 1B 34
LEICESTER 4D 4 (1B 28)
Leicester Abbey (remains) 4A 20
LEICESTER AIRPORT 2G 39
Leicester Bowling Club 2E 37
Leicester Castle Mound 5A 5 (2A 28)
Leicester Cathedral 4C 4 (2B 28)
Leicester City FC 5A 28
LEICESTER FOREST EAST 5F 25
LEICESTER FOREST EAST SERVICE AREA
    . . . . .5H 25
LEICESTER FRITH HOSPITAL 3D 18
    (within Glenfield Hospital)
LEICESTER GENERAL HOSPITAL 3A 30
Leicester Guildhall 4B 4
Leicester La. LE9: Des 6A 24
    LE19: End 6H 33
Leicester Leys Leisure Cen. 6A 12
Leicester Monarchs (Speedway) 1A 4
Leicester North Station
    Great Central Railway 6F 13
LEICESTER NUFFIELD HEALTH HOSPITAL
    . . . . .5B 22
Leicester Outdoor Pursuits Cen. 1C 20
Leicester Racecourse 4G 37
Leicester Rd. LE2: G Par 2B 44
    LE2: Leic, Oad 2G 37
    LE2: Oad 4A 38
    LE3: Glen 3B 18
    LE4: Leic 2D 12
    LE6: Groby 2F 17
    LE7: Anst 5G 11
    LE7: Crop, Thurc 1B 12
    LE8: Bla .2B 44
    LE8: Count 1F 55
    LE8: Flec 4B 58
    LE8: Kib H 1G 59
    LE9: Sap 6B 50
    LE16: Mkt H 1B 64
    LE17: Lut 1G 63
    LE18: Wig 4E 37
    LE19: End, Nar 4E 43
    LE67: Mark 2C 8
LEICESTER ROYAL INFIRMARY
    . . . . .7C 5 (3B 28)
Leicestershire County Cricket Ground
    . . . . .2A 36
Leicestershire Lawn Tennis Club 6E 29
LEICESTER SPIRE HOSPITAL 6A 30
Leicester Station (Rail) 5F 5 (2C 28)
Leicester St. LE5: Leic 1F 29
Leicester Tigers RFC 8D 5 (4B 28)
Leicester Western By-Pass
    LE4: Beau L, Leic 6H 11
    LE6: Groby 6F 17
    LE7: Anst 1A 18
    LE7: Sys, Wan 2E 13
LEIRE 6B 60

Leire La. LE9: B Ast 3A 60
   LE17: D Bas 6D 60
   LE17: Leire 6B 60
Leire Rd. LE17: Leire 6A 60
Leire St. LE4: Leic 3D 20
Lema Cl. LE4: Leic 6C 14
Lena Dr. LE6: Groby 6G 9
Len Hollis Ct. LE2: Leic 2D 28
               (off Barnard Cl.)
Lenthall Sq. LE16: Mkt H 5D 64
Leopold Cl. LE8: Count 1D 54
Leopold Rd. LE2: Lelc 6C 28
Leopold St. LE18: Wig 1F 45
Letchworth Rd. LE3: Leic 1E 27
Lethbridge Cl. LE1: Leic 1F 4 (6C 20)
Leveret Dr. LE8: Whet 6H 43
Leveric Rd. LE5: Leic 5G 21
Lewis Cl. LE4: Leic 3F 19
Lewis Ct. LE19: End 4B 34
Lewisher Rd. LE4: Leic 2H 21
Lewis Way LE8: Count 2F 55
Lewitt Cl. LE4: Leic 1H 19
Lexham St. LE4: Leic 3D 20
Leybury Way LE7: Scra 1F 31
Leycroft Rd. LE4: Beau L 5B 12
Leyland Rd. LE3: Brau 2D 34
Leys, The LE7: E Gos 1H 7
   LE8: Count 2C 54
   LE8: Kib B 4A 62
Leys Cl. LE2: Oad 3C 38
Leysdale Cl. LE4: Leic 2F 19
Leyton Cl. LE17: Lut 5H 63
Liberty Pk. LE2: Leio 8A 5
Liberty Rd. LE3: Glen, Leic 1B 26
Lichfield Av. LE9: B Ast 5A 52
Lichfield Dr. LE8: Bla 5B 44
Lichfield Ct. LE1: Leic 1C 4 (6B 20)
Lidster Cl. LE5: Leic 5B 22
Lilac Av. LE5: Leic 4C 22
Lilac Dr. LE17: Lut 4E 63
Lilac Wlk. LE5: Leic 4C 22
Lillingstone Cl. LE67: Mark 2C 8
Limber Cres. LE3: Leic 4C 26
Lime Av. LE6: Groby 3E 17
Lime Cl. LE7: Sys 6F 7
Lime Dr. LE7: Sys 1F 15
Lime Gro. LE8: Bla 3B 44
   LE9: K Mux 2D 24
Lime Gro. Cl. LE4: Leic 1G 19
Limehurst Rd. LE5: Leic 4D 22
Lime Kilns LE18: Wig 3C 46
Limes, The LE18: Wig 1B 46
Limes Cl. LE7: Thurn 2G 31
Limetree Av. LE4: Birs 3G 13
Lime Tree Rd. LE19: End 1F 43
Linacres Rd. LE3: Leic 4C 26
Lincoln Ct. LE16: Mkt H 1E 65
Lincoln Dr. LE7: Sys 1G 15
   LE8: Bla 5B 44
   LE18: Wig 1F 45
Lincoln St. LE2: Leic 5F 5 (2D 28)
Linden Av. LE8: Count 1C 54
Linden Dr. LE5: Leic 4H 29
   LE17: Lut 4F 63
Linden Dr. Fr.
   LE8: Count 1D 54
Linden Farm Rd. LE5: Leic 1C 30
Linden La. LE9: K Mux 3F 25
Linden St. LE5: Leic 2F 29
Lindfield Rd. LE3: Leic 6E 19
Lindisfarne Rd. LE7: Sys 6D 6
Lindrick Dr. LE5: Leic 5G 29
Lindsay Rd. LE3: Leic 6F 27
Lindsey Gdns. LE16: Mkt H 6C 64
Lindum Cl. LE7: Sys 1D 14
Lineker Rd. LE2: Leic 8A 5 (4A 28)
Linford Cl. LE18: Wig 1C 46
Linford Cres. LE67: Mark 3C 8
Linford St. LE4: Leic 2C 20
Ling Dale LE7: E Gos 2H 7
Lingdale Lodge
   LE7: E Gos 2H 7
Link Ri. LE67: Mark 3D 8

Link Rd. LE2: Leic 2G 37
   LE7: Anst 5E 11
   LE7: Quen 4H 7
Links Rd. LE8: Kib B 5B 62
   LE9: K Mux 3C 24
Linkway Gdns. LE3: Leic 2G 27
Linley Grn. LE9: Cosb 2F 53
Linnett Cl. LE19: Nar 4C 42
Linney Rd. LE4: Leic 3G 19
Lintlaw Cl. LE4: Leic 1F 21
Linton St. LE5: Leic 3E 29
Linwood La. LE2: Leic 3B 36
Lipton Rd. LE4: Beau L 5A 12
Lismore Wlk. LE4: Leic 2F 19
Lit. Barley Cl. LE4: Leic 2F 19
LITTLE BOWDEN 4F 65
Lit. Bowden Mnr. LE16: L Bow 3E 65
Lit. Connery Leys LE4: Birs 2F 13
Little Dale LE18: Wig 2C 46
Lit. Dunmow Rd. LE5: Leic 5H 21
Lit. Easton Cl. LE5: Leic 5H 21
Littlefare, The LE3: Brau 5B 26
Littlegarth LE2: Leic 4B 36
Lit. Glen Rd. LE2: G Par 2C 44
Little Hill LE18: Wig 1B 46
LITTLE HILL ESTATE, THE 2B 46
Lit. Holme St. LE3: Leic 5A 5 (2H 27)
Lit. John Rd. LE5: Leic 5H 35
Little La. LE17: Leire 6B 60
Little Lunnon LE17: D Bas 6E 61
Lit. Markfield LE67: Mark 3A 8
Lit. Masons Cl. LE3: Brau 6B 26
Littlemeer Cl. LE3: Brau 6B 26
Littlemore Cl. LE5: Leic 1H 29
Lit. Pool Rd. LE3: Leic 1G 27
Little Theatre 5E 5
LITTLETHORPE 5D 42
Littleton St. LE4: Leic 6H 19
Littleway, The LE5: Leic 1H 29
             (not continuous)
Lit. Wood Cl. LE4: Leic 1G 19
Livesey Cl. LE9: Sap 6A 50
Livesey Dr. LE9: Sap 6A 50
Livingstone St. LE3: Leic 3G 27
Llewellyn Ct. LE2: Leic 6F 29
Lobbs Wood Cl. LE5: Leic 5B 22
Lobbs Wood Ct. LE5: Leic 5B 22
Lobelia Cl. LE19: Nar 3B 42
Locke Av. LE4: Leic 6B 14
Lockerbie Av. LE4: Leic 1E 21
Lockerbie Wlk. LE4: Leic 1F 21
Lock Ga. Cl. LE18: Wig 3G 45
Lockhouse Cl. LE2: Leic 5F 35
Lock Keeper Cl. LE18: Wig 3G 45
Lockley Cl. LE6: Ratby 5D 16
Lockley Gdns. LE9: Sap 6C 50
Lockside Cl. LE2: G Par 1A 44
Loddington Cl. LE7: Sys 6G 7
Lodge Cl. LE4: Thurm 5D 14
   LE7: Sys 5G 7
   LE8: Kib H 3H 59
   LE9: Hun 3H 41
Lodge Farm LE19: Litt 5D 42
Lodge Farm Rd. LE5: Leic 1C 30
Lodge M. LE7: Thurn 3E 31
Lodge Rd. LE8: Flec 6E 59
Lodgewood Av. LE4: Birs 4F 13
Logan Av. LE2: Leic 3G 35
Logan Cl. LE16: Mkt H 2C 64
Logan Cres. LE16: Mkt H 2B 64
Logan St. LE16: Mkt H 3C 64
Lombardy Ri. LE5: Leic 6E 21
Lomond Cres. LE4: Leic 3G 19
London Rd. LE1: Leic 6F 5 (3C 28)
   LE2: Leic 6F 5 (3C 28)
   LE2: Oad 6D 38
               (Gorse La.)
   LE2: Oad 4A 38
            (Leicester Rd.)
   LE8: Bur O, G Gle 4D 48
   LE67: Mark 3B 8

London St. LE5: Leic 1F 29
Long Brimley Cl. LE16: L Bow 3G 65
Longcliffe Rd. LE5: Leic 6E 21
Long Cl. LE7: Anst 4E 11
Longfellow Rd. LE2: Leic 1C 36
Longford Cl. LE18: Wig 3A 46
Long Furrow LE7: E Gos 2H 7
Long Grey LE8: Flec 4A 58
Longhade Furlong LE7: Anst 4H 11
Longhurst Cl. LE4: Leic 6C 14
Longlands, The LE16: L Bow 3G 65
Long La. LE1: Leic 2B 4 (1A 28)
   LE18: Wig 1B 46
Longleat Cl. LE5: Leic 5F 21
   LE16: L Bow 3G 65
Long Meadow LE18: Wig 3C 46
Long Mdw. Way LE4: Birs 2F 13
Long Roses Way LE4: Birs 2F 13
Longstone Grn. LE5: Leic 6E 23
Long St. LE9: S Stan 2C 50
   LE18: Wig 1A 46
Lonsdale Rd. LE4: Thurm 5C 14
Lonsdale St. LE2: Leic 3E 29
Lord Bassett Cl. LE9: Sap 6B 50
Lord Byron St. LE2: Leic 1C 36
Lord Cl. LE19: Nar 4D 42
Lords Av. LE4: Beau L 4C 12
Lorne Rd. LE2: Leic 6C 28
LOROS HOSPICE 3E 19
Lorraine Rd. LE2: Leic 2H 35
Lorrimer Rd. LE2: Leic 1A 36
Loseby La. LE1: Leic 4C 4 (2B 28)
Loseby Wlk. LE1: Leic 4C 4
      (within St Martins Sq. Shop. Cen.)
Lothair Rd. LE2: Leic 6A 28
Loughborough Rd. LE4: Birs, Leic . . .6F 13
   LE4: Birs, Wan 1G 13
   LE7: R'ley, Wan 1G 13
Loughland Cl. LE8: Bla 3A 44
Louise Av. LE6: Groby 3F 17
Lound Rd. LE9: Sap 5B 50
Lovelace Way LE8: Flec 6C 58
Loves La. LE17: D Bas 6F 61
Lowcroft Dr. LE2: Oad 5C 38
Lwr. Brown St. LE1: Leic 5C 5 (3B 28)
Lwr. Church St. LE7: Sys 5F 7
Lwr. Free La. LE1: Leic 3D 4 (1B 28)
Lwr. Hastings St. LE1: Leic . . .7E 5 (3C 28)
Lwr. Hill St. LE1: Leic 2D 4 (1B 28)
Lwr. Keyham La. LE5: Leic 4E 23
           (Hamilford Cl.)
   LE5: Leic 5A 22
              (Main St.)
Lwr. Lee St. LE1: Leic 2D 4 (1B 28)
Lwr. Leicester Rd. LE17: Lut 4H 63
Lwr. Willow St. LE1: Leic 6C 20
Lowick Dr. LE18: Wig 1C 46
Lowland Av. LE3: Leic E 5G 25
Loxley Rd. LE3: Glen 4A 18
LUBBESTHORPE 2H 33
Lubbesthorpe Bridle Rd. LE3: Brau . . .6C 26
   LE19: End 1F 33
Lubbesthorpe Rd. LE3: Brau 2C 34
Lubbesthorpe Way LE3: Brau 1B 34
           (Dominus Way)
   LE3: Brau 4B 26
        (Kingsway Nth.)
   LE19: Brau 1B 34
Lubenham Hill LE16: Mkt H 3A 64
Lubenham Rd. LE16: E Farn 4A 64
Lucas' Marsh Nature Reserve 5A 38
Ludgate Cl. LE4: Birs 3E 13
Ludlam Cl. LE8: Count 1C 54
Ludlow Cl. LE2: Oad 4C 38
Lulworth Cl. LE5: Leic 3H 29
   LE18: Wig 4B 46
Lunsford Rd. LE5: Leic 5F 21
Luther St. LE3: Leic 3G 27
LUTTERWORTH 5G 63
Lutterworth One Stop Shop 4H 63
Lutterworth Rd. LE2: Leic 5G 35
   LE8: Whet, Bla 6A 44
   LE9: Cosb 6G 61

Lutterworth Rd. LE17: Bitt 2F 63
  LE17: Lut, D Bas, Cosb 6G 61
  LE17: Lut, Mist 6H 63
Lutterworth Sports Cen. 4G 63
Lychgate Cl. LE7: Crop 1G 11
Lydall Rd. LE2: Leic 5A 36
Lydford Rd. LE4: Leic 3G 21
Lyle Cl. LE4: Leic 6C 14
Lyme Rd. LE2: Leic 4E 29
Lymington Rd. LE5: Leic 5D 22
Lyn Cl. LE3: Leic 2D 18
Lyncote Rd. LE3: Leic 1F 35
Lyncroft Leys LE7: Scra 6E 23
Lyndale Cl. LE4: Thurm 5C 14
Lyndale Rd. LE3: Brau 1D 34
Lyndhurst LE2: Leic 5E 29
Lyndhurst Rd. LE2: Oad 3A 38
Lyndon Dr. LE2: Oad 3H 37
Lyndwood Ct. LE2: Leic 6F 29
Lyngate Av. LE4: Birs 3G 13
Lynholme Rd. LE2: Leic 3D 36
Lynmouth Cl. LE3: Glen 6A 18
Lynmouth Dr. LE18: Wig 4C 36
Lynmouth Rd. LE5: Leic 5D 22
Lyon Cl. LE18: Wig 5C 36
Lytham Rd. LE2: Leic 6C 28
Lytton Rd. LE2: Leic 5D 28
              (not continuous)

M

Mablowe Fld. LE18: Wig 3C 46
Macaulay Rd. LE17: Lut 2G 63
Macaulay St. LE2: Leic 1B 36
Macdonald Rd. LE4: Leic 4C 20
McDowell Way LE19: Nar 4D 42
Machin Dr. LE9: B Ast 3C 60
McKenzie Wlk. LE5: Leic 2A 30
Mackenzie Way LE1: Leic 1F 4 (6C 20)
McVicker Cl. LE5: Leic 1A 30
Madeline Cl. LE16: G Bow 1F 65
Madeline Rd. LE4: Beau L 5C 12
Madras Rd. LE1: Leic 1D 28
Magazine Wlk. LE1: Leic 5B 5 (2A 28)
Magistrates' Court
  Leicester 5C 5 (2B 28)
Magna Rd. LE18: Wig 2G 45
Magna Rd. Ind. Est. LE18: Wig 2G 45
Magnolia Cl. LE2: Leic 4G 35
  LE3: Leic E 5E 25
Magnolia Dr. LE17: Lut 3F 63
Magnus Rd. LE4: Leic 3E 21
Maiden St. LE7: Sys 6D 6
Maidenwell Av. LE5: Leic, Ham 4C 22
Maidstone Rd. LE2: Leic 2D 28
Maidwell Cl. LE18: Wig 1D 46
Maino Cres. LE17: Lut 5E 63
Main St. LE3: Brau 5C 26
  LE3: Glen 4H 17
  LE5: Leic .5B 30
              (School La.)
  LE5: Leic .5A 30
              (Warren Cl.)
  LE6: New L 2H 9
  LE6: Ratby 5C 16
  LE7: Bark 3G 15
  LE7: Bush, Thurn 3F 31
  LE7: Coss 1A 6
  LE7: Scra 5F 23
  LE8: Bur O 3H 49
  LE8: Count 2F 55
  LE8: Flec .6B 58
  LE8: G Gle 3D 48
  LE8: Kib H 3A 62
  LE8: Peat M 6G 55
  LE8: Smee W 6H 59
  LE9: B Ast 6A 52
  LE9: Cosb 2F 53
              (not continuous)
  LE9: Hun .4H 41
  LE9: K Mux 2D 24
  LE9: Thurl 6A 32

Main St. LE16: E Farn 6A 64
  LE17: D Bas 5F 61
  LE17: Leire 6B 60
  LE18: Kilby 2D 56
  LE67: Mark 3B 8
Malabar Rd. LE1: Leic 2F 4 (1D 28)
Malcolm Arc. LE1: Leic 3C 4
Malham Cl. LE4: Leic 2G 19
Malham Way LE2: Oad 4D 38
Mallard Av. LE6: Groby 2E 17
Mallard Dr. LE7: Sys 5D 6
Mallard Way LE3: Leic E 5E 25
Malling Av. LE9: B Ast 6H 51
Malling Cl. LE4: Birs 2H 13
Malvern Rd. LE2: Leic 5F 29
Mandarin Way LE8: Whet 1H 53
Mandervell Rd. LE2: Oad 4H 37
Mandora La. LE2: Leic 3D 28
Manitoba Rd. LE1: Leic 1E 4 (6C 20)
Mann Cl. LE3: Brau 5B 26
Manners Rd. LE2: Leic 2A 36
Mnr. Brook Cl. LE9: S Stan 2C 50
Manor Cl. LE2: Oad 1B 38
Manor Ct. LE8: Bla 3C 44
Manor Dr. LE4: Beau L 6A 12
Mnr. Farm Cl. LE9: B Ast 1B 60
Mnr. Farm Way LE3: Glen 6A 18
Manor Gdns. LE3: Glen 5A 18
Manor Ho. Gdns. LE5: Leic 4C 30
Manor Rd. LE2: Oad 1H 37
  LE4: Thurm 5B 14
  LE8: Flec .6C 58
  LE9: Cosb 1F 53
  LE9: Sap .5B 50
  LE17: Bitt .2F 63
Manor Rd. Extension
  LE2: Oad .2B 38
Manor Road Sports Hall 2A 38
Manor St. LE18: Wig 1H 45
Manor Wlk. LE16: Mkt H 3D 64
Mansfield St. LE1: Leic 2C 4 (1B 28)
Manston Cl. LE4: Leic 6E 15
Mantle Rd. LE3: Leic 1H 27
Manton Cl. LE9: B Ast 1D 60
Manton Way LE7: Sys 1G 15
Maple Av. LE3: Brau 4A 26
  LE8: Bla .5B 44
  LE8: Count 1F 55
Maple Cl. LE4: Leic 3A 20
Maple Ct. LE2: Leic 2D 28
Maple Dr. LE17: Lut 4F 63
Maple Rd. LE4: Thurm 5B 14
Mapleton Rd. LE18: Wig 6E 37
Maple Tree Wlk. LE19: Litt 4E 43
Maplewell Dr. LE4: Beau L 5A 12
Maplin Rd. LE5: Leic 4E 23
Marble St. LE1: Leic 5C 5 (2B 28)
Marcus Cl. LE7: Sys 1C 14
Marefield Cl. LE7: Thurn 1G 31
Marfitt St. LE4: Leic 3D 20
Margam Cl. LE3: Leic 3F 19
Margaret Anne Rd. LE2: Oad 5B 38
Margaret Cl. LE4: Thurm 3C 14
Margaret Cres. LE18: Wig 6D 36
Margaret Rd. LE5: Leic 2G 29
              (not continuous)
Marigold Way LE19: Nar 3B 42
Marina Dr. LE6: Groby 2G 17
Marina Rd. LE5: Leic 3F 29
Marions Way LE9: Crof 1H 51
Marjorie St. LE4: Leic 4C 20
Markam Ct. LE4: Thurm 5C 14
MARKET GDN. Cl. LE4: Thurm 5C 14
MARKET HARBOROUGH 3D 64
MARKET HARBOROUGH &
  DISTRICT HOSPITAL 3C 64

Market Harborough Old Grammer School
  . . . . .3D 64
          (off Adam & Eve St.)
Market Harborough Station (Rail) 3F 65
Market Pl. LE1: Leic 4C 4 (2B 28)
Market Pl. App. LE1: Leic 4D 4 (2B 28)
Market Pl. Sth. LE1: Leic 4C 4 (2B 28)
Market St. LE1: Leic 4C 4 (2B 28)
  LE17: Lut .4G 63
MARKFIELD 3C 8
Markfield Community Sports Cen. 3C 8
Markfield Ct. Retirement Village
  LE67: Mark 5C 8
Markfield Ind. Est. LE67: Mark 1A 8
Markfield La. LE6: New L 2D 8
  LE67: Mark, New L 2D 8
Markfield Rd. LE6: Groby 1D 16
  LE6: Ratby 3B 16
Markland LE2: Leic 5G 35
Marlborough Dr. LE8: Flec 6F 59
Marlborough Pl. LE17: Lut 5G 63
Marlborough St. LE1: Leic 5D 5 (2B 28)
Marlborough Way LE16: Mkt H 1D 64
Marlow Rd. LE3: Leic 5H 27
Marmion Cl. LE8: Flec 6F 59
Maromme Sq. LE18: Wig 6F 37
Marquis St. LE1: Leic 6D 5 (3B 28)
Marriott Cl. LE3: Leic E 5H 25
Marriott Dr. LE8: Kib H 5B 62
Marriott Rd. LE2: Leic 4A 36
Marriot Wlk. LE2: Leic 3B 36
Marsden Av. LE7: Quen 4H 7
Marsden La. LE2: Leic 3F 35
Marshall Cl. LE3: Brau 5A 26
Marshall Ct. LE16: Mkt H 4E 65
Marsh Av. LE8: Kib H 4B 62
Marsh Cl. LE4: Leic 6C 14
Marsh Dr. LE8: Kib H 4A 62
Marston Cl. LE2: Oad 6A 38
Marston Cres. LE8: Count 2E 55
Marston Dr. LE6: Groby 2F 17
Marston Rd. LE4: Leic 3G 21
  LE9: Crof .6F 41
Marstown Av. LE18: Wig 1F 45
Martel Ho. LE8: G Gle 2D 48
Martin Av. LE2: Oad 4B 38
  LE9: Leic E 4F 25
Martin Cl. LE4: Leic 5D 20
  LE9: S Stan 4B 50
Martin Ct. LE7: Anst 6F 11
Martindale Cl. LE2: Leic 8B 5 (4A 28)
Martin Dr. LE7: Sys 5C 6
Martin Ryan Wlk. LE3: Leic 6A 5 (3H 27)
Martinshaw Cl. LE3: Leic 2C 18
Martinshaw La. LE6: Groby 2E 17
Martin Sq. LE6: Ratby 5D 16
Martin St. LE4: Leic 5D 20
Martins Yd. LE16: Mkt H 3D 64
Martival LE5: Leic 5G 21
Marvin Cl. LE3: Leic 6F 19
Marwell Cl. LE4: Leic 1B 20
Marwell Wlk. LE4: Leic 1B 20
Marwood Rd. LE4: Leic 1H 19
Mary Ct. LE3: Leic 5F 19
Marydene Ct. LE5: Leic 4C 30
Marydene Dr. LE5: Leic 4C 30
Mary Gee Ho's. LE2: Leic 1F 37
Marylebone Dr. LE17: Lut 4H 63
Mary Rd. LE3: Leic 5F 19
Mary's Ct. LE7: Anst 5F 11
Masefield Av. LE19: End 1C 42
Mason Row LE5: Ham 2D 22
Masons Cl. LE19: Nar 4D 42
Matlock Av. LE18: Wig 2G 45
Matlock St. LE2: Leic 1E 29
Matts Cl. LE2: Leic 4H 35
Maura Cl. LE8: Whet 6H 43
Maurice Dr. LE8: Count 2D 54
Maurice Rd. LE16: Mkt H 6C 64
Mavis Av. LE3: Leic 5G 27
Mawby Cl. LE8: Whet 6A 44

Maxfield Ho. LE2: Leic 2D 28
Maxwell Way LE17: Lut 2G 63
May Cl. LE3: Leic 3E 27
Mayfield Dr. LE18: Wig 5F 37
Mayfield Rd. LE2: Leic 4E 29
Mayflower Cl. LE67: Mark 3C 8
Mayflower Ct. LE67: Mark 3C 8
Mayflower Rd. LE5: Leic 4G 29
Mayflower Wlk. LE67: Mark 3C 8
(off Mayflower Cl.)
Maynard Rd. LE2: Leic 1D 28
(not continuous)
Mayns La. LE8: Bur O 5F 49
Mayor's Wlk. LE1: Leic 4C 28
Mayre Cl. LE9: B Ast 2D 60
Mays Farm Dr. LE9: S Stan 1B 50
Maytree Cl. LE9: Leic E 4E 25
Maytree Ct. LE9: Leic E 4E 25
Maytree Dr. LE9: Leic E 4E 25
Meadhurst Rd. LE3: Leic 2E 27
Meadow, The LE9: B Ast 2C 60
Meadowbrook Rd. LE8: Kib B 5H 59
Meadow Cl. LE6: Ratby 5D 16
LE9: S Stan 2B 50
LE16: Mkt H 2E 65
(off Meadow St.)
Meadow Ct. LE2: Leic 2G 35
LE18: Wig 1C 46
LE19: Nar 2C 42
Meadow Ct. Rd. LE6: Groby 2F 17
Meadowcourt Rd. LE2: Leic 2H 37
Meadowcroft Cl. LE3: Glen 6H 17
Meadowdale Rd. LE16: L Bow 2G 65
Meadow Gdns. LE2: Leic 3C 36
Meadow Hill LE8: G Gle 2C 48
Meadow La. LE4: Birs 3H 13
LE7: Sys 5B 6
LE67: Mark 2C 8
Meadows, The LE16: Litt 4F 43
Meadows Edge LE19: End 1C 42
MEADOWS ESTATE, THE 1D 46
Meadow St. LE16: Mkt H 2D 64
Meadowsweet Rd. LE5: Ham 3C 22
Meadow Vw. LE2: Oad 4B 38
Meadow Way LE6: Groby 2F 17
LE18: Wig 1C 46
Meads, The LE3: Leic 2C 26
Meadvale Rd. LE2: Leic 2D 36
Meadway LE3: Leic 1E 27
Meadway, The LE4: Birs 3G 13
LE7: Sys 1D 14
Meadwell Rd. LE3: Leic 3B 26
Medhurst Cl. LE8: Whet 6A 44
Medina Rd. LE3: Leic 5H 19
Medway Cl. LE16: L Bow 3F 65
Medway St. LE2: Leic 3E 29
Meer, The LE8: Flec 6F 59
Megazone Laser Cen. 1D 4
Melba Way LE4: Birs 2H 13
Melbourne Cl. LE8: Kib B 5H 59
Melbourne Rd. LE2: Leic 2E 29
Melbourne St. LE2: Leic 1D 28
Melcombe Wlk. LE4: Leic 2B 20
Melcroft Av. LE3: Leic 2F 27
Melford St. LE5: Leic 6H 21
Melland Pl. LE2: Leic 4A 36
Mellerstain Wlk. LE5: Leic 6G 21
Mellier Cl. LE19: Nar 1C 42
Mellor Rd. LE3: Leic 2E 27
Melody Av. LE7: Anst 5G 11
Melrose St. LE4: Leic 4D 20
Melton Av. LE4: Leic 6A 14
Melton Dr. LE9: B Ast 5A 52
Melton Rd. LE4: Leic, Thurm 4D 20
LE4: Thurm 5B 14
LE7: E Gos, Quen, Sys 5F 7
Melton St. LE1: Leic 6C 20
Memory La. LE1: Leic 6C 20
Mendip Av. LE4: Leic 4G 19
Mennecy Cl. LE8: Count 2D 54
Mensa Cl. LE2: Leic 2E 29
Menzies Rd. LE4: Leic 3A 20
Mercer's Way LE7: E Gos 2H 7

Merchants Comn. LE7: E Gos 2H 7
Mercia Dr. LE2: Oad 3H 37
Mercury Cl. LE2: Leic 2D 28
Mere, The LE8: G Gle 3C 48
Mere Cl. LE5: Leic 1E 29
Meredith Rd. LE3: Leic 6F 27
Mere La. LE2: Oad 1H 47
Mere Rd. LE2: Gt Stret 4H 39
LE5: Leic 6E 21
LE8: Peat M 6E 55
LE18: Wig 6G 37
Meres Wlk. LE18: Wig 6H 37
Mereworth Cl. LE5: Leic 5F 21
Meridian Bus. Pk. LE19: Brau 3B 34
(Meridian Sth.)
LE19: Brau 1B 34
(Tiber Way)
Meridian E. LE19: Brau 6B 26
Meridian Leisure Pk.
LE19: Brau 6C 26
Meridian Nth. LE19: Brau 2B 34
Meridian Sth. LE19: Brau 3B 34
Meridian Way LE19: Brau 6B 26
Meridian W. LE19: Brau 2B 34
Meriton Rd. LE17: Lut 5F 63
Merlin Cl. LE3: Leic E 5G 25
LE9: B Ast 6A 52
Merrydale Ct. LE5: Leic 5G 21
Merton Av. LE3: Leic 2G 27
LE7: Sys 6F 7
Merton Cl. LE9: B Ast 6H 51
Merton Way LE8: Kib H 4H 59
Merus Cl. LE19: Brau 6B 26
Mervyn Rd. LE5: Lelc 3F 29
Metcalf Cl. LE9: S Stan 3B 50
Methuen Av. LE4: Thurm 3C 14
Meynell Cl. LE2: Oad 5C 38
Meynell Rd. LE5: Leic 6F 21
Meynells Gorse (Park & Ride) 3A 26
Michael Lewis Ho. LE3: Leic 1F 27
Michael Ramsey Ct.
LE2: G Par 6G 35
Mickleton Dr. LE5: Leic 4B 30
Middlebrook Cl. LE6: Ratby 5D 16
Middlebrook Grn.
LE16: Mkt H 2E 65
Middledale Rd. LE16: L Bow 3F 65
Middlefield Rd. LE7: Coss 2B 6
Middlesex Rd. LE2: Leic 2H 35
Middleton Cl. LE9: S Stan 3C 50
LE18: Wig 6H 37
Middletons Cl. LE8: Flec 5B 58
Middleton St. LE2: Leic 2G 35
Midhurst Av. LE3: Brau 1D 34
Midland Cotts. LE18: Wig 1G 45
Midland Ct. LE17: Lut 2H 63
Midland St. LE1: Leic 3F 4 (1C 28)
Midway Rd. LE5: Leic 5F 29
Milestone Cl. LE8: Kib H 5B 62
Milford Cl. LE19: Nar 3C 42
Milford Rd. LE2: Leic 1D 36
Millbrook Cl. LE4: Leic 2B 20
Millbrook Dr. LE9: B Ast 2B 60
Millbrook Wlk. LE4: Leic 2B 20
Mill Cl. LE4: Birs 5H 13
LE8: Smee W 6H 59
LE9: Sap 5C 50
LE18: Wig 3F 45
Millday Cl. LE8: Kib H 4H 59
Mill Dr. LE6: Ratby 6D 16
Miller Cl. LE4: Leic 6C 14
Millers Cl. LE3: Glen 5G 17
LE7: Sys 6E 7
Millersdale Av. LE5: Leic 3D 30
Millers Gdns. LE16: Mkt H 4A 64
Millers Grange LE9: B Ast 2B 60
Millers Yd. LE16: Mkt H 3D 64
Millfield Cl. LE7: Anst 6F 11
Millfield Cres. LE3: Brau 3D 34
Mill Gro. LE17: Lut 5H 63
Mill Hill LE4: Leic 3C 20
LE19: End 5G 33
Mill Hill Cl. LE8: Whet 4A 44

Mill Hill Ind. Est. LE19: End 4G 33
(Feldspar Cl.)
LE19: End 5G 33
(Quarry La.)
Mill Hill La. LE2: Leic 3D 28
LE67: Mark 2B 8
Mill Hill Rd. LE16: Mkt H 3E 65
Milligan Rd. LE2: Leic 3A 36
Mill La. LE2: Leic 6A 5 (3A 28)
LE4: Thurm 3B 14
LE7: Sys 4D 6
LE8: Bla 3C 44
LE8: Kib B, Smee W 6G 59
LE9: Earl S, Thurl 3A 40
LE19: End 6H 33
Mill La., The LE3: Glen 5G 17
Mill La. Ind. Est. LE3: Glen 4F 17
Milll Fld. Av. LE8: Count 1D 54
Mill Rd. LE7: Thurc 1B 12
Millstone La. LE1: Leic 5B 5 (2B 28)
LE7: Sys 4G 7
Mill St. LE1: Leic 6D 5 (3B 28)
Mill Vw. LE7: Anst 6G 11
LE9: Hun 4H 41
Millwood Cl. LE4: Leic 6E 13
Milnroy Rd. LE5: Leic 1E 31
Milton Cl. LE18: Wig 1C 46
Milton Cres. LE4: Leic 2F 19
Milton Gdns. LE2: Oad 4A 38
LE19: Nar 2C 42
Milton Ho. LE4: Leic 2F 19
Milton St. LE19: Nar 2C 42
Milverton Av. LE4: Leic 4G 19
Milverton Cl. LE18: Wig 5E 37
Milverton Dr. LE18: Wig 5E 37
Minehead St. LE3: Leic 2F 27
Minster Ct. LE1: Leic 5C 5
Minster Cres. LE4: Leic 4H 19
Minstrel's Wlk. LE7: E Gos 2H 7
Mint Rd. LE2: Leic 7A 5 (3H 27)
Misterton Way LE17: Lut 5H 63
Mitchell Gro. LE7: Scra 5G 23
Mitchell Rd. LE19: End 6G 33
Moat Cl. LE9: Thurl 6A 32
Moat St. LE5: Leic 5C 22
Moat Gdns. LE9: Sap 6B 50
Moat Rd. LE5: Leic 2F 29
Moat St. LE18: Wig 1A 46
Modbury Av. LE4: Leic 1A 20
Moira St. LE4: Leic 4D 20
Monal Cl. LE8: Whet 1H 53
Monarch Cl. LE4: Birs 3A 14
Monar Cl. LE4: Leic 1F 21
Monckton Cl. LE1: Leic 1F 4 (6C 20)
Monica Rd. LE3: Brau 2D 34
Monks Cres. LE4: Leic 3C 12
Monmouth Dr. LE2: Leic 1C 44
Monroe Cl. LE16: Mkt H 1C 64
Monsell Dr. LE2: Leic 4G 35
Montague Av. LE7: Sys 1F 15
Montague Rd. LE2: Leic 5D 28
LE9: B Ast 6B 52
Monterey Ct. LE5: Leic 6A 22
Montgomery Cl. LE17: Lut 6E 63
Montreal Rd. LE1: Leic 1F 4 (6C 20)
Montrose Cl. LE16: Mkt H 5C 64
Montrose Ct. LE5: Leic 5A 22
Montrose Rd. LE2: Leic 4G 35
Montrose Rd. Sth. LE2: Leic 4G 35
Montvale Gdns. LE4: Leic 5H 19
Moon Cl. LE2: Leic 2D 28
Moores Cl. LE18: Wig 1E 45
Moores La. LE19: End 6H 33
Moores Rd. LE4: Leic 3D 20
Moorfields LE5: Leic 5D 22
Moorgate Av. LE4: Birs 3F 13
Moorgate St. LE4: Leic 5C 20
Moorland Rd. LE7: Sys 6C 6
Morban Rd. LE2: Leic 3F 35
Morcote Rd. LE3: Leic 4C 26
Moreton Rd. LE5: Leic 5H 21
Morland Av. LE2: Leic 1G 37

Morledge St. LE1: Leic 3F 4 (1C 28)
Morley Arc. LE1: Leic 3D 4
Morley Rd. LE5: Leic 1E 29
LE9: Sap 6C 50
Morley St. LE16: Mkt H 3C 64
Mornington St. LE5: Leic 6F 21
Morpeth Av. LE4: Leic 6D 12
Morpeth Dr. LE2: Oad 5D 38
Morris Cl. LE3: Brau 5B 26
Morrison Ct. LE8: Kib B 6A 62
Morris Rd. LE2: Leic 6C 28
Mortiboys Way LE9: S Stan 3B 50
Mortimer Pl. LE3: Leic 6F 27
Mortimer Rd. LE19: Nar 4C 42
Mortimer Way LE3: Leic 6E 27
Mortoft Rd. LE4: Leic 2D 20
Morton Wlk. LE5: Leic 5F 21
Morwoods, The LE2: Oad 4B 38
Mossdale Rd. LE3: Brau 1C 34
Mosse Way LE2: Oad 3C 38
Mossgate LE3: Leic 6E 19
Mosswithy LE8: Flec 6E 59
Mostyn Av. LE7: Sys 5G 7
Mostyn St. LE3: Leic 2F 27
Mottisford Rd. LE4: Leic 1B 20
Mottisford Wlk. LE4: Leic 1B 20
Moulton Rd. LE5: Ham 1B 22
Mount, The LE7: Scra 5F 23
LE17: D Bas 6E 61
Mountain Rd. LE4: Leic 1A 22
Mount Av. LE5: Leic 1F 29
Mountbatten Way LE17: Lut 5F 63
Mountcastle Rd. LE3: Leic 5G 27
Mt. Pleasant LE2: Oad 5D 38
Mount Rd. LE2: Oad 4B 38
LE5: Leic 1E 29
LE9: Cosb 2F 53
Mount Vw. LE8: G Gle 2E 49
Mowbray Dr. LE7: Sys 5G 7
Mowmacre Community & Sports Cen.
.......................6E 13
MOWMACRE HILL 6D 12
Mowmacre Hill LE4: Leic 6E 13
Mowsley End LE18: Wig 1B 46
Muirfield Cl. LE3: Leic 1A 26
Mulberry Av. LE3: Leic 1A 26
Mulberry Cl. LE17: Lut 3F 63
Mull Way LE8: Count 2F 55
Muncaster Cl. LE9: B Ast 3C 60
Mundella St. LE2: Leic 4E 29
Mundesley Rd. LE5: Ham 3B 22
Municipal Sq. W. LE1: Leic 4D 4
Munnings Cl. LE4: Leic 5D 20
Muntjack Rd. LE8: Whet 5H 43
Murby Way LE3: Brau 5A 26
Muriel Rd. LE3: Leic 2G 27
Murray Cl. LE9: B Ast 3B 60
Murrayfield Rd. LE3: Leic 2A 26
Murray St. LE2: Leic 1D 28
Mus. of Science & Technology 3B 20
Museum Sq. LE1: Leic 6E 5 (3C 28)
Musgrove Cl. LE3: Leic 2H 27
Musson Rd. LE3: Leic 6C 18
Muston Gdns. LE2: Leic 2D 36
MW House LE19: End 4C 34
Myrtle Av. LE4: Birs 2H 13
Myrtle Rd. LE2: Leic 3E 29

N

Nagle Gro. LE4: Leic 6B 14
Namur Rd. LE18: Wig 6A 36
Nansen Rd. LE5: Leic 3G 29
NARBOROUGH 3D 42
Narborough Bogs Nature Reserve 3F 43
Narborough Rd. LE3: Leic 6F 27
LE9: Cosb 6E 43
LE9: Hun 4H 41
Narborough Rd. Nth. LE3: Leic 2H 27
Narborough Rd. Sth. LE3: Brau 3D 34
LE19: End 5C 34
(not continuous)

Narborough Station (Rail) 4E 43
Narborough Wood Bus. Pk.
LE19: End 2E 33
Narrow Boat Cl. LE18: Wig 3G 45
Narrow La. LE2: Leic 3G 35
Naseby Cl. LE16: Mkt H 4D 64
LE18: Wig 1C 46
Naseby Rd. LE4: Leic 3G 21
Naseby Sq. LE16: Mkt H 4D 64
Naseby Way LE8: G Gle 3D 48
National Diving Cen. 4C 50
National Gas Mus., The 6A 28
National Space Cen. 3B 20
Navigation Dr. LE2: G Par 1A 44
Navigation St. LE1: Leic 1D 4 (6B 20)
Naylor Rd. LE7: Sys 4G 7
Neal Av. LE3: Brau 5C 26
Neale Ho. LE8: G Gle 2D 48
Necton St. LE7: Sys 6E 7
Nedham St. LE2: Leic 1D 28
Ned Ludd Cl. LE7: Anst 5G 11
Needham Av. LE2: G Par 6E 35
Needham Cl. LE2: Oad 5E 39
Needlegate LE1: Leic 1B 4 (6A 20)
Needwood Way LE19: Nar 1B 42
Nelot Way LE5: Leic 2B 30
Nelson St. LE1: Leic 6F 5 (3C 28)
LE7: Sys 6F 7
LE16: Mkt H 3C 64
Nene Ct. LE2: Oad 4C 38
Nene Dr. LE2: Oad 4C 38
Neptune Cl. LE2: Leic 2E 29
Neston Gdns. LE2: Leic 3B 36
Neston Rd. LE2: Leic 3B 36
Netherfield Cl. LE9: B Ast 1D 60
Netherfield Rd. LE7: Anst 4F 11
Nether Fld. Way LE3: Brau 6B 26
NETHER HALL 4D 22
Nether Hall La. LE4: Birs 5H 13
Netherhall Rd. LE5: Leic 5C 22
Netton Cl. LE18: Wig 3A 46
Nevanthon Rd. LE3: Leic 2F 27
Neville Dr. LE67: Mark 3B 8
Neville Rd. LE3: Leic 2F 27
Neville Smith Cl. LE9: Sap 6B 50
Newall Cl. LE17: Lut 4G 63
Newarke, The LE2: Leic 5A 5 (2A 28)
Newarke Cl. LE2: Leic 6A 5 (3A 28)
Newarke Grn. LE2: Leic 5B 5 (2A 28)
Newarke Houses Mus. & Gardens 5B 5
Newarke Point LE2: Leic ...6A 5 (3A 28)
Newarke St. LE1: Leic 5C 5 (2B 28)
Newark Rd. LE4: Thurm 3C 14
Newbiggin Pl. LE4: Leic 2G 19
New Bond St. LE1: Leic 3C 4 (1B 28)
New Bri. Rd. LE2: G Par 1A 44
New Bri. St. LE2: Leic 8B 5 (4A 28)
Newbury Cl. LE18: Wig 2A 46
Newby Cl. LE8: Whet 2H 43
Newby Gdns. LE2: Oad 5D 38
New Cl. LE5: Leic 3F 29
Newcombe Rd. LE3: Leic 5F 27
Newcombe St. LE16: Mkt H 4D 64
New Flds. Av. LE3: Leic 5E 27
New Flds. Sq. LE3: Leic 6F 27
New Forest Cl. LE18: Wig 3B 46
NEWFOUNDPOOL 6G 19
Newgate End LE18: Wig 1A 46
Newham Cl. LE4: Leic 6E 15
Newhaven Rd. LE5: Leic 4C 30
New Henry St. LE3: Leic 1A 4 (6A 20)
NEW HUMBERSTONE 6H 21
Newington St. LE4: Leic 3D 20
Newington Wlk. LE4: Leic 3D 20
New Inn Cl. LE9: B Ast 2C 60
Newlyn Pde. LE5: Leic 4D 22
Newmarket St. LE2: Leic 1D 36
Newmarket Wlk. LE2: Leic 1D 36
New Pk. Rd. LE2: Leic 1A 36
NEW PARKS 5C 18
New Parks Blvd. LE3: Leic 2B 26
(not continuous)
New Parks Cres. LE3: Leic 5E 19

New Parks Leisure Cen. 5D 18
New Pk. St. LE3: Leic 5A 5 (2H 27)
New Parks Way LE3: Leic 2B 26
New Parliament St.
LE1: Leic 2D 4 (1B 28)
New Pingle St. LE3: Leic 1A 4 (6A 20)
Newpool Bank LE2: Oad 5E 39
Newport Pl. LE1: Leic 5E 5 (2C 28)
Newport St. LE3: Leic 1G 27
Newquay Dr. LE3: Glen 4A 18
New Rd. LE1: Leic 2C 4 (1B 28)
LE8: Kib B, Kib H 5A 62
LE9: S Stan 3B 50
New Romney Cl. LE5: Leic 5E 23
New Romney Cres. LE5: Leic 5E 23
Newry, The LE2: Leic 4B 36
New Star Rd. LE4: Leic 1H 21
Newstead Av. LE3: Leic 4G 19
LE7: Bush 3G 31
LE18: Wig 5E 37
Newstead Rd. LE2: Leic 1E 37
New St. LE1: Leic 4C 4 (2B 28)
LE2: Oad 3A 38
LE7: Quen 4H 7
LE8: Bla 3B 44
LE8: Count 1F 55
LE9: S Stan 2B 50
LE17: Lut 4G 63
Newton Dr. LE4: Birs 3H 13
NEWTON HARCOURT 5H 47
Newton La. LE8: G Gle 4C 48
LE8: New H 4F 47
LE18: Wig 1B 46
Newton Way LE9: B Ast 3B 60
New Town Cl. LE8: Kib B 5H 59
NEWTOWN LINFORD 3A 10
Newtown Linford La. LE6: Groby 5A 10
Newtown St. LE1: Leic 7D 5 (3B 28)
New Wlk. LE1: Leic 5D 5 (2B 28)
(not continuous)
LE9: Sap 6B 50
New Walk Mus. & Art Gallery
.....................6E 5 (3C 28)
New Way Rd. LE5: Leic 5F 29
New Wharf LE2: Leic 5A 5 (2A 28)
New Wycliffe Home LE4: Leic 2F 21
New Zealand La. LE7: Quen 3G 7
Nicholas Dr. LE6: Ratby 5D 16
Nichols St. LE1: Leic 3F 4 (1C 28)
Nicklaus Rd. LE4: Leic 1F 21
Nidderdale Rd. LE18: Wig 1D 46
Nine Leys Sq. LE4: Wan 2F 13
Nine Riggs Sq. LE4: Wan 2G 13
Nithsdale Av. LE16: Mkt H 4D 64
Nithsdale Cres. LE16: Mkt H 4E 65
Nixon Ct. LE2: Leic 6C 28
Noble Cl. LE17: Lut 2G 63
Noble St. LE3: Leic 1H 27
Nock Verges LE9: S Stan 3B 50
Noel St. LE3: Leic 4H 27
Nook, The LE7: Anst 5G 11
LE8: G Gle 3C 48
LE8: Whet 4H 43
LE9: Cosb 3F 53
LE17: Bitt 2F 63
LE19: End 6H 33
LE67: Mark 2B 8
Nook Cl. LE6: Ratby 4C 16
Nook St. LE3: Leic 6F 19
Norbury Av. LE4: Leic 4E 21
Norbury Cl. LE16: Mkt H 2C 64
Norfolk Lodge LE4: Leic 5D 20
Norfolk Rd. LE18: Wig 6B 36
Norfolk St. LE3: Leic 2H 27
Norfolk Wlk. LE3: Leic 2H 27
Norman Ct. LE2: Oad 5D 38
Normandy Cl. LE3: Glen 6A 18
Norman Rd. LE4: Thurm 3B 14
Norman St. LE3: Leic 3H 27
Normanton Gro. LE9: Thurl 1E 41
Normanton Rd. LE5: Leic 3E 29
NORMANTON TURVILLE 1C 40
Norris Cl. LE4: Leic 2E 19

Northampton Rd. LE16: Mkt H 3D 64
Northampton Sq. LE1: Leic ...4E 4 (2C 28)
Northampton St. LE1: Leic 5E 5 (2C 28)
North Av. LE2: Leic 5E 29
Northbank LE16: Mkt H 3D 64
North Bri. Pl. LE3: Leic 1A 4 (6H 19)
Northcote Rd. LE2: Leic 1D 36
North Deepdale LE5: Leic 1H 29
Northdene Rd. LE2: Leic 4C 36
Northdown Dr. LE4: Thurm 5C 14
North Dr. LE5: Leic 5A 22
North End Cl. LE5: Leic 3B 36
NORTH EVINGTON 1G 29
Northfield Av. LE4: Birs 3H 13
    LE18: Wig 5D 36
Northfield Rd. LE4: Leic 4G 21
    LE8: Bla 2B 44
NORTHFIELDS 3F 21
Northfields LE7: Sys 5F 7
Northfold Rd. LE2: Leic 3E 37
Northgates LE1: Leic 2A 4 (1A 28)
Northgate St. LE3: Leic 1A 4 (6A 20)
Northleigh Gro. LE16: Mkt H 2C 64
North Mills LE3: Leic 1A 4 (6H 19)
North St. LE2: Oad 3A 38
    LE7: Sys 5E 7
    LE18: Wig 6F 37
Northumberland Av. LE4: Leic 3E 21
Northumberland Rd. LE18: Wig 6B 36
Northumberland St.
    LE1: Leic 1A 4 (6A 20)
Norton St. LE1: Leic 6C 5 (3B 28)
Norwich Rd. LE4: Leic 2H 19
Norwood Rd. LE5: Leic 4G 29
Nottingham Rd. LE5: Leic 1F 29
Nowell Cl. LE2: G Par 2D 44
Nuffield Health Club
    Leicester 5C 28
Nugent St. LE3: Leic 1H 27
Nunneley Way LE16: Mkt H 1E 65
Nursery Cl. LE4: Thurm 5B 14
    LE7: Quen 4H 7
    LE9: Thurl 1E 41
Nursery Ct. LE8: Kib H 5C 62
Nursery Gdns. LE17: D Bas 5F 61
Nursery Hollow LE2: G Par 6E 35
Nursery Rd. LE5: Leic 6D 22
Nutfield Rd. LE3: Leic 4G 27
Nuthall Gro. LE2: G Par 5F 35

O

OADBY 3A 38
Oadby Hill Dr. LE2: Oad 3H 37
Oadby Ind. Est. LE2: Oad 4H 37
Oadby Racecourse (Park & Ride) ...2G 37
Oadby Rd. LE18: Wig 6G 37
Oadby Swimming Pool 3H 37
Oak & Ash Bus. Pk. LE5: Leic 6E 21
Oak Av. LE17: Leire 6A 60
Oakberry Rd. LE17: Lut 2H 63
Oakberry Rd. Ind. Est. LE17: Lut ..2H 63
Oak Cl. LE9: Thurl 6A 32
    LE16: Mkt H 2E 65
Oak Cres. LE3: Brau 5A 26
Oakcroft Av. LE9: K Mux 1E 25
Oakdale Cl. LE3: Leic 1A 26
Oakdene Rd. LE2: Leic 3C 36
Oak Dr. LE7: Sys 1F 15
Oakenshaw Cl. LE4: Leic 6E 13
Oakfield Av. LE3: Glen 3B 18
    LE4: Birs 4F 13
    LE17: Lut 4F 63
    LE67: Mark 3B 8
Oakfield Cl. LE8: G Gle 2D 48
Oakfield Ct. LE3: Glen 3B 18
Oakfield Cres. LE8: Bla 5C 44
Oakfield Rd. LE2: Leic 4E 29
Oak Grn. LE67: Mark 5C 8
Oakhill Trad. Est. LE2: Leic 6B 28
Oakland Av. LE4: Leic 6H 13
Oakland Rd. LE2: Leic 6C 28

Oaklands Pk. LE16: L Bow 4E 65
Oakleigh Av. LE2: G Par 2E 45
Oakley Rd. LE5: Leic 6F 21
Oakmeadow LE3: Glen 6H 17
Oakmeadow Way LE6: Groby 3E 17
Oakpool Gdns. LE2: Leic 6H 35
Oakridge Cl. LE5: Ham 2C 22
Oak Rd. LE19: Litt 5E 43
Oaks Ct. LE19: Nar 3C 42
Oaks Dr. LE8: Bla 4C 44
Oakside Cl. LE6: Leic 3C 30
Oakside Cres. LE5: Leic 2C 30
Oaks Ind. Est. LE17: Lut 3H 63
    LE19: Nar 4C 42
Oak Spinney Pk. LE3: Leic E 3H 25
Oaks Rd. LE8: G Gle 3D 48
Oak St. LE5: Leic 6E 21
Oaks Way LE2: Oad 1H 37
Oakthorpe Av. LE3: Leic 3F 27
Oaktree Cl. LE5: Ham 3C 22
    LE6: Groby 2E 17
    LE8: Kib B 4B 62
Oakwood Cl. LE3: Leic E 5F 37
Oakwood Dr. LE2: Leic 5F 25
Oakwood Rd. LE4: Leic 4H 19
Oasis, The LE3: Glen 5H 17
Oban St. LE3: Leic 1G 27
Occupation Rd. LE9: S Stan 6B 40
Ocean Cl. LE5: Leic 6C 22
Ocean Rd. LE5: Leic 1C 30
Ocean Wlk. LE5: Leic 1C 30
Odam Cl. LE3: Leic 5D 26
Odeon Arc. LE1: Leic 4C 4
Odeon Cinema
    Leicester 5B 28
Offranville Cl. LE4: Thurm 5D 14
Ogwen Cl. LE5: Leic 1D 30
Okehampton Av. LE5: Leic 4H 29
Okehampton Wlk. LE5: Leic 4H 29
Old Barn Wlk. LE4: Leic 2G 19
Old Charity Farm LE2: S'ton 6E 31
Old Church Rd. LE19: End 6C 34
Old Church St. LE2: Leic 3G 35
Old Coach Rd., The LE17: D Bas ..5F 61
Old Coffee Mills, The LE16: Mkt H ..4E 65
Old Field Cl. LE8: Count 1C 54
Old Forge Rd. LE19: Nar 5H 61
Old Garden Cl. LE8: Bla 4B 44
Old Grammar School, The
    LE8: Kib B 5A 62
Old Hall Cl. LE4: Thurm 3C 14
    LE6: Groby 3F 17
Old House Cl. LE19: Litt 4E 43
Old Mill Cl. LE9: B Ast 2B 60
Old Mill La. LE1: Leic 1A 4 (6A 20)
Old Mill Rd. LE9: B Ast 2B 60
Old Milton St. LE1: Leic 1E 4 (6C 20)
Old Rectory Cl. LE9: B Ast 1A 60
Old Saffron La. LE2: Leic 6A 28
Old School Ct. LE8: Kib B 5A 62
Old School M. LE16: Mkt H 3D 64
Old School Yd. LE9: Sap 6B 50
Old Station Cl. LE8: Whet 3H 43
Old Station Rd. LE7: Sys 6C 7
Oliver Cl. LE7: Sys 1C 14
Oliver Ct. LE2: Leic 6E 29
Oliver Rd. LE4: Leic 3F 21
Oliver St. LE2: Leic 1A 36
Olphin St. LE4: Leic 5C 20
Olympic Cl. LE3: Glen 5B 18
Onslow St. LE2: Leic 3E 29
Ontario Cl. LE1: Leic 1E 4 (6C 20)
Opal Ct. LE1: Leic 7E 5 (4C 28)
Orange Hill LE17: Lut 5H 63
Orange St. LE18: Wig 3F 45
Orohard, The LE2: Leic 2F 37
    LE6: Groby 2D 16
    LE9: S Stan 3C 50
Orchard Av. LE2: G Par 6F 35
Orchard Cl. LE2: Oad 5A 38
    LE7: Scra 6F 23
    LE9: Cosb 2F 53
Orchard Gdns. LE4: Thurm 5D 14

Orchard La. LE8: Count 2F 55
    LE8: G Gle 4D 48
Orchard M. LE8: Bla 3B 44
Orchard Mobile Home Pk.
    LE7: Sys 5F 7
Orchard Rd. LE4: Birs 4H 13
    LE9: B Ast 6A 52
    LE17: Lut 5F 63
Orchards, The LE5: Leic 5E 23
Orchards Dr. LE18: Wig 1H 45
Orchards Nature Reserve, The ...4F 19
Orchardson Av. LE4: Leic 5C 20
Orchard St. LE1: Leic 1D 4 (6B 20)
    LE8: Flec 6B 58
    LE16: Mkt H 2D 64
Orchard Way LE7: Sys 6G 7
Orchid Cl. LE5: Ham 3D 22
    LE19: Nar 2C 42
Orchid Pl. LE9: B Ast 3D 60
Oriel Dr. LE7: Sys 6F 7
Orkney Way LE8: Count 2F 55
Orlando Rd. LE2: Leic 5D 28
Orme Cl. LE4: Leic 2E 19
Ormen Grn. LE3: Leic 1B 26
Oronsay Rd. LE4: Leic 2F 19
Orpine Rd. LE5: Ham 2B 22
Orsett Cl. LE5: Leic 5A 22
Orson Dr. LE18: Wig 6D 36
Orson St. LE5: Leic 2F 29
Orton Rd. LE4: Leic 2A 20
Orwell Dr. LE4: Beau L 1E 19
Osborne Rd. LE5: Leic 2F 29
Osbourne Ct. LE8: Whet 3H 43
Osiers, The LE3: Brau 2D 34
Osiers Bus. Cen., The LE19: Brau ..3C 34
Osmaston Rd. LE5: Leic 3E 29
Osprey Cl. LE9: B Ast 6A 52
Osprey Rd. LE4: Beau L 5A 12
Oswin Rd. LE3: Leic 2C 26
Ottawa Rd. LE1: Leic 2F 4 (6C 20)
Otter Way LE8: Whet 6H 43
Oulston La. LE5: Ham 1C 22
Outfields Dr. LE7: Crop 1H 11
Outwood Cl. LE3: Leic 2B 26
Oval, The LE1: Leic 7F 5 (3C 28)
    LE2: Oad 5H 37
    LE9: S Stan 3C 50
    LE16: Mkt H 2D 64
Overdale Av. LE3: Glen 3H 17
Overdale Cl. LE3: Glen 3H 17
    LE16: L Bow 3F 65
Overdale Rd. LE2: Leic 3D 36
    LE4: Thurm 5D 14
Overfield Av. LE16: Mkt H 1E 65
Overfield Cl. LE6: Ratby 5D 16
    LE19: Nar 4C 42
Overfield Wlk. LE6: Ratby 4D 16
Overing Cl. LE4: Leic 2C 20
Overpark Av. LE3: Leic 3D 26
Overseal Rd. LE3: Leic 5C 18
Overstrand Rd. LE5: Ham 3B 22
Overton Rd. LE5: Leic 6F 21
Owen Cl. LE3: Brau 6B 26
    LE4: Leic 6C 14
Owston Dr. LE18: Wig 6D 36
Oxendon St. LE2: Leic 2D 28
Oxendon Wlk. LE2: Leic 2D 28
Oxford Av. LE2: Leic 4D 28
Oxford Ct. LE1: Leic 6C 5 (3B 28)
    LE7: Sys 5G 7
Oxford Dr. LE18: Wig 6B 36
Oxford Rd. LE2: Leic 5D 28
Oxford St. LE1: Leic 5B 5 (2A 28)
    LE7: Sys 5G 7
Oxon Way LE5: Leic 2A 30
Oxted Ri. LE2: Oad 6A 38

P

Packer Av. LE3: Leic E 3H 25
Packhorse Dr. LE19: End 1F 43
Packhorse Grn. LE2: Leic 6H 35

Packhorse Rd.—Pleasant Cl.

Packhorse Rd. LE2: Leic 6H **35**
Packman Grn. LE8: Count 2F **55**
Packwood Rd. LE4: Leic 2A **20**
Paddock, The LE8: Kib B 5A **62**
LE67: Mark 2C **8**
Paddock Cl. LE2: Oad 3H **37**
LE8: Bla 3B **44**
LE8: Count 1E **55**
Paddock Ct. LE16: Mkt H 2D **64**
Paddocks, The LE19: Litt 4E **43**
Paddock St. LE18: Wig 1B **46**
Paddock Vw. LE7: Sys 6D **6**
Padgate Cl. LE7: Scra 6F **23**
Padside Cl. LE5: Ham 1D **22**
Padside Row LE5: Ham 1C **22**
Padstow Rd. LE4: Leic 2G **21**
Padwell La. LE7: Bush 3G **31**
Page Cl. LE17: Lut 2G **63**
Paget Av. LE4: Birs 3H **13**
Paget Rd. LE3: Leic 1G **27**
Paget St. LE2: Leic 3G **35**
LE8: Kib B 5A **62**
Paigle Rd. LE2: Leic 3G **35**
Painter St. LE1: Leic 5C **20**
Palfreyman La. LE2: Oad 6D **38**
Palmer Dr. LE17: Lut 5G **63**
Palmer Sq. LE4: Birs 2G **13**
Palmerston Blvd. LE2: Leic 3E **37**
Palmerston Cl. LE7: Anst 5G **11**
LE8: Kib B 5H **59**
Palmerston Way LE2: Leic 3E **37**
Palmer St. LE4: Leic 2C **20**
Pamela Pl. LE4: Leic 1A **20**
Pankhurst Rd. LE4: Beau L 5A **12**
Paper Mill Cl. LE7: Anst 5F **11**
Parade, The LE2: Oad 3A **38**
LE8: Flec .6B **58**
Paramore Cl. LE8: Whet 6A **44**
Parham Cl. LE3: Leic 4F **19**
Park & Ride
Birstall 2G 13
Enderby 5C 34
Meynells Gorse 3A 26
Oadby Racecourse 2G 37
Park Av. LE2: Leic 1A **36**
LE67: Mark 2B **8**
Park Cl. LE9: Cosb 3F **53**
Park Cres. LE2: Oad 5C **38**
Parkdale Rd. LE4: Thurm 5C **14**
Park Dr. LE3: Glen 5A **18**
LE3: Leic E 4A **26**
LE16: Mkt H 2D **64**
Parker Dr. LE4: Leic 3H **19**
Parkfield Cl. LE6: Ratby 5D **16**
Parkhill LE2: Leic 1H **35**
Park Hill Av. LE2: Leic 2H **35**
Park Hill Dr. LE2: Leic 2H **35**
Park Ho. LE16: Mkt H 2D **64**
Park Ho. Cl. LE4: Birs 6G **13**
Park Ho. Ct. LE8: Bla 3B **44**
LE9: Sap 6B **50**
Parkland Dr. LE2: Oad 3A **38**
Parklands Av. LE6: Groby 2D **16**
Parklands Leisure Cen. 5H 37
Park La. LE2: Leic 5F **29**
Park M. LE16: Mkt H 2D **64**
LE18: Wig .3F **45**
Park Ri. LE3: Leic 2C **26**
Park Rd. LE4: Birs 5F **13**
LE6: Ratby 6D **16**
LE7: Anst .6F **11**
LE8: Bla 3A **44**
LE9: Cosb .3F **53**
LE9: Sap 6B **50**
LE18: Wig .3F **45**
LE19: Nar .4D **42**
Parkside LE6: Groby 1F **17**
Parkside Cl. LE4: Beau L 5A **12**
Parkstone Cl. LE18: Wig 3A **46**
Parkstone Rd. LE5: Leic 5D **22**
LE7: Sys 4F **7**
Park St. LE1: Leic 5D **5** (2B **28**)
LE8: Flec .5B **58**
Park Va. Rd. LE5: Leic 2E **29**
Park Vw. LE3: Leic 1C **26**
Park Vw. Cl. LE9: B Ast 1B **60**
Parkway, The LE5: Leic 6B **22**
Parlour Cl. LE18: Wig 1A **46**
Parnell Cl. LE19: Litt 5E **43**
Parry St. LE5: Leic 6E **21**
Parsons Dr. LE2: G Par 6E **35**
Partridge Cl. LE7: Sys 5D **6**
Partridge Rd. LE4: Thurm 5D **14**
Parvian Rd. LE2: Leic 5C **36**
Pasley Cl. LE2: Leic 5H **35**
Pasley Rd. LE2: Leic 5H **35**
Pasture La. LE1: Leic 1B **4** (6A **20**)
Pastures, The LE2: Oad 5E **39**
LE7: Anst .6G **11**
LE7: Sys 6C **6**
LE9: B Ast .2B **60**
LE16: Mkt H 3B **64**
LE19: Nar .2C **42**
Paterson Cl. LE4: Beau L 5A **12**
Paton St. LE3: Leic 3H **27**
Patrick St. LE16: Mkt H 4E **65**
Patterdale Rd. LE4: Thurm 5C **14**
Paul Dr. LE4: Leic 1H **21**
Pauline Av. LE4: Leic 1D **20**
Pavilion, The
Huncote 3G 41
Pawley Cl. LE8: Whet 5A **44**
Pawley Gdns. LE2: Leic 5H **35**
Pawley Grn. LE2: Leic 5H **35**
Payne St. LE4: Leic 2D **20**
Peacock Dr. LE8: Whet 6H **43**
Peacock La. LE1: Leic 4B **4** (2A **28**)
Peakdale LE18: Wig 2D **46**
Peake Rd. LE4: Leic 4F **21**
Pear Tree Cl. LE17: Lut 4E **63**
Peartree Cl. LE3: Glen 6H **17**
LE7: Anst .6F **11**
Pear Tree Gdns. LE16: Mkt H 4C **64**
Peatling La. LE8: Count 3F **55**
PEATLING MAGNA 6G 55
Peatling Rd. LE8: Count 2F **55**
Pedlars Cl. LE4: Leic 2F **19**
Pedlars Way LE7: E Gos 2H **7**
Peebles Way LE4: Leic 2F **21**
Peel Cl. LE8: Kib B 5H **59**
Peewit Cl. LE2: G Par 6E **35**
Pegasus Cl. LE2: Leic 2D **28**
Pegasus Ct. LE16: Mkt H 2C **64**
Peldon Cl. LE4: Leic 3H **19**
Pelham St. LE1: Leic 6C **5** (3B **28**)
LE2: Oad 3A **38**
Pelham Way LE1: Leic 6C **5** (3B **28**)
Pells Cl. LE8: Flec 5B **58**
Pembroke Av. LE7: Sys 1F **15**
LE18: Wig .1F **45**
Pembroke St. LE5: Leic 6E **21**
Pembroke Wlk. *LE5: Leic 6E 21*
(off Pembroke St.)
Pembury Cl. LE8: G Gle 2D **48**
Pen Cl. LE2: Leic 5A **36**
Penclose Rd. LE8: Flec 5A **58**
Pendene Rd. LE2: Leic 6E **29**
Pendlebury Dr. LE2: Leic 2C **36**
Pendragon Way LE3: Leic E 5G **25**
Penfold Cl. LE9: Sap 5B **50**
Penfold Dr. LE8: Count 2D **54**
Penhale Rd. LE3: Brau 1D **34**
Penkridge Wlk. LE4: Leic 1A **20**
Pen La. Av. LE4: Wan 2G **13**
Penman Way LE19: End 4C **34**
Pennant Cl. LE3: Glen 6B **18**
Penney Cl. LE18: Wig 6E **37**
Pennine Cl. LE2: Oad 4D **38**
Penny Long La. LE3: Leic E 4F **25**
Penrith Rd. LE4: Leic 3E **21**
Penryn Dr. LE18: Wig 2A **46**
Pensilva Cl. LE18: Wig 2A **46**
Pentridge Cl. LE18: Wig 3A **46**
Penzance Av. LE18: Wig 2A **46**
Peppercorn Cl. LE4: Leic 2G **19**
Peppercorn Wlk. LE4: Leic 2H **19**
Percival St. LE5: Leic 6F **21**
Percival Way LE6: Groby 2H **17**
Percy Rd. LE2: Leic 2A **36**
Percy St. LE3: Brau 1E **35**
Peregrine Ri. LE4: Beau L 5A **12**
Peregrine Rd. LE9: B Ast 5A **52**
Perkins Cl. LE16: Mkt H 2E **65**
Perkyn Rd. LE5: Leic 1C **30**
Perseverance Rd. LE4: Birs 6G **13**
Perth Av. LE3: Leic 6E **19**
(not continuous)
Peter's Cl. LE9: S Stan 3A **50**
Peters Dr. LE5: Leic 6B **22**
Petersfield LE9: Crof 1G **51**
Petunia Cl. LE3: Leic E 5F **25**
Petworth Dr. LE3: Leic 1F **27**
LE16: L Bow 4G **65**
Pevensey Av. LE5: Leic 4D **30**
Peverel Ct. LE3: Brau 6C **26**
Peverel Rd. LE3: Leic 5E **27**
Peveril Rd. LE17: Ash M 5H **61**
Phillip Dr. LE2: G Par 2E **45**
Phillips Cres. LE4: Beau L 5A **12**
Phipps Cl. LE8: Whet 5A **44**
Phoenix Arts Cen.
Leicester 5C 5 (2B 28)
Phoenix Cl. LE3: Leic 6F **19**
Phoenix Sq. LE1: Leic 3F **4**
Piccadilly Cinema 6F 21
Piccaver Ri. LE3: Leic 1B **26**
Pickering Cl. LE4: Leic 4F **21**
LE9: S Stan 3B **50**
Pickering Rd. LE9: B Ast 3B **60**
Pickhill Rd. LE5: Ham 2D **22**
Picks Cl. LE16: L Bow 3G **65**
Pickwell Cl. LE3: Leic 5C **18**
Pickwell Dr. LE7: Sys 6G **7**
Picton Cl. LE5: Ham 1C **22**
Piers Rd. LE3: Glen 4A **18**
Pilgrim Gdns. LE5: Leic 4A **30**
Pilkington Rd. LE3: Leic 4C **26**
Pimpernel Cl. LE19: Nar 2B **42**
Pindar Rd. LE3: Leic 5E **19**
Pine Cl. LE17: Lut 4E **63**
Pine Dr. LE7: Sys 1F **15**
Pinehurst Cl. LE3: Leic 1A **26**
Pinel Cl. LE9: B Ast 3C **60**
Pine Rd. LE3: Glen 5A **18**
Pines, The LE7: Bush 3H **31**
Pine Tree Av. LE5: Leic 6A **22**
LE6: Groby 3F **17**
Pine Tree Cl. LE2: Oad 5B **38**
Pine Tree Gdn. LE2: Oad 5B **38**
Pine Tree Gro. LE9: Leic E 5E **25**
Pine Tree Wlk. LE5: Leic 5A **22**
Pine Vw. LE3: Leic E 3H **25**
Pinewood Av. LE4: Thurm 6C **14**
Pinewood Cl. LE4: Beau L 6A **12**
LE8: Count 1E **55**
Pinewood Ct. LE67: Mark 5C **8**
Pinewood Dr. LE67: Mark 5C **8**
Pinfold LE3: Brau 2D **34**
Pinfold, The LE6: Ratby 5C **16**
LE67: Mark 3C **8**
Pinfold Cl. LE4: Birs 2G **13**
Pinfold Rd. LE4: Thurm 5B **14**
Pingle La. LE9: Pott M 5C **40**
Pingle St. LE3: Leic 1A **4** (6A **20**)
Pinnacle, The LE19: Nar 4D **42**
Pintail Cl. LE8: Whet 1H **53**
Pioneer Cl. LE4: Leic 4A **20**
Piper Cl. LE3: Leic 6E **19**
Piper Way LE3: Leic 6E **19**
Pipewell Wlk. LE4: Leic 2A **20**
Pipistrelle Way LE2: Oad 5E **39**
Pitchens Cl. LE4: Beau L 6H **11**
Pits Av. LE3: Brau 2C **34**
Pitton Cl. LE18: Wig 3A **46**
Plantation, The LE8: Count 1E **55**
Plantation Av. LE2: Leic 3G **35**
Platts La. LE7: Coss 2A **6**
Player Cl. LE4: Leic 6B **14**
Pleasant Cl. LE3: Leic E 5F **25**

94 A-Z Leicester

Plough Cl. LE3: Leic E 6F 25
  LE9: B Ast .3C 60
Ploughmans' Lea LE7: E Gos 2H 7
Plover Cres. LE4: Beau L 5B 12
Plowman Cl. LE3: Glen 4A 18
Plumtree Way LE7: Sys 1F 15
Pluto Cl. LE2: Leic 2D 28
Plymouth Dr. LE5: Leic 4H 29
Plymstock Cl. LE3: Leic 1F 27
Poachers Cl. LE3: Glen 5H 17
Poachers Pl. LE2: Oad 5D 38
Pochin Dr. LE16: Mkt H 1D 64
Pochin's Bri. Rd. LE18: Wig 3G 45
Pochins Cl. LE18: Wig 2A 46
Pochin St. LE9: Crof 1G 51
Pocklingtons Wlk. LE1: Leic 5C 5 (2B 28)
Point, The LE16: L Bow 2G 65
Polaris Cl. LE2: Leic 2D 28
Polebrook Cl. LE3: Brau 2C 18
Pollard Cl. LE2: Leic 5F 29
Pollard Rd. LE3: Leic 4C 26
Pomeroy Dr. LE2: Oad 4H 37
Pontylue Way LE7: Sys 1C 14
Pool Rd. LE3: Leic 1F 27
Pope Cres. LE19: End 6G 33
Pope St. LE2: Leic 1C 36
Poplar Av. LE4: Birs 3G 13
  LE8: Count .2E 55
  LE17: Lut 4F 63
  LE67: Mark 3B 8
Poplar Rd. LE19: Litt 5D 42
Poplars, The LE3: Brau 2E 35
  LE6: Ratby 4B 16
Poplars Cl. LE6: Groby 2E 17
Poplars Ct. LE16: Mkt H 2C 64
Poplars Farm Ct. LE8: Count 1E 55
Poppins, The LE4: Beau L 5B 12
Popple Cl. LE9: B Ast 2C 60
Poppy Cl. LE2: Leic 5B 36
  LE6: Groby 2G 17
Porlock St. LE3: Leic 2F 27
Portcullis Rd. LE5: Leic 4E 23
Portgate LE18: Wig 2C 46
Portishead Rd. LE5: Leic 5G 21
Portland Gdns. LE2: Cosb 1F 53
Portland Rd. LE2: Leic 6E 29
  LE9: K Mux .3E 25
Portland St. LE9: Cosb 1F 53
Portland Towers LE2: Leic 1G 37
Portland Wlk. LE2: Oad 6C 38
Portloc Dr. LE18: Wig 3B 46
Portman St. LE4: Leic 3D 20
Portmore Cl. LE4: Leic 3G 19
Portsdown Rd. LE2: Leic 3F 37
Portslade Ho. LE3: Glen 1A 26
Portsmouth Rd. LE4: Leic 4C 20
Portwey, The LE5: Leic 5G 21
Post Office La. LE8: New H 4H 47
  LE16: Mkt H 3E 65
Post Rd. LE4: Thurm 2C 14
POTTERS MARSTON 6D 40
Potters Marston La. LE9: Thurl 3C 40
Potter St. LE1: Leic 2E 4 (1C 28)
Potterton Rd. LE4: Leic 1H 19
Pougher Cl. LE9: Sap 6C 50
Powys Av. LE2: Leic 6G 29
Powys Gdns. LE2: Leic 6G 29
Poynings Av. LE3: Leic 1E 27
Prebend St. LE2: Leic 6F 5 (3C 28)
Preston Cl. LE6: Ratby 5E 17
Preston Ri. LE5: Leic 4C 22
Prestwold Rd. LE5: Leic 5E 21
Pretoria Cl. LE4: Beau L 4C 12
Pretoria Rd. LE9: K Mux 2D 24
Price Way LE4: Thurm 4E 15
Pride Pl. LE16: Mkt H 4C 64
Priestley Rd. LE3: Leic 2E 27
Priestman Rd. LE3: Brau 6A 26
Priest Mdw. LE8: Flec 5B 58
PRIMETHORPE 6A 52
Primethorpe Wlk. LE9: B Ast 6A 52
Primrose Cl. LE6: Groby 2G 17
  LE19: Nar 3C 42

Primrose Hill LE2: Oad 3H 37
Primrose Way LE7: Quen 3H 7
  LE9: K Mux 1F 25
Prince Albert Dr. LE3: Glen 6A 18
Prince Dr. LE2: Oad 4C 38
Princes Cl. LE7: Anst 5G 11
Princess Av. LE2: Oad 5C 38
Princess Dr. LE9: K Mux 2D 24
Princess Rd. Backways
  LE1: Leic 6D 5 (3B 28)
Princess Rd. E. LE1: Leic 7E 5 (3C 28)
Princess Rd. W. LE1: Leic 6D 5 (3B 28)
Princess St. LE19: Nar 3E 43
Print Works, The LE16: Mkt H 5E 65
Priory Bus. Pk. LE8: Kib H 3G 59
Priory Cl. LE7: Sys 6D 6
Priory Cres. LE3: Leic 2C 26
Priory Wlk. LE3: Leic E 4G 25
Private Rd. LE9: S Stan 2B 50
Progress Way LE4: Leic 2A 22
Prospect Hill LE5: Leic 1E 29
Prospect Rd. LE5: Leic 1F 29
Pulford Dr. LE7: Scra, Thurn 1F 31
Pullen Ct. LE8: Whet 4H 43
Pullman Rd. LE18: Wig 6D 36
Purbeck Cl. LE18: Wig 3B 46
Purcell Rd. LE4: Leic 5C 20
Purley Rd. LE4: Leic 4E 21
Putney Rd. LE2: Leic 5B 28
Putney Rd. E. LE2: Leic 6C 28
Putney Rd. W. LE2: Leic 5B 28
Pymm Ley Cl. LE6: Groby 2F 17
Pymm Ley Gdns. LE6: Groby 2F 17
Pymm Ley La. LE6: Groby 3F 17
Pytchley Cl. LE4: Leic 6E 13

Q

Quad, The LE1: Leic 3B 4
Quadrant, The LE4: Leic 3B 4
Quainton Rd. LE2: Leic 4H 27
Quarry La. LE19: End 5G 33
Quarrymans Ct. LE67: Mark 2B 8
Quarry Vw. Cl. LE9: Hun 3H 41
Quartz Cl. LE19: End 4H 33
Quebec Rd. LE1: Leic 2F 4 (1C 28)
Queen Elizabeths Wlk. LE3: Leic 1H 27
Queens Dr. LE3: Leic E 4G 25
  LE18: Wig 1H 45
  LE19: End 1F 43
Queensferry Pde. LE2: Leic 6G 35
Queensgate Dr. LE4: Birs 3E 13
Queensmead Cl. LE6: Groby 3E 17
Queens Pk. Way LE2: Leic 1D 44
                         (not continuous)
Queens Rd. LE2: Leic 5D 28
  LE8: Bla 4A 44
Queen St. LE1: Leic 3E 4 (2C 28)
  LE2: Oad 3B 38
  LE7: Bark T 4G 15
  LE16: L Bow .4F 65
  LE67: Mark 3B 8
Quemby Cl. LE4: Leic 3C 20
Quenby Cres. LE7: Sys 6G 7
Quenby St. LE5: Leic 6F 21
QUENIBOROUGH 4H 7
Queniborough Ind. Est. LE7: Quen . . .4H 7
Queniborough Rd. LE4: Leic 4E 21
  LE7: Bark, Sys 3H 15
Quickthorns LE2: Oad 3H 37
Quiney Way LE2: Oad 3C 38
Quinton Ri. LE2: Oad 5A 38
Quorn Av. LE2: Oad 3B 38
Quorndon Ri. LE6: Groby 3E 17
Quorn Rd. LE5: Leic 6F 21

R

Radar Rd. LE3: Leic 2B 26
Radcot Lawns LE2: Leic 6H 35

Radford Dr. LE3: Brau 4A 26
Radford Ho. LE3: Brau 4A 26
Radiant Rd. LE5: Leic 6C 22
Radnor Ct. LE19: Nar 1B 42
Radnor Rd. LE18: Wig 6C 36
Radstone Wlk. LE5: Leic 1H 29
Raeburn Rd. LE2: Leic 6D 28
Ragdale Rd. LE4: Leic 4F 21
Railway St. LE18: Wig 3F 45
Raine Way LE2: Oad 6D 38
Rainsborough Gdns. LE16: Mkt H 5C 64
Rainsford Cres. LE4: Leic 2A 20
Ralphs Cl. LE17: D Bas 5F 61
Ramsbury Rd. LE2: Leic 4D 36
Ramsdean Av. LE18: Wig 6E 37
Ramsey Cl. LE17: Lut 4H 63
Ramsey Gdns. LE5: Leic 4E 23
Ramsey Way LE5: Leic 4E 23
Ramson Cl. LE5: Ham 3C 22
Rancliffe Cres. LE3: Leic 3E 27
Randles Cl. LE7: Bush 3G 31
Rannoch Cl. LE4: Leic 2G 19
Ranton Way LE3: Leic 5G 19
Ranworth Wlk. LE4: Leic 1A 20
RATBY 5C 16
Ratby La. LE3: Leic E 2G 25
  LE9: K Mux, Leic E 6E 17
  LE67: Mark 4C 8
Ratby Mdw. La. LE19: End 6C 34
Ratby Rd. LE6: Groby 3E 17
  LE6: Ratby 1A 24
Ratcliffe LE2: Leic 1E 37
Ratcliffe Ct. LE2: Leic 1F 37
Ratcliffe Dr. LE9: Hun 4H 41
Ratcliffe Rd. LE2: Leic 1E 37
Ratcliffe St. LE4: Leic 3D 20
Ravenhurst Rd. LE3: Brau 6D 26
Raven Rd. LE3: Leic 4C 26
Ravensbridge Dr. LE4: Leic 5H 19
Ravensthorpe Rd. LE18: Wig 1C 46
Raw Dykes 5A 28
Raw Dykes Rd. LE2: Leic 5A 28
Rawlings Ct. LE2: Oad 5E 39
Rawlings Pas. LE2: Oad 3A 38
Rawlinson Wlk. LE4: Leic 2G 19
Rawson St. LE1: Leic 6D 5 (3C 28)
  LE19: End 6H 33
Rawsthorne Wlk. LE4: Leic 5C 20
Rayleigh Grn. LE5: Leic 4E 23
Rayleigh Way LE5: Leic 4E 23
Raymond Rd. LE3: Leic 4G 27
Rayner Rd. LE4: Leic 1H 21
Rayns Way LE7: Sys 1C 14
Rearsby Rd. LE4: Leic 4E 21
Rectory Cl. LE18: Wig 2B 46
Rectory End LE8: Bur O 2H 49
Rectory Gdns. LE2: Leic 5B 30
Rectory La. LE7: Thurc 1B 12
  LE8: Kib B 4A 62
  LE16: L Bow .4F 65
Rectory Rd. LE7: Wan 1H 13
  LE67: Mark 2C 8
Redcar Rd. LE4: Leic 4D 20
Redcomb Bus. Pk. LE19: End 4F 33
Red Hill LE4: Birs 6F 13
Red Hill Av. LE19: Nar 3C 42
Red Hill Circ. LE4: Leic 1C 20
Red Hill Cl. LE4: Thurm 3C 14
Red Hill La. LE4: Thurm 3C 14
                         (not continuous)
Red Hill Way LE4: Leic 6D 12
Red Ho. Cl. LE2: Leic 5G 35
Red Ho. Gdns. LE2: Leic 5G 35
Red Ho. Ri. LE2: Leic 5G 35
Red Ho. Rd. LE2: Leic 5G 35
Redlioh Cl. LE16: L Bow 3G 65
Redmarle Rd. LE3: Leic 4E 27
Redpath Cl. LE4: Leic 6D 20
Redruth Av. LE18: Wig 2A 46
Redruth Cl. LE18: Wig 3A 46
                 (off Launceston Rd.)
Redruth Rd. LE4: Beau L 4C 12
Redwing Wlk. LE5: Leic 6E 21

Redwood Ct.—Ryderway

Redwood Ct. LE18: Wig .6F **37**
Redwood Wlk. LE5: Leic .6E **21**
Reed Pool Cl. LE8: Count .1F **55**
Rees Gro. LE4: Leic .6B **14**
Reeth Cl. LE4: Leic .2G **19**
Reeves Cl. LE8: Whet .6H **43**
Regal Ct. LE19: End .1F **43**
Regency Cl. LE2: G Par .2D **44**
Regency Ct. LE3: Leic .2G **27**
Regent Cl. LE18: Wig .1H **45**
Regent Ct. LE17: Lut .5G **63**
Regent Rd. LE1: Leic .6D **5** (3B **28**)
LE8: Count .1F **55**
Regent St. LE1: Leic .6F **5** (3C **28**)
LE2: Oad .3A **38**
LE17: Lut .5G **63**
LE19: Nar .3E **43**
Regent St. Ind. Est. LE19: Nar .4F **43**
Regents Wlk. LE3: Leic E .4G **25**
Rendell Rd. LE4: Leic .4C **20**
Renfrew Rd. LE5: Leic .5E **23**
Renishaw Dr. LE5: Leic .5G **29**
Repington Row LE2: Leic .4B **36**
Repton Rd. LE18: Wig .5D **36**
Repton St. LE3: Leic .6H **19**
Reservoir Rd. LE7: Crop .1G **11**
Retail Fish Mkt. *LE1: Leic* .*4C* **4**
(off Market Pl.)
Retreat, The LE5: Leic .2H **29**
Reynolds Chase LE18: Wig .6F **37**
Reynolds Pl. LE3: Leic .5E **27**
Rhodes Cl. LE16: Mkt H .4B **64**
Ribble Av. LE2: Oad .3D **38**
Richard III Rd. LE3: Leic .3A **4** (1H **27**)
Richard Cl. LE3: Brau .4A **26**
Richardson Cl. LE9: S Stan .4B **50**
Richardsons Cl. LE9: B Ast .2C **60**
Richmond Av. LE2: Leic .1A **36**
Richmond Cl. LE2: Leic .1A **36**
LE8: Flec .6B **58**
LE9: Cosb .3E **53**
Richmond Dr. LE2: G Par .2E **45**
Richmond Rd. LE2: Leic .1A **36**
Richmond St. LE2: Leic .6B **5** (3A **28**)
Richmond Way LE2: Oad .6C **38**
Richmore Rd. LE5: Ham .2D **22**
Riddington Rd. LE3: Brau .2D **34**
LE19: Litt .5E **43**
Ridgemere Cl. LE7: Sys .5H **7**
Ridgemere La. LE7: Sys .6H **7**
Ridge Vw. LE16: Mkt H .1D **64**
Ridgeway LE2: Oad .6B **38**
LE19: Litt .5E **43**
Ridgeway, The LE3: Leic .6E **19**
LE16: Mkt H .1E **65**
Ridgeway Dr. LE4: Thurm .5D **14**
Ridgeway W. LE16: Mkt H .1D **64**
Ridgway Rd. LE2: Leic .1F **37**
Riding, The LE4: Beau L .5B **12**
Ridings, The LE7: Quen .4H **7**
Ridley Cl. LE7: Crop .1H **11**
LE8: Bla .5A **44**
Ridleys Cl. LE8: Count .1D **54**
Ridley St. LE3: Leic .3H **27**
Riley Cl. LE9: S Stan .4B **50**
LE16: Mkt H .4A **64**
Ringers Cl. LE2: Oad .1A **38**
Ringers Spinney LE2: Oad .1A **38**
Ring Rd. LE2: Leic .3F **37**
(not continuous)
Ringwood Cl. LE18: Wig .2A **46**
Ringwood Rd. LE5: Leic .4E **23**
Ripley Cl. LE16: L Bow .3G **65**
Ripon Dr. LE8: Bla .5B **44**
Ripon St. LE2: Leic .4E **29**
Rise, The LE19: Nar .1C **42**
Riseholme Cl. LE3: Brau .2D **34**
Riston Cl. LE2: Oad .6B **38**
Ritchie Pk. LE16: Mkt H .6D **64**
Riverdale Cl. *LE7: Sys* .*5E* **7**
(off Brookside)
Riversdale Cl. LE4: Birs .5H **13**
Riverside LE16: Mkt H .3F **65**
Riverside Cl. LE8: G Gle .2D **48**
Riverside Ct. LE4: Birs .5H **13**
LE9: Crof .1G **51**
LE19: Litt .4E **43**
Riverside Dr. LE2: Leic .3G **35**
Riverside Ind. Est. LE16: Mkt H .2F **65**
Riverside M. LE7: Wan .1A **14**
Riverside Pl. LE16: Mkt H .2F **65**
Riverside Rd. LE17: Lut .5H **63**
Riverside Wlk. LE16: Mkt H .3E **65**
Riverside Way LE4: Leic .4B **20**
LE19: Litt .4E **43**
Rivers St. LE3: Leic .1H **27**
Rivet's Mdw. Cl. LE3: Brau .6B **26**
Robert Hall St. LE4: Leic .2B **20**
Robertsbridge Av. LE4: Leic .2A **20**
Robertsbridge Wlk. LE4: Leic .2A **20**
Robertson Cl. LE9: S Stan .3B **50**
Roberts Rd. LE4: Leic .4C **20**
Robin Cl. LE2: Leic .2A **36**
Robinia Cl. LE17: Lut .5E **63**
Robins Fld. LE6: Ratby .5D **16**
Robinson Rd. LE5: Leic .6H **21**
Robinson Way LE67: Mark .3D **8**
Roborough Grn. LE5: Leic .1E **31**
Robotham Cl. LE9: Hun .4A **42**
LE19: Nar .4D **42**
Roche Cl. LE2: Leic .5G **35**
Rochester Cl. LE8: Kib H .3H **59**
Rochester Gdns. LE16: Mkt H .5C **64**
Rockbridge Rd. LE2: Oad .5D **38**
Rockery Cl. LE5: Leic .6A **22**
Rockingham Cl. LE5: Leic .1B **30**
LE8: Bla .5B **44**
Rockingham Ind. Est. LE16: Mkt H .2G **65**
Rockingham Rd. LE16: L Bow, Mkt H .3F **65**
Rockley Rd. LE4: Leic .4G **19**
Roebuck Cl. LE8: Whet .6H **43**
Roecliffe Cl. LE3: Leic .3D **18**
LE67: Mark .3C **8**
Roehampton Dr. LE18: Wig .4D **36**
Rogerstone Rd. LE5: Leic .3D **30**
Rolleston Cl. LE16: L Bow .3F **65**
Rolleston Rd. LE18: Wig .6D **36**
Rolleston St. LE5: Leic .1F **29**
Roman Hill LE18: Wig .3C **46**
Roman Rd. LE4: Birs .6G **13**
Roman St. LE3: Leic .3H **27**
Roman Way LE7: Sys .1C **14**
LE16: Mkt H .3D **64**
Romulus Ct. LE19: Brau .1B **34**
Romway Av. LE5: Leic .5G **29**
Romway Rd. LE5: Leic .5G **29**
Rona Gdns. LE5: Leic .6E **23**
Ronald Ct. LE2: Leic .6E **29**
Rookery, The LE6: Groby .2F **17**
Rookery Cl. LE8: Kib B .5B **62**
Rookery La. LE4: Thurm .5B **14**
LE6: Groby .2E **17**
Rookwell Dr. LE16: L Bow .5E **65**
Rosamund Av. LE3: Brau .1E **35**
Rose Acre Cl. LE7: Scra .6F **23**
Rosebank Rd. LE8: Count .2F **55**
Rosebarn Way LE5: Leic .4D **22**
Rosebery Av. LE8: Kib B .5H **59**
Rosebery Rd. LE7: Anst .5G **11**
Rosebery St. LE5: Leic .1F **29**
Rose Cres. LE3: Leic E .5F **25**
Rosedale Av. LE4: Leic .3F **21**
Rosedale Rd. LE18: Wig .1D **46**
Rosedene Av. LE4: Thurm .5B **14**
Rose Farm Bus. Pk. LE8: Count .5F **45**
Rose Farm Cl. LE3: Leic .3D **26**
Rosemead Dr. LE2: Oad .4A **38**
Rosemoor Cl. LE16: L Bow .3G **65**
Rosendene Cl. LE9: K Mux .3F **25**
Roseneath Av. LE4: Leic .3G **21**
Rose St. LE4: Leic .3B **20**
Rosetree Av. LE4: Birs .3G **13**
Roseway LE4: Leic .2F **21**
Roslyn St. LE2: Leic .3E **29**
Rossett Dr. LE4: Leic .3H **19**
Rossetti Rd. LE19: End .6G **33**
Rosshill Cres. LE5: Leic .6E **23**
Ross's La. LE18: Wig .1B **46**
Ross' Wlk. LE4: Leic .5C **20**
(not continuous)
Rotherby Av. LE4: Leic .4F **21**
Rothley St. LE4: Leic .4C **20**
Roughton St. LE4: Leic .3C **20**
Roundhay Rd. LE3: Leic .5G **27**
Roundhill LE9: K Mux .2E **25**
Roundhill Cl. LE7: Sys .1D **14**
LE16: L Bow .4G **65**
Roundhill Rd. LE5: Leic .4F **29**
Roundway, The LE4: Leic .6D **14**
Rowan Av. LE16: Mkt H .5D **64**
(not continuous)
Rowanberry Av. LE3: Leic .1A **26**
Rowan Dr. LE17: Lut .4F **63**
Rowans, The LE8: Count .1E **55**
Rowan St. LE3: Leic .1G **27**
Rowlandson Cl. LE4: Leic .2D **12**
Rowlands Way LE2: G Par .1B **44**
Rowlatts Hill Rd. LE5: Leic .1H **29**
Rowley Cl. LE8: Flec .6F **59**
ROWLEY FIELDS .**5F 27**
Rowley Flds. Av. LE3: Leic .6F **27**
Rowley's Ct. LE2: Oad .3H **37**
Rowlinson Ct. LE3: Leic .4E **19**
Rowsley Av. LE5: Leic .3F **29**
Rowsley St. LE5: Leic .4E **29**
Royal Arc. LE1: Leic .3C **4**
Royal Ct. LE19: Nar .3E **43**
Royal E. St. LE1: Leic .1D **4** (6B **20**)
Royal Kent St. LE1: Leic .1B **4** (6A **20**)
Royal Rd. LE4: Leic .3D **20**
Royce Cl. LE3: Brau .5A **26**
Roy Cl. LE19: Nar .3E **43**
Roydene Cres. LE4: Leic .3G **19**
Royston Cl. LE2: Leic .1D **44**
Ruby St. LE3: Leic .1G **27**
Ruddington Wlk. LE4: Leic .1A **20**
Ruding Rd. LE3: Leic .3H **27**
Ruding St. LE3: Leic .3A **4** (1A **28**)
Ruding Ter. *LE3: Leic* .*3H* *27*
(off Ruding Rd.)
Rufford St. LE5: Leic .1G **29**
Rugby Cl. LE16: Mkt H .4C **64**
Rugby Rd. LE17: C'ach, Lut .5G **63**
Rugby St. LE3: Leic .6H **19**
Rumsey Dr. LE8: Whet .3A **44**
Runcorn Cl. LE2: Leic .6G **35**
Runcorn Rd. LE2: Leic .6H **35**
Runnymede Gdns. LE3: Glen .6B **18**
Rupert Rd. LE16: Mkt H .5D **64**
Rupert St. LE1: Leic .5C **5** (2B **28**)
Ruperts Way LE8: G Gle .3D **48**
Rushden Ho. LE3: Glen .1A **26**
Rushes, The LE67: Mark .2C **8**
Rushey Cl. LE4: Leic .1E **21**
RUSHEY MEAD .**6C 14**
Rushford Cl. LE4: Leic .4F **21**
Rushford Dr. LE4: Leic .4F **21**
Rushmere Wlk. LE3: Leic E .5G **25**
Rushton Dr. LE2: Leic .5F **35**
Rushy Cl. LE3: Brau .6A **26**
Ruskin Av. LE7: Sys .1G **15**
Ruskin Fld. LE7: Anst .4E **11**
Ruskington Dr. LE18: Wig .4F **37**
Russell Ct. LE2: Leic .3G **35**
Russell Sq. LE1: Leic .1E **4** (6C **20**)
Russet Cl. LE16: Mkt H .1E **65**
Russett Way LE4: Birs .2A **14**
Rutherford Rd. LE4: Beau L .6A **12**
Rutland Av. LE2: Leic .6A **28**
LE18: Wig .6D **36**
Rutland Cen. LE1: Leic .3E **4** (1C **28**)
Rutland Cl. LE3: Leic E .4G **25**
Rutland Dr. LE4: Thurm .4C **14**
Rutland St. LE1: Leic .4D **4** (2B **28**)
Rutland Wlk. LE16: Mkt H .1E **65**
Rydal St. LE2: Leic .7A **5** (3A **28**)
Ryde Av. LE2: Leic .2F **37**
Ryder Rd. LE3: Leic .1A **26**
Ryderway LE17: Lut .5F **63**

96 A-Z Leicester

Rye Cl. LE2: Leic 5A **36**
Ryegate Cres. LE4: Birs 3F **13**
Rye Hill Av. LE17: Lut 5H **63**
Ryelands Cl. LE16: L Bow 2G **65**

S

Sacheverell Way LE6: Groby 4D **16**
Sacheverel Rd. LE3: Leic 1B **26**
Sackville Gdns. LE8: Leic 1E **37**
Saddington Rd. LE8: Flec 6B **58**
Saddler Rd. LE5: Ham 2C **22**
Saddlers Cl. LE3: Glen 5H **17**
  LE7: E Gos 2H **7**
Saffron Ct. LE2: Leic 4B **36**
Saffron Hill Rd. LE2: Leic 1A **36**
Saffron La. LE2: Leic 5A **28**
Saffron Lane Sports Cen. 6B **28**
Saffron Rd. LE18: Wig 6A **36**
Saffron Way LE2: Leic 3A **36**
Sage Rd. LE2: Leic 7A **5** (3H **27**)
Sahara Cl. LE4: Leic 2D **20**
St Aidan's Av. LE7: Sys 6D **6**
St Albans Rd. LE2: Leic 3D **28**
St Andrews Dr. LE2: Leic 6H **29**
St Andrew's Rd. LE2: Leic 2A **36**
St Annes Cl. LE7: Sys 1G **15**
St Anne's Dr. LE2: Leic 3H **35**
St Augustine Rd. LE3: Leic . . .4A **4** (2H **27**)
  (not continuous)
St Austell Rd. LE5: Leic 6E **23**
St Barnabas Rd. LE5: Leic 1G **29**
St Bernard's Av. LE4: Leic 2D **20**
St Bernard St. LE4: Leic 3D **20**
Saintbury Rd. LE3: Glen 4B **18**
St Columba Way LE7: Sys 5D **6**
St Crispins Way LE4: Thurm 2C **14**
St Cuthbert's Av. LE8: G Gle 3D **48**
St Davids Cl. LE3: Leic E 4F **25**
St David's Cres. LE2: Leic 6G **29**
St David's Rd. LE3: Leic 1A **26**
St Denys Rd. LE5: Leic 3B **30**
St Dunstan Rd. LE3: Leic 1G **27**
St George's Retail Pk.
  LE1: Leic 3F **4** (1D **28**)
St George St. LE1: Leic 4F **4** (2C **28**)
St George's Way LE1: Leic 4F **4** (2C **28**)
St Helens Cl. LE4: Leic 4G **19**
St Helens Dr. LE4: Leic 4H **19**
St Hilda's Dr. LE7: Sys 1G **15**
St Ives Rd. LE4: Leic 3G **21**
  LE18: Wig 2A **46**
St James Cl. LE2: Oad 6C **38**
  LE9: Hun .4H **41**
St James Ct. *LE2: Leic* *4E 29*
  (off St James Rd.)
  LE4: Birs .4H **13**
St James Rd. LE2: Leic 4E **29**
St James St. LE1: Leic 2E **4** (1C **28**)
St James Ter. LE2: Leic 4E **29**
St Johns LE19: End 1F **43**
St John's Av. LE7: Sys 6G **7**
St Johns Bus. Pk. LE17: Lut 5H **63**
St John's Ct. LE17: Lut 5F **63**
St Johns Rd. LE2: Leic 5E **29**
St John St. LE1: Leic 1C **4** (6B **20**)
St Johns Wlk. LE1: Leic 5E **5**
St Leonard's Ct. LE2: Leic 5D **28**
St Leonard's Rd. LE2: Leic 5D **28**
St Luke's Cl. LE7: Thurn 3F **31**
ST LUKES HOSPITAL 1C **64**
St Margarets Dr. LE17: Leire 6A **60**
St Margarets Pastures Sports Cen.
. . . . .1A **4** (6A **20**)
St Margaret's St. LE1: Leic . .1C **4** (6B **20**)
St Margaret's Way LE1: Leic . .1B **4** (6A **20**)
  LE4: Leic .5A **20**
St Mark's St. LE1: Leic 1E **4** (6C **20**)
St Martins LE1: Leic 4C **4** (2B **28**)
St Martin's E. LE1: Leic 4C **4** (2B **28**)
St Martins Sq. *LE1: Leic* 4C **4**
  (within St Martin's Sq. Shop. Cen.)

St Martins Sq. Shop. Cen.
  LE1: Leic 4C **4** (2B **28**)
St Martins Wlk. *LE1: Leic* *4C 4*
  (within St Martins Sq. Shop. Cen.)
St Martins W. LE1: Leic 4B **4** (2A **28**)
St Mary's Av. LE3: Brau 4A **26**
  LE5: Leic .5C **22**
St Mary's Bus. Pk. LE16: Mkt H 2E **65**
St Marys Cl. LE9: B Ast 1A **60**
St Mary's Ct. LE3: Brau 4A **26**
  LE5: Leic .5C **22**
  LE16: Mkt H *2F 65*
  (off Middlebrook Grn.)
St Mary's Pl. LE16: Mkt H 3E **65**
St Mary's Rd. LE2: Leic 5D **28**
  LE16: Mkt H 3D **64**
  LE17: Lut .4F **63**
ST MATTHEW'S 1F **4** (6C **20**)
St Matthews Bus. Cen.
  LE1: Leic .1E **4**
St Matthew's Way LE1: Leic . .1E **4** (6C **20**)
St Maxine Ct. LE2: Leic 6E **29**
St Mellion Cl. LE4: Beau L 4B **12**
St Michael's Av. LE4: Leic 2D **20**
St Michael's Cl. LE67: Mark 2B **8**
St Michaels Ct. LE4: Thurm 4B **14**
  LE9: S Stan 3B **50**
St Nicholas Circ. LE1: Leic . . .4A **4** (2A **28**)
St Nicholas Cl. LE16: L Bow 4E **65**
St Nicholas Pl. LE1: Leic 4B **4** (2A **28**)
St Nicholas Wlk. *LE1: Leic* *3A 4*
  (off Welles St.)
St Nicholas Way LE16: L Bow 4E **65**
St Oswalds Rd. LE3: Leic 6D **18**
St Pauls Cl. LE2: Oad 3D **38**
St Pauls Ct. LE7: Sys 5F **7**
St Paul's Dr. LE7: Sys 1E **15**
St Paul's Rd. LE3: Leic 1G **27**
St Peter's Cl. LE3: Glen 5H **17**
  LE17: Leire 6B **60**
St Peter's Ct. LE7: Sys 5F **7**
St Peter's Dr. LE8: Whet 3H **43**
St Peter's La. LE1: Leic 2C **4** (1B **28**)
St Peters Path LE2: Oad 4A **38**
St Peter's Sq. LE1: Leic 3B **4**
St Peter's St. LE7: Sys 6E **7**
St Phillips Rd. LE5: Leic 4F **29**
St Saviour's Hill LE5: Leic 1E **29**
St Saviour's Rd. LE5: Leic 1E **29**
St Saviour's Wlk. LE5: Leic 2H **29**
St Stephens Rd. LE2: Leic 3E **29**
St Swithin's Rd. LE5: Leic 2D **30**
St Thomas Rd. LE18: Wig 2E **45**
St Thomas's Rd. LE8: G Gle 2E **49**
St Wilfrid's Cl. LE8: Kib B 4A **62**
St Wolstan's Cl. LE18: Wig 6F **37**
Salcombe Cl. LE18: Wig 2A **46**
Salcombe Dr. LE3: Glen 5A **18**
Salisbury Av. LE1: Leic 3D **28**
  LE9: Crof .1G **51**
Salisbury Cl. LE8: Bla 5B **44**
Salisbury Rd. LE1: Leic 8F **5** (4D **28**)
Salisbury Rd. Backways LE1: Leic 7F **5**
Salisbury Rd. Houses *LE1: Leic* *4D 28*
  (off Salisbury Rd.)
Salkeld Rd. LE2: Leic 1C **44**
Saltash Cl. LE18: Wig 2A **46**
Saltcoates Av. LE4: Leic 1E **21**
Saltersagte Dr. LE4: Birs 3G **13**
Saltersford Rd. LE5: Leic 6H **21**
Saltersgate Dr. LE4: Birs 3G **13**
Salts Cl. LE19: End 1D **42**
Samphire Cl. LE5: Ham 3D **22**
Samson Rd. LE3: Leic 6E **18**
Samuel St. LE1: Leic 3F **4** (1D **28**)
Sandacre St. LE1: Leic 2C **4** (1B **28**)
Sanderson Cl. LE8: Whet 5A **44**
Sandfield Cl. LE4: Leic 6C **14**
Sandford Cl. LE5: Leic 1A **30**
Sandford Ct. LE5: Leic 1A **30**
Sandford Rd. LE7: Sys 6E **7**
Sandgate Av. LE4: Birs 3F **13**

Sandham Bri. Rd. *LE7: Crop* *1H 11*
  (off Station Rd.)
Sandhill Dr. LE19: End 2F **43**
Sandhills Av. LE5: Ham 2A **22**
Sandhurst Cl. LE3: Leic 1F **27**
Sandhurst Gdns. LE3: Leic 1F **27**
Sandhurst Rd. LE3: Leic 6F **19**
Sandhurst St. LE2: Oad 3A **38**
Sandiacre Dr. LE4: Thurm 3D **14**
Sandown Ct. LE3: Glen 4A **18**
Sandown Rd. LE2: Leic 6F **29**
  LE3: Glen .4A **18**
  LE18: Wig 5F **37**
Sandpiper Cl. LE2: Leic 6E **21**
Sandringham Av. LE4: Leic 2D **20**
Sandringham Rd. LE2: G Par 2E **45**
Sandringham Way LE16: L Bow 4G **65**
Sandy Ri. LE18: Wig 5H **37**
Sanvey Cl. LE2: Leic 3G **35**
Sanvey Ga. LE1: Leic 2A **4** (1A **28**)
Sanvey La. LE2: Leic 3F **35**
SAPCOTE 6B **50**
Sapcote Rd. LE9: S Stan 3C **50**
Saunderson Rd. LE4: Leic 1H **19**
Savernake Rd. LE4: Leic 4G **19**
Saville Rd. LE8: Bla 5C **44**
Saville St. LE5: Leic 1G **29**
Sawbrook LE8: Flec 6C **58**
Sawday Dr. LE2: Leic 8B **5** (4A **28**)
Sawley St. LE5: Leic 4F **29**
Saxby Dr. LE7: Sys 1G **15**
Saxby St. LE2: Leic 6F **5** (3D **28**)
Saxon Cl. LE16: Mkt H 2E **65**
Saxon Dale LE2: G Par 1C **44**
Saxondale Rd. LE18: Wig 3C **46**
Saxons Ri. LE6: Ratby 4C **16**
Saxon St. LE3: Leic 3H **27**
Saxthorpe Rd. LE5: Ham 3B **22**
Scalborough Cl. LE8: Count 1C **54**
Scalpay Cl. LE4: Leic 2F **19**
Scarborough Rd. LE4: Leic 3D **20**
Scholars Cl. LE8: Count 2F **55**
Scholars Wlk. LE2: Leic 5E **29**
School Cl. LE9: Crof 2G **51**
School Cres. LE9: B Ast 6A **52**
Schoolgate LE2: Leic 4B **36**
School Ho. Cl. LE7: Anst 6F **11**
School La. LE4: Birs 5G **13**
  LE5: Leic .5B **30**
  LE7: Bark .3H **15**
  LE9: Hun .4H **41**
  LE16: Mkt H 3D **64**
  LE19: Nar .4E **43**
School Rd. LE8: Kib B 5A **62**
School St. LE7: Sys 5F **7**
  LE8: Flec .6B **58**
School Wlk. LE8: Kib B 5A **62**
Scotland End LE16: L Bow 5E **65**
Scotland La. LE8: Bur O 2H **49**
Scotland Rd. LE16: L Bow 5E **65**
Scotland Way LE8: Count 2F **55**
Scotswood Cres. LE2: Leic 6G **35**
Scott Cl. LE16: Mkt H 1D **64**
Scott Ct. LE2: Leic 1C **36**
Scott St. LE2: Leic 1C **36**
SCRAPTOFT 5F **23**
Scraptoft La. LE5: Leic 6A **22**
  LE7: Bee .2H **23**
  LE7: Scra .6A **22**
Scraptoft M. LE5: Leic 6A **22**
  LE7: Scra .5F **23**
Scraptoft Ri. LE7: Scra 5F **23**
Scraptoft Wlk. LE5: Leic 5D **22**
Scrivener Cl. LE7: Bush 2G **31**
Scudamore Rd. LE3: Leic 2H **25**
Seacole Cl. LE3: Brau 5B **26**
Seaford Rd. LE2: Leic 4H **35**
Seagrave Dr. LE2: Oad 3H **37**
Seaton Ri. LE5: Leic 4E **23**
Seaton Rd. LE3: Brau 6A **26**
  LE18: Wig 2A **46**
Seddons Cl. LE4: Leic 1H **19**
Sedgebrook Cl. LE5: Leic 3E **31**

Sedgebrook Rd. LE5: Leic 3D 30
Sedgefield Dr. LE7: Sys 6C 6
LE7: Thurn 1F 31
Segrave Rd. LE3: Leic 5F 27
Seine La. LE19: End 5F 33
Selbury Dr. LE2: Oad 4H 37
Selby Av. LE5: Leic 4D 22
Selby Cl. LE16: Mkt H 6D 64
Selkirk Rd. LE4: Leic 1F 21
Senator Cl. LE7: Sys 1D 14
Sence Cres. LE8: G Gle 3C 48
Sence Ho. LE16: Mkt H 3E 65
Severn Cl. LE9: Cosb 2F 53
Severn Rd. LE2: Oad 4C 38
Severn St. LE2: Leic 3D 28
Sextant Rd. LE5: Leic 6C 22
Seymour Cl. LE2: Leic 6D 28
Seymour St. LE2: Leic 3D 28
Seymour Way LE3: Leic E 5F 25
Shackerdale Rd. LE2: Leic 4D 36
LE18: Wig 5C 36
Shackleton St. LE1: Leic ...1E 4 (6C 20)
Shades Cl. LE9: Crof 1G 51
Shadrack Cl. LE9: S Stan 4B 50
Shady La. LE5: Leic 6B 30
Shaeffer Ct. LE4: Leic 3F 19
Shaftesbury Av. LE4: Leic 3D 20
Shaftesbury Rd. LE3: Leic 3G 27
Shakespeare Cl. LE3: Brau 6C 26
Shakespeare Dr. LE3: Brau 6D 26
Shakespeare St. LE2: Leic 1B 36
Shalford Rd. LE5: Leic 5H 21
Shanklin Av. LE2: Leic 2F 37
Shanklin Dr. LE2: Leic 2F 37
Shanklin Gdns. LE2: Leic 2F 37
LE3: Leic E 5H 25
Shanklin Wlk. LE2: Leic 3F 37
Shanti Margh LE4: Leic 3E 21
Shardlow Rd. LE18: Wig 6E 37
Sharmon Cres. LE3: Leic 1B 26
Sharow Rd. LE5: Ham 2C 22
Sharpe Way LE19: Nar 4D 42
Sharpland LE2: Leic 4G 35
Sharpley Dr. LE4: Beau L 5A 12
Sharpley Hill LE6: New L 1H 9
Shaw Cl. LE8: Whet 5H 43
Shaw Wood Cl. LE6: Groby 2E 17
Shearer Cl. LE4: Leic 1G 21
Shearsby Cl. LE18: Wig 1B 46
Sheene Rd. LE4: Beau L 1E 19
Sheepwash La. LE7: Anst 5G 11
Sheffield St. LE3: Leic 4H 27
Sheldon St. LE5: Leic 1E 29
Shelduck Cl. LE8: Whet 1H 53
Shelford Wlk. LE4: Leic 2A 20
Shelland Cl. LE16: L Bow 4H 65
Shelley Dr. LE17: Lut 3G 63
Shelley Rd. LE19: End 1C 42
Shelley St. LE2: Leic 1C 36
Shenley Rd. LE18: Wig 5G 37
Shenton Cl. LE4: Thurn 5E 15
LE8: Whet 4H 43
LE18: Wig 6E 37
Shepherd Cl. LE5: Ham 2C 22
LE9: Leic E 4E 25
Shepherd's Wlk. LE7: E Gos 2H 7
Sherard Way LE3: Brau 6B 26
Sherborne Av. LE18: Wig 3A 46
Sheridan Cl. LE19: End 1C 42
Sheridan St. LE2: Leic 1B 36
Sheringham Rd. LE4: Leic 3H 19
Sherloyd Cl. LE2: Leic 1H 21
Sherrard Rd. LE5: Leic 1E 29
LE16: Mkt H 1D 64
Sherrier Way LE17: Lut 2G 63
Sherwood St. LE5: Leic 1G 29
Shetland Rd. LE4: Leic 3E 21
Shetland Way LE8: Count 1F 55
Shield Cres. LE2: Leic 1C 44
Shipley Rd. LE5: Leic 3F 29

Shipman Rd. LE3: Brau 3D 34
Shipston Hill LE2: Oad 5A 38
Shipton Cl. LE18: Wig 1D 46
Shipton Rd. LE5: Ham 2C 22
Shire Cl. LE3: Leic 2C 26
Shires La. LE1: Leic 3B 4 (1A 28)
Shires Wlk. LE1: Leic 3C 4 (1B 28)
Shirley Av. LE2: Leic 1F 37
Shirley Dr. LE7: Sys 4F 7
Shirley Rd. LE2: Leic 1F 37
Shirley St. LE4: Leic 3C 20
Shoemakers, The LE7: Anst 5F 11
Short Cl. LE8: Flec 6C 58
Shortridge La. LE19: End 6H 33
Short St. LE1: Leic 2C 4 (1B 28)
Shottens Cl. LE4: Leic 3F 19
Shottery Av. LE3: Brau 6D 26
Shoulbard LE8: Flec 5A 58
Shrewsbury Av. LE2: Leic 3C 36
LE16: L Bow 4G 65
Shropshire Cl. LE16: Mkt H 2D 64
Shropshire Pl. LE16: Mkt H 2D 64
Shropshire Rd. LE2: Leic 2H 35
Shuttleworth La. LE9: Cosb 4E 53
Sibson Rd. LE4: Birs 4G 13
Sibton La. LE2: Oad 5A 38
Sickleholm Dr. LE5: Leic 5G 29
Siddons Wlk. LE1: Leic 3D 4
Sidings, The LE4: Leic 1B 20
LE8: Whet 3H 43
Sidmouth Av. LE5: Leic 4A 30
Sidney Rd. LE2: Leic 2F 37
Sidwell St. LE5: Leic 2G 29
Silbury Rd. LE4: Leic 4G 19
Silsden Ri. LE2: Leic 6H 35
Silver Arc. LE1: Leic 3C 4
Silver Birch Way LE7: E Gos 1H 7
Silverdale Dr. LE4: Thurn 5D 14
Silverstone Dr. LE4: Leic 6B 14
Silver St. LE1: Leic 3C 4 (1B 28)
Silverton Rd. LE2: Oad 3C 38
Silver Wlk. LE1: Leic 3C 4
(off Silver St.)
Silverwood Cl. LE5: Leic 2C 30
Simborough Way LE16: L Bow 3G 65
Simmins Cl. LE2: Leic 5H 35
Simmins Cres. LE2: Leic 5H 35
Simons Cl. LE18: Wig 3C 46
Simpson Cl. LE7: Sys 1C 14
LE8: Whet 5A 44
Siskin Hill LE2: Oad 5A 38
Sitch Cl. LE9: B Ast 2C 60
Sitwell Wlk. LE5: Leic 5H 29
Six Acre Cl. LE6: Ratby 5D 16
Six Acres LE9: B Ast 1A 60
Skampton Grn. LE5: Leic 2B 30
Skampton Rd. LE5: Leic 2B 30
Skelton Dr. LE2: Leic 3C 36
Sketchley Cl. LE5: Leic 1D 30
Skippon Cl. LE16: Mkt H 4C 64
Skipworth St. LE2: Leic 3E 29
Skye Way LE8: Count 2F 55
Slade Cl. LE3: Brau 5A 26
Slade Greens, The LE2: Leic 5G 35
Slade Pl. LE2: Leic 5G 35
Slate Brook Cl. LE6: Groby 2F 17
Slate Cl. LE3: Glen 5H 17
Slate Pit La. LE6: Groby 1A 16
Slater St. LE1: Leic 1B 4 (6A 20)
LE3: Leic 1A 4 (6A 20)
Slate St. LE2: Leic 5F 5 (2C 28)
Sloane Cl. LE19: End 6G 33
(not continuous)
Smart Cl. LE3: Brau 5B 26
Smedmore Rd. LE5: Leic 5F 21
Smeeton Ct. LE8: Kib B 5A 62
Smeeton Rd. LE8: Kib B 6A 62
SMEETON WESTERBY 6H 59
Smith Av. LE4: Thurn 5D 14
Smith Dorrien Rd. LE5: Leic 6G 21
Smith Way LE19: End 5C 34
Smithy Farm Dr. LE9: S Stan 3A 50
Smore Slade Hills LE2: Oad 5E 39

Smyth Cl. LE16: Mkt H 1D 64
Snape Cl. LE5: Ham 1D 22
Snowdens End LE18: Wig 2C 46
Snowdrop Cl. LE19: Nar 3B 42
Snow Hill LE4: Leic 4G 19
Soar Ho. LE16: Mkt H 3F 65
Soar La. LE3: Leic 2A 4 (1H 27)
Soar Mill La. LE9: B Ast 5H 51
Soar Rd. LE4: Thurn 2C 14
Soar Valley Way LE2: Leic 5D 34
LE3: Leic 5D 34
LE19: End 5D 34
Sockburn Cl. LE5: Ham 2D 22
Somerby Dr. LE2: Oad 4C 38
Somerby Rd. LE7: Thurn 1F 31
Somerfield Wlk. LE4: Leic 3F 19
Somerfield Way LE3: Leic E 5F 25
Somerscales Wlk. LE4: Leic 6D 20
Somerset Av. LE4: Leic 3H 19
Somerton Dr. LE3: Glen 5A 18
Somers Rd. LE5: Leic 1C 30
Somerville Rd. LE3: Leic 6F 27
Sonning Way LE2: G Par 1C 44
Sopers Rd. LE9: Crof 2G 51
Sorrel Rd. LE5: Ham 3C 22
Sorrel Way LE19: Nar 2B 42
Sth. Albion St. LE1: Leic 5E 5 (2C 28)
Southampton St. LE1: Leic ..3E 4 (1C 28)
South Av. LE3: Leic E 4H 25
LE18: Wig 1A 46
South Charnwood Leisure Cen. ...4G 7
Sth. Church Ga. LE1: Leic ..1B 4 (6A 20)
Southdown Dr. LE4: Thurn 6C 14
Southdown Rd. LE5: Leic 1F 29
South Dr. LE5: Leic 5A 22
LE9: S Stan 4C 50
Southernhay Av. LE2: Leic 1E 37
Southernhay Cl. LE2: Leic 6E 29
Southernhay Rd. LE2: Leic 1E 37
Southey Cl. LE4: Leic 5D 20
LE19: End 1C 42
Southfield Av. LE7: Sys 6F 7
Southfield Cl. LE2: G Par 6E 35
LE7: Scra 6F 23
SOUTH FIELDS 4A 28
South Flds. LE1: Leic 7E 5 (3C 28)
Southfields Av. LE2: Oad 3H 37
Southfields Dr. LE2: Leic 4A 36
(not continuous)
Southfields Drive Sports Cen. 4B 36
Southfields Wlk. LE2: Leic 4B 36
Southgates LE1: Leic 4B 4 (2A 28)
Southgates Underpass
LE1: Leic 4B 4 (2A 28)
Sth. Kingsmead Rd. LE2: Leic 3E 37
SOUTH KNIGHTON 2F 37
Sth. Knighton Rd. LE2: Leic 2F 37
Southland Rd. LE2: Leic 3F 37
Southleigh Gro. LE16: Mkt H 2C 64
Southmeads Cl. LE2: Leic 2A 38
Southmeads Rd. LE2: Leic, Oad ..2H 37
Southside Rd. LE3: Brau 3D 34
South St. LE2: Oad 3A 38
Southview Ct. LE5: K Mux 5A 22
Southview Dr. LE5: Leic 5H 29
South Wlk. LE6: Ratby 4C 16
South Way LE5: Kib B 4B 62
Southway LE8: Bla 5B 44
SOUTH WIGSTON 2F 45
South Wigston Station (Rail) 1F 45
Sovereign Pk. LE16: Mkt H 5E 65
Sovereign Pk. Ind. Est.
LE16: Mkt H 5E 65
Spa Dr. LE9: Sap 5B 50
Spa La. LE18: Wig 1B 46
Spalding St. LE5: Leic 1G 29
Sparkenhoe LE2: Crof 2G 51
Sparkenhoe St. LE2: Leic 4F 4 (2D 28)
Sparsis Gdns. LE19: End 2F 43
Speedwell Cl. LE19: Nar 2B 42
Speedwell Dr. LE5: Ham 2B 22
LE9: B Ast 3C 60
Speers Rd. LE3: Leic 5C 18

Spencefield Dr. LE5: Leic 4B 30
Spencefield Gdns. LE5: Leic 2C 30
Spencefield La. LE5: Leic 4B 30
Spencer Av. LE4: Thurm 4C 14
Spencer Rd. LE17: Lut 4G 63
Spencer St. LE2: Oad 3A 38
  LE16: Mkt H 3C 64
Spence St. LE5: Leic 6F 21
Spence Street Swimming Pool 6F 21
Spendlow Gdns. LE2: Leic 5A 36
Spendlow Grn. LE2: Leic 5A 36
Spiers Cl. LE19: Nar 4D 42
Spinner Cl. LE9: B Ast 1D 60
Spinney, The LE2: Oad 5G 39
  LE7: Thurn 3E 31
Spinney Av. LE8: Count 1F 55
Spinney Cl. LE2: G Par 6E 35
  LE3: Brau 5A 26
  LE6: Groby 3E 17
  LE7: Sys 6C 6
  LE16: Mkt H 3B 64
Spinney Ct. LE9: Crof 1G 51
Spinney Dr. LE8: Kib H 4A 62
Spinney Halt LE8: Whet 4G 43
Spinney Hill Rd. LE5: Leic 6E 21
SPINNEY HILLS 1F 29
Spinney Ri. LE4: Birs 4F 13
Spinney Side LE6: Groby 3E 17
Spinney Vw. LE8: G Gle 2E 49
Spion Kopje LE2: Oad 2A 48
Sponne Ri. LE2: Leic 5A 36
Sports Fld. La. LE9: Hun 3H 41
Sports Rd. LE3: Glen 5A 18
Springbrook Dr. LE7: Scra 1F 31
Spring Cl. LE2: Leic 4H 35
  LE6: Ratby 5D 16
  LE17: Lut 5G 63
Springdale Rd. LE4: Thurm 5C 14
Springfield Cl. LE3: Glen 6H 17
  LE8: Kib B 6B 62
  LE9: B Ast 2B 60
Springfield Ct. LE16: Mkt H 4E 65
Springfield Cres. LE8: Kib B 6A 62
Springfield La. LE8: Smee W 6A 62
Springfield Rd. LE2: Leic 5E 29
Springfield St. LE16: Mkt H 4E 65
Spring Gdns. LE9: Sap 5C 50
  LE19: Litt 5E 43
Springhill Gdns. LE16: Mkt H 4B 64
Spring La. LE18: Wig 6F 37
Springs, The LE8: Flec 6B 58
  LE9: B Ast 1A 60
Springway Cl. LE5: Leic 2E 31
Springwell Cl. LE8: Count 1E 55
Springwell Dr. LE8: Count 1D 54
Springwell La. LE8: Whet 6H 43
Spruce Way LE17: Lut 3F 63
Square, The LE3: Glen 4H 17
  LE7: Thurn 3F 31
  LE8: Count 1F 55
  LE8: New H 5H 47
  LE9: Sap 6B 50
  LE16: Mkt H 3D 64
  LE19: Litt 5E 43
Square Ct. LE4: Birs 4H 13
Squire's Ride LE7: E Gos 1H 7
Squirrel Cl. LE19: Nar 4C 42
Squirrel's Cnr. LE7: E Gos 1H 7
Stable Cl. LE19: Litt 4E 43
Stablegate Way LE16: L Bow 3F 65
Stackley Rd. LE8: G Gle 2D 48
Stackyard Cl. LE3: Leic E 5H 25
Stadium Pl. LE4: Leic 3A 20
Stadium Ri. LE4: Leic 3H 19
Stadon Rd. LE7: Anst 5F 11
Stafford Dr. LE18: Wig 1F 45
Stafford Leys LE3: Leic E 4F 25
Stafford St. LE4: Leic 2E 21
Staindale LE18: Wig 1D 46
Stainmore Av. LE19: Nar 1C 42
Stamford Cl. LE3: Glen 5H 17
  LE6: Ratby 4C 16
  LE16: Mkt H 4D 64

Stamford Dr. LE6: Groby 3F 17
  LE7: Crop 1H 11
Stamford Hall LE2: Leic 1H 37
Stamford Ri. LE6: New L 3A 10
Stamford Rd. LE9: K Mux 3E 25
Stamford St. LE1: Leic 5D 5 (2B 28)
  LE3: Glen 4H 17
  LE6: Ratby 4B 16
Stanbrig LE18: Wig 3C 46
Stancliff Rd. LE4: Leic 6D 14
Stanfell Rd. LE2: Leic 1C 36
Stanhope Rd. LE18: Wig 2C 46
Stanhope St. LE5: Leic 2F 29
Stanier Dr. LE4: Leic 1H 21
Stanier Rd. LE9: B Ast 1C 60
Stanley Burroughs Almshouses
  LE9: Sap 6B 50
Stanley Dr. LE5: Leic 5A 22
Stanley Rd. LE2: Leic 4E 29
Stanton La. LE9: Crof, Pott M 1D 50
  LE9: Sap, S Stan 5A 50
Stanton Rd. LE9: Sap 6B 50
Stanton Row LE2: Leic 3B 36
Stanway Cl. LE16: L Bow 3F 65
Stanyon Cl. LE8: Count 1E 55
Stapleford Rd. LE4: Leic 1H 19
Staplehurst Av. LE3: Brau 1C 34
Star Cotts. LE9: S Stan 1B 50
Starmer Cl. LE9: Cosb 2G 53
Station Cl. LE9: K Mux 3E 25
Station Dr. LE9: K Mux 3E 25
Station Hollow LE8: Kib B 5A 62
Station La. LE7: Scra 1F 31
  LE17: Leire 6A 60
Station Rd. LE3: Glen 4H 17
  LE4: Birs 6F 13
  LE6: Ratby 5C 16
  LE7: Crop, R'ley 1G 11
  LE7: Thurn 2F 31
  LE8: Count 2D 54
  LE8: G Gle, Wist 1B 58
  LE9: B Ast 1B 60
  LE9: Crof 1G 51
  LE9: K Mux 2D 24
  LE9: S Stan 2A 50
  LE16: G Bow 1F 65
  LE17: D Bas 5G 61
  LE17: Lut 5H 63
  LE18: Wig 1H 45
  LE19: Litt, Nar 4E 43
Station St. LE2: Leic 5F 5 (2C 28)
  LE8: Kib B 5A 62
  LE8: Whet 3G 43
  LE18: Wig 1G 45
Staveley Cl. LE18: Wig 1C 46
Staveley Rd. LE5: Leic 4F 29
Staythorpe Rd. LE4: Leic 6E 15
Steadman Av. LE9: Cosb 2G 53
Stebbings Rd. LE2: Leic 4H 35
Steele Cl. LE5: Leic 2A 30
Steeple Cl. LE18: Wig 5G 37
Steins La. LE5: Leic 5B 22
Stelle Way LE3: Glen 2B 18
Stemborough La. LE17: Leire 6B 60
Stenor Cl. LE8: Flec 5A 58
Stenson Rd. LE3: Leic 4E 19
Stephenson Cl. LE6: Groby 2E 17
  LE9: B Ast 3C 60
Stephenson Ct. LE3: Glen 3A 18
Stephenson Dr. LE3: Leic 6F 19
Stephenson Way LE6: Groby 2E 17
Stevens Cl. LE9: S Stan 3C 50
Stevens St. LE16: Mkt H 3C 64
Stevenson Gdns. LE9: Cosb 1F 53
Stevenstone Cl. LE2: Oad 4D 38
Stewart Av. LE19: End 2C 42
Steyning Cres. LE3: Glen 4B 18
Stiles, The LE7: Sys 5F 7
Stiles Cl. LE9: B Ast 2B 60
Stillington Cres. LE5: Ham 1C 22
Stinford Leys LE16: L Bow 3G 65
Stirling Dr. LE7: Thurn 1F 31
Stockland Rd. LE2: Leic 5A 36

Stocks Rd. LE7: Scra 5F 23
Stockton Ho. LE3: Glen 1B 26
Stockton Rd. LE4: Leic 4G 21
Stockwell Cl. LE16: L Bow 3G 65
Stockwell Rd. LE2: Leic 2F 37
Stokesby Ri. LE2: Leic 2C 44
Stokes Cl. LE8: Bla 3A 44
Stokes Dr. LE3: Leic 5F 19
Stonebridge St. LE5: Leic 1F 29
Stonechat Wlk. LE5: Leic 1E 29
Stone Cl. LE4: Beau L 5A 12
Stonecroft LE8: Count 2C 54
Stonecrop Rd. LE5: Ham 3C 22
Stonehaven Rd. LE4: Leic 1F 21
Stonehill Av. LE4: Birs 2G 13
Stonehill Ct. LE8: G Gle 2E 49
Stonehill Dr. LE8: G Gle 2E 49
Stonehurst Rd. LE3: Brau 1D 34
Stoneleigh Mnr. LE2: Leic 5F 29
Stoneleigh Way LE3: Leic 5F 19
Stonelodge Rd. LE6: Groby 2H 17
Stonesby Av. LE2: Leic 4A 36
Stonesby Wlk. LE2: Leic 4B 36
STONEYGATE 6F 29
Stoneygate Av. LE2: Leic 6E 29
Stoneygate Cl. LE2: Leic 5E 29
Stoneygate Rd. LE2: Leic 5E 29
Stoney Hollow LE17: Lut 5G 63
Stoney La. LE67: S Bar 2A 8
STONEY STANTON 3C 50
Stoneywell Rd. LE4: Beau L 6H 11
Stores La. LE8: Flec 6B 58
Storey St. LE3: Leic 6H 19
Stornaway Rd. LE5: Leic 6D 22
STOUGHTON 6E 31
Stoughton Av. LE2: Leic 6F 29
Stoughton Cl. LE2: Oad 3B 38
Stoughton Dr. LE5: Leic 5H 29
Stoughton Dr. Nth. LE5: Leic 4F 29
Stoughton Dr. Sth. LE2: Leic 6H 29
Stoughton La. LE2: Leic 5B 30
Stoughton Lodge Farm LE2: S'ton 5D 30
Stoughton Rd. LE2: Leic 6H 29
  (Gartree Rd.)
  LE2: Leic 6F 29
  (London Rd.)
  LE2: Leic 4E 31
  (Thurnby La.)
  LE2: Oad 3A 38
Stoughton St. LE2: Leic 2D 28
Stoughton St. Sth. LE2: Leic 2D 28
Stour Cl. LE2: Oad 3D 38
Stowe Cl. LE3: Leic 4E 19
Strand, The LE2: Leic 6C 28
Strasbourg Dr. LE4: Leic 2F 19
Stratford Rd. LE3: Brau 6D 26
Strathaven Rd. LE4: Leic 1F 21
Strathern Rd. LE3: Leic 3D 18
Strathmore Av. LE4: Leic 3F 21
Stratton Cl. LE16: Mkt H 5C 64
Strawberry Gdns. LE19: End 5F 33
Streamside LE9: B Ast 2B 60
Strensall Rd. LE2: Leic 6H 35
Stretton Cl. LE8: G Gle 3D 48
Stretton Hall Dr. LE2: Oad 6F 39
Stretton Karting Circuit 2G 39
Stretton Rd. LE3: Leic 2G 27
  LE8: G Gle 2D 48
Strollers Way LE7: E Gos 2H 7
Stroma Way LE8: Count 2F 55
Stroud Rd. LE5: Leic 6F 21
Strudwick Way LE8: Whet 2A 44
Stuart Ct. LE2: Leic 6E 29
  LE8: Kib B 5A 62
Stuart Rd. LE2: G Par 6G 35
  LE16: Mkt H 5C 64
Stuart St. LE3: Leic 4H 27
  LE8: Kib B 5A 62
Stubbs Rd. LE4: Leic 5D 20
Sturdee Cl. LE2: Leic 5H 35
Sturdee Grn. LE2: Leic 5G 35
Sturdee Rd. LE2: Leic 5G 35
Sturrock Cl. LE7: Thurn 1F 31

Styon Rd. LE3: Leic 4C 18
Sudeley Av. LE4: Leic 3A 20
Suffolk Cl. LE18: Wig 6C 36
Suffolk St. LE5: Leic 2G 29
Sulgrave Rd. LE5: Leic 6F 21
Summerbridge La. LE5: Ham 1C 22
Summerlea Rd. LE5: Leic 1C 30
Summers Way LE16: Mkt H 4C 64
Sunbury Grn. LE5: Leic 6E 23
Sunbury Ri. LE8: Count 1C 54
Sundew Rd. LE5: Ham 3C 22
Sundial Rd. LE5: Ham 2C 22
Sunningdale Ind. Pk.
    LE3: Leic 3A 26
Sunningdale Rd. LE3: Leic 3H 25
Sunnycroft Rd. LE3: Leic 2E 27
Sunnyfield Cl. LE5: Leic 2C 30
Sunnyside LE2: Oad 5C 38
Sunnyside Cl. LE8: Whet 2H 43
Sun Way LE3: Brau 4B 26
Surrey St. LE4: Leic 4D 20
Susan Av. LE5: Leic 4B 30
Sussex Rd. LE18: Wig 6B 36
Sussex St. LE5: Leic 1D 28
Sutherington Way LE7: Anst 4G 11
Sutherland St. LE2: Leic 3E 29
Sutton Av. LE4: Leic 4E 21
Sutton Cl. LE2: Oad 6B 38
Sutton Ct. LE9: B Ast 5A 52
    LE16: Mkt H 5D 64
SUTTON IN THE ELMS 5A 52
Sutton La. LE9: B Ast 4H 51
Sutton Pl. LE4: Leic 3E 21
Sutton Rd. LE2: Leic 1C 36
    LE16: G Bow 1H 65
Swainson Rd. LE4: Leic 5G 21
Swain St. LE1: Leic 4F 4 (2C 28)
    LE2: Leic 4F 4 (2D 28)
Swale Cl. LE2: Oad 3D 38
Swallow Cl. LE3: Leic E 6E 25
Swallowdale Dr. LE4: Beau L 5B 12
Swallow Dr. LE7: Sys 5C 6
Swallows Dale LE7: E Gos 1H 7
Swan Cl. LE2: G Par 1A 44
Swannington Rd. LE3: Leic 6G 19
    LE9: B Ast 1C 60
Swanscombe Rd. LE2: Leic 6H 27
Swan St. LE3: Leic 2A 4 (1A 28)
Swan Way LE7: Sys 5C 6
Sweetbriar Rd. LE3: Leic 4G 27
Swift Cl. LE7: Sys 5D 6
Swift Ho. LE16: Mkt H 3E 65
Swiftway LE17: Lut 3G 63
Swindale Cl. LE2: Leic 7B 5 (3A 28)
Swinford Av. LE2: Leic 1D 44
Swinford Ct. LE2: Leic 1D 44
Swinford Rd. LE17: C'ach, Lut 6H 63
Swinstead Rd. LE5: Leic 3D 30
Swinton Cl. LE5: Ham 2D 22
Swithland Av. LE4: Leic 4A 20
Swithland Cl. LE67: Mark 3C 8
Swithland Ct. LE3: Brau 2D 34
Sword Cl. LE3: Glen 6A 18
Sybil Rd. LE5: Leic 6F 27
Sycamore Cl. LE2: Leic 6H 29
    LE2: Oad 6G 39
    LE7: Sys 1F 15
Sycamore Dr. LE6: Groby 2F 17
    LE17: Lut 4E 63
Sycamore Gro. LE6: Groby 2F 17
Sycamore Rd. LE4: Birs 2G 13
Sycamore St. LE8: Bla 3B 44
Sycamore Way LE19: Litt 5D 42
Sykefield Av. LE3: Leic 3G 27
Sylvan Av. LE5: Leic 1F 29
Sylvan St. LE3: Leic 1G 27
Sylvan Way LE3: Leic E 3H 25
Symington Way LE16: Mkt H 3D 64
SYSTON 5F 7
Syston By-Pass LE4: Thurm 4C 6
    LE7: Coss, Rat W, Sys 4C 6
Syston Northern By-Pass
    LE7: Quen, Rat W 3E 7

Syston Rd. LE7: Coss 2A 6
    LE7: Quen 3H 7
Syston Station (Rail) 6E 7
Syston St. E. LE1: Leic 6D 20
Syston St. W. LE1: Leic 5C 20
Sywell Dr. LE18: Wig 1C 46

T

Tadcaster Av. LE2: Leic 6H 35
Tadcaster Grn. LE2: Leic 6H 35
Tailby Av. LE5: Leic 5G 21
Tailors Link LE7: E Gos 2H 7
Talbot La. LE1: Leic 4A 4 (2A 28)
Talbot St. LE4: Leic 2C 20
Talbott Cl. LE9: B Ast 3C 60
Talbot Yd. LE16: Mkt H 3D 64
Tamar Rd. LE2: Oad 4D 38
    LE4: Leic 3G 21
Tamerton Rd. LE2: Leic 4A 36
Tannery Ter. LE7: Anst 5G 11
Tansey Cres. LE9: S Stan 3A 50
Tansley Av. LE18: Wig 2G 45
Tarbat Rd. LE5: Leic 6D 22
Tarragon Rd. LE2: Leic 7A 5 (3H 27)
Tatlow Ho. LE3: Glen 1B 26
Tatlow Rd. LE3: Leic 1A 26
Tatton Cl. LE3: Leic 4E 19
Taunton Cl. LE18: Wig 2A 46
Taunton Rd. LE3: Leic 2F 27
Taurus Cl. LE2: Leic 2D 28
Taverner Dr. LE6: Ratby 6D 16
Taverners Rd. LE4: Beau L 4C 12
Tavistock Dr. LE5: Leic 4H 29
Taylor Cl. LE7: Sys 6E 7
    LE9: S Stan 3B 50
Taylor Rd. LE1: Leic 1F 4 (6C 20)
Taylor's Bri. Rd.
    LE18: Wig 2G 45
Teal Cl. LE3: Leic E 5E 25
Teal Way LE7: Sys 5C 6
Teasel Cl. LE19: Nar 3C 42
Tebbs Cl. LE8: Count 1C 54
Tedder Cl. LE17: Lut 5E 63
Tedworth Grn. LE4: Leic 6D 12
Teignmouth Cl. LE5: Leic 4H 29
Teignmouth Wlk. LE5: Leic 4H 29
Telford Way LE5: Leic 2E 31
Tempest Rd. LE4: Birs 6F 13
Temple Rd. LE5: Leic 2G 29
Tendring Dr. LE18: Wig 6H 37
Tennis Ct. Dr. LE5: Leic 6A 22
Tennyson Rd. LE17: Lut 3G 63
Tennyson St. LE2: Leic 4E 29
    LE19: Nar 2C 42
Tentercroft Av. LE7: Sys 5G 7
Terrace Cotts. LE9: Crof 1G 51
Tetuan Rd. LE3: Leic 1F 27
Tewkesbury St. LE3: Leic 1H 27
Thackeray St. LE2: Leic 1B 36
Thackney Leys LE8: Kib H 4H 59
Thames St. LE1: Leic 1D 4 (6B 20)
Thatcher Cl. LE4: Leic 1F 19
Thatchers Cnr. LE7: E Gos 2H 7
Thatch Mdw. Dr. LE16: L Bow 3G 65
The . . . .
    Names prefixed with 'The' for example
    'The Albany' are indexed under the
    main name such as 'Albany, The'
Theatre Mall LE1: Leic 3D 4
    (off Haymarket Cen.)
Thirlmere Rd. LE18: Wig 6G 37
Thirlmere St. LE2: Leic 8B 5 (4A 28)
Thistle Cl. LE7: Crop 1H 11
    LE19: Nar 3C 42
Thistley Cl. LE3: Brau 5A 26
Thomas Cl. LE3: Brau 1E 35
Thomas Dr. LE8: Count 1D 54
Thomasson Rd. LE5: Leic 1B 30
Thomson Ct. LE4: Leic 5B 14
Thomson Ct. LE67: Mark 3D 8
Thoresby St. LE5: Leic 1G 29

Thornborough Cl. LE16: L Bow 4F 65
    LE19: Nar 4B 42
Thornborough Way LE5: Ham 1B 22
Thornby Gdns. LE18: Wig 1C 46
Thorndale Rd. LE4: Thurm 4D 14
Thorneycroft Cl. LE9: B Ast 3D 60
Thornhills LE19: Nar 1C 42
Thornhills Gro. LE19: Nar 1C 42
Thornholme Cl. LE4: Leic 1G 19
Thornton Cl. LE3: Leic 4B 26
    LE7: Sys 5E 7
    LE9: B Ast 3C 60
Thornton Dr. LE19: Nar 3E 43
Thornton La. LE67: Mark 6A 8
Thornton Wlk. LE1: Leic 4B 4
Thorntree Cl. LE3: Leic 3D 18
Thornville Cl. LE4: Leic 4G 21
THORPE ASTLEY 5B 26
Thorpe Dr. LE18: Wig 5F 37
Thorpe Fld. Dr. LE4: Thurm 3D 14
Thorpe La. LE7: Bark 4G 15
Thorpe St. LE3: Leic 2H 27
Thorpe Way LE19: End 5B 34
Thorpewell LE5: Leic 1H 29
Thorpewell Wlk. LE5: Leic 1H 29
Threadgold Cl. LE4: Beau L 5B 12
Thresher's Wlk. LE7: E Gos 2H 7
THURCASTON 1B 12
Thurcaston Rd. LE4: Leic 4D 12
    (Greengate La.)
    LE4: Leic 1B 20
    (Red Hill Way, not continuous)
Thurcroft Cl. LE2: G Par 6H 35
THURLASTON 6A 32
Thurlaston La. LE9: Crof 4E 41
    LE9: Earl S 2A 40
Thurlaston Rd. LE9: Hun, Nar 6D 32
Thurlby Rd. LE5: Leic 6F 21
Thurlington Rd. LE3: Leic 4E 27
Thurlow Cl. LE2: Oad 5D 38
Thurlow Rd. LE2: Leic 6C 28
THURMASTON 5C 14
Thurmaston Blvd. LE4: Leic 1G 21
    (not continuous)
Thurmaston Footpath LE4: Leic 1G 21
Thurmaston La. LE4: Leic 1H 21
    LE5: Leic 5A 22
THURNBY .3F 31
Thurnby Hill LE7: Bush, Thurn 2E 31
Thurnby La. LE2: S'ton 6E 31
THURNBY LODGE 1E 31
Thurn Ct. LE5: Leic 6D 22
Thurncourt Cl. LE5: Leic 6C 22
Thurncourt Gdns. LE5: Leic 1F 31
Thurncourt Rd. LE5: Leic 6C 22
Thurnview Rd. LE5: Leic 4C 30
Thyme Cl. LE2: Leic 7A 5 (3A 28)
Tiber Way LE19: Brau 1B 34
Tichborne Cl. LE2: Leic 3D 28
Tichborne St. LE2: Leic 3D 28
Tiffany Cl. LE2: Leic 5F 29
Tigers Cl. LE18: Wig 1E 45
Tigers Rd. LE18: Wig 1E 45
Tigers Way LE1: Leic 8D 5 (4B 28)
Tilbury Cres. LE4: Leic 6E 15
Tilford Cres. LE2: Leic 1D 44
Tillett Rd. LE3: Brau 5B 26
Tilley Cl. LE3: Brau 6B 26
Tillingham Rd. LE5: Leic 5H 21
Tilling Rd. LE4: Leic 2G 19
Tilling Wlk. LE4: Leic 1G 19
Tilton Dr. LE2: Oad 6A 38
Timber St. LE18: Wig 2F 45
Timberwood Dr.
    LE6: Groby 3E 17
Timble Rd. LE5: Ham 1D 22
Timson Cl. LE16: Mkt H 1C 64
Tinkers Dell LE7: E Gos 1H 7
Tiptree Cl. LE4: Leic 3H 19
Tithe Cl. LE4: Wan 2F 13
Tithe St. LE5: Leic 6G 21
Tithings, The LE8: Kib B 4A 62
Tiverton Av. LE4: Leic 3E 21

Tiverton Cl.—Vinehouse Cl.

Tiverton Cl. LE2: Oad .4C **38**
LE19: Nar .3B **42**
Tiverton M. LE4: Leic .3E **21**
Tofts, The LE18: Wig .2B **46**
Tolcarne Rd. LE5: Leic .5C **22**
Tolchard Cl. LE5: Leic .2A **30**
Tollemache Av. LE4: Leic .3A **20**
Toller Rd. LE2: Leic .6E **29**
Tollerton Cl. LE5: Ham .1D **22**
Tolton Rd. LE4: Leic .1H **19**
Tolwell Rd. LE4: Beau L .6C **12**
Tomlin Rd. LE4: Leic .4G **21**
Tomlinson Ct. LE2: Oad .3A **38**
Tom Paine Cl. LE3: Brau .5B **26**
Topcliffe Wlk. LE4: Leic .2A **20**
Top Cl. LE3: Brau .6B **26**
Tophall Dr. LE8: Count .2E **55**
Torch Way LE16: Mkt H .6E **65**
Torcross Cl. LE3: Glen .5C **18**
Toronto Cl. LE1: Leic .1F **4** (6C **20**)
Torridon Cl. LE4: Leic .2H **19**
Torrington Cl. LE18: Wig .3B **46**
Totland Rd. LE3: Leic .5G **19**
Tourist Info. Cen.
Leicester .4D 4 (2B 28)
Market Harborough .3D 64
Wigston .6F 37
Tournament Rd. LE3: Glen .6B **18**
Tovey Cres. LE2: Leic .5H **35**
Towers Cl. LE9: K Mux .3E **25**
Towers Dr. LE9: K Mux .3E **25**
Tower St. LE1: Leic .7D **5** (3B **28**)
Towle Rd. LE3: Leic .5C **18**
Town End Cl. LE2: Leic .1E **37**
Town Hall Sq. *LE1: Leic .4D 4*
(off Every St.)
Townsend Cl. LE4: Leic .6B **14**
LE9: B Ast .2D **60**
Townsend Ct. LE2: Leic .3G **35**
Townsend Rd. LE9: S Stan .4B **50**
LE19: End .6H **33**
Town Sq. *LE7: Sys .5F 7*
(off Walkers Way)
Town Sq. Shop. Cen. LE7: Sys .5F **7**
Town St. LE8: Bur O .3H **49**
Towpath Link LE18: Wig .3G **45**
Trading Est. LE2: Leic .1D **28**
Trafalgar Cl. LE7: Sys .6E **7**
Trafalgar Way LE2: G Par .2D **44**
Trafford Rd. LE5: Leic .6H **21**
Tranter Pl. LE4: Leic .3F **21**
Treasure Cl. LE3: Glen .6A **18**
Treaty Rd. LE3: Glen .6B **18**
Tredington Rd. LE3: Glen .4B **18**
Treetops Cl. LE5: Leic .6A **22**
Trefoil Cl. LE5: Ham .3C **22**
LE9: B Ast .3D **60**
Tremaine Dr. LE18: Wig .2A **46**
Trenant Rd. LE2: Leic .5A **36**
Trent Av. LE4: Beau L .4D **12**
Trent Cl. LE2: Oad .4D **38**
LE9: B Ast .1C **60**
Trescoe Ri. LE3: Leic .2C **26**
Tressell Way LE3: Brau .5B **26**
Trevanth Rd. LE4: Leic .2H **21**
Trevino Dr. LE4: Leic .6C **14**
Trevose Gdns. LE5: Leic .6D **22**
Trigo Cl. LE4: Beau L .1E **19**
Trillium Cl. LE5: Ham .2C **22**
Trinity Cl. LE7: Sys .6F **7**
Trinity La. LE1: Leic .6D **5** (3B **28**)
Trinity Rd. LE8: Whet .3H **43**
LE19: End .1G **43**
Tristram Cl. LE3: Leic E .5G **25**
Triumph Rd. LE3: Glen .6A **18**
Trojan Way LE7: Sys .1C **14**
Troon Ind. Est. LE4: Leic .1A **22**
(not continuous)
Troon Way LE4: Leic .6B **14**
Troon Way Bus. Cen. LE4: Leic .1H **21**
Trueway Rd. LE5: Leic .5G **29**
Truro Dr. LE18: Wig .2B **46**
Tuckey Cl. LE9: Sap .5C **50**
Tudor Cl. LE3: Leic .2H **27**
Tudor Dr. LE2: Oad .3B **38**
LE9: Cosb .3F **53**
Tudor Gro. LE6: Groby .4E **17**
Tudor Rd. LE3: Leic .6H **19**
Tudor Wlk. LE3: Leic .2H **27**
Tuffleys Way LE3: Brau .6A **26**
Tungstone Way LE16: Mkt H .5D **64**
Tunstall Cres. LE4: Leic .5G **21**
Turnbull Dr. LE3: Brau .1D **34**
Turnbury Way LE5: Leic .6G **29**
Turner Ri. LE2: Oad .5B **38**
Turner Rd. LE5: Leic .6H **21**
Turner St. LE1: Leic .7D **5** (3B **28**)
Turner Wlk. LE5: Leic .1A **30**
Turnpike Cl. LE16: Mkt H .1C **64**
LE17: Lut .2H **63**
Turnpike Way LE67: Mark .3C **8**
Turnstone Wlk. LE5: Leic .6E **21**
Turn St. LE7: Sys .5E **7**
Turville Cl. LE18: Wig .3C **46**
Turville Rd. LE3: Leic .4F **27**
Tuskar Rd. LE5: Leic .6D **22**
Tuxford Rd. LE4: Leic .2A **22**
Twickenham Rd. LE2: Leic .1C **44**
Twitten, The LE2: G Par .2D **44**
Two Steeples Sq. LE18: Wig .6F **37**
Twycross St. LE2: Leic .2E **29**
Tyburn Cl. LE3: Leic .2D **18**
Tyers Cl. LE9: Thurl .6A **32**
Tyes End LE4: Leic .2E **19**
Tyler Rd. LE6: Ratby .5D **16**
Tymecrosse Gdns. LE16: Mkt H .1C **64**
Tyndale St. LE3: Leic .3H **27**
Tynedale Cl. LE2: Oad .4D **38**
Tyringham Rd. LE18: Wig .1C **46**
Tyrrell St. LE3: Leic .1H **27**
Tysoe Hill LE3: Glen .4B **18**
Tythorn Dr. LE18: Wig .4C **36**

U

Ullesthorpe Rd. LE17: Bitt .1E **63**
Ullswater Dr. LE2: Oad .4C **38**
Ullswater St. LE2: Leic .7A **5** (3A **28**)
Ullswater Wlk. LE2: Oad .4C **38**
Ulverscroft Dr. LE6: Groby .3F **17**
Ulverscroft La. LE6: New L .1G **9**
Ulverscroft Rd. LE4: Leic .5D **20**
Ulverscroft Way LE67: Mark .2C **8**
Una Av. LE3: Brau .1E **35**
Underwood Ct. LE3: Glen .5H **17**
Underwood Cres. LE9: Sap .5C **50**
Underwood Dr. LE9: S Stan .4A **50**
Unicorn Pk. LE4: Thurm .3B **14**
Unicorn St. LE4: Thurm .3B **14**
Union Wharf LE16: Mkt H .2C **64**
Unity Rd. LE3: Glen .5A **18**
University Cl. LE7: Sys .6F **7**
University of Leicester
at Leicester Royal Infirmary .7C 5
Main Campus .5C 28
Princess Rd. W. .6D 5
Princess Rd. E. .7F 5 (3C 28)
University of Leicester Botanic Gdns.
.1H 37
University Rd. LE1: Leic .8F **5** (5C **28**)
Upex Cl. LE8: Whet .1H **53**
Upland Cl. LE67: Mark .2B **8**
Upland Dr. LE67: Mark .2B **8**
Uplands Rd. LE2: Leic .4B **36**
LE2: Oad .3B **38**
Uplands Wlk. LE2: Leic .4B **36**
Up. Brown St. LE1: Leic .5C **5** (2B **28**)
Up. Charnwood St. LE2: Leic .1D **28**
Up. Church St. LE7: Sys .5F **7**
Up. George St. LE1: Leic .1E **4** (6C **20**)
Up. Hall Cl. LE5: Leic .5C **22**
Up. Hall Grn. LE5: Leic .5C **22**
Up. King St. LE1: Leic .7D **5** (3B **28**)
Up. Nelson St. LE1: Leic .6F **5** (3C **28**)
Up. New Wlk. LE1: Leic .3D **28**
Up. Temple Wlk. LE4: Leic .2E **19**
Up. Tichborne St. LE2: Leic .3D **28**
Upperton Ri. LE3: Leic .3G **27**
Upperton Rd. LE2: Leic .8A **5** (3G **27**)
LE3: Leic .8A **5** (3G **27**)
Uppingham Cl. LE5: Leic .2C **30**
Uppingham Dr. LE9: B Ast .5H **51**
Uppingham Rd. LE5: Leic .6F **21**
LE7: Bush, Hou H .2G **31**
Upton Dr. LE18: Wig .1D **46**
Utah Cl. LE3: Glen .6A **18**
Uttoxeter Cl. LE4: Leic .6B **14**
Uxbridge Rd. LE4: Leic .1E **21**

V

Vale Cl. LE5: Leic .6C **22**
Vale End LE7: Thurn .2F **31**
Valence Rd. LE3: Leic .4F **27**
Valentine Dr. LE2: Oad .3H **37**
Valentine Rd. LE5: Leic .2D **30**
Valiant Cl. LE3: Glen .6B **18**
Valjean Cres. LE9: Leic E .4E **25**
Valley Dr. LE3: Brau .5A **26**
(not continuous)
Valley La. LE17: Bitt .2F **63**
Valley Rd. LE5: Ham .1B **22**
LE67: Mark .3C **8**
Valley Way LE16: L Bow .2G **65**
Vancouver Rd. LE1: Leic .1F **4** (6C **20**)
Vandyke Rd. LE2: Oad .5B **38**
Vann Wlk. LE4: Leic .3C **20**
Vaughan Cl. LE16: Mkt H .6D **64**
Vaughan Rd. LE2: Leic .2A **36**
Vaughan St. LE3: Leic .1H **27**
Vaughan Way LE1: Leic .3B **4** (1A **28**)
Ventnor Rd. LE2: Leic .2F **37**
Ventnor Rd. Sth. LE2: Leic .3F **37**
Ventnor St. LE5: Leic .2F **29**
Verdale Av. LE4: Leic .6D **14**
Vernon Rd. LE2: Leic .2A **36**
Vernon St. LE3: Leic .1H **27**
Vestry Ho. LE1: Leic .3E **4** (1C **28**)
Vestry St. LE1: Leic .3E **4** (1C **28**)
Vetch Cl. LE19: Nar .3B **42**
Vicarage Cl. LE7: Sys .5F **7**
LE9: K Mux .1E **25**
Vicarage La. LE4: Leic .2C **20**
LE5: Leic .5B **22**
LE7: Bark .3H **15**
LE8: Whet .3H **43**
Victoria Av. LE2: Leic .3D **28**
LE16: Mkt H .2C **64**
Victoria Ct. LE2: Leic .5E **29**
LE2: Oad .2H **37**
Victoria Dr. LE6: Groby .3F **17**
Victoria Gdns. LE2: Leic .4E **29**
Victoria Hall LE1: Leic .4B **4**
Victoria M. LE1: Leic .6F **5**
Victorian Lawn Tennis Club .5F 29
Victoria Pde. LE1: Leic .3D **4** (1B **28**)
Victoria Pk. Rd. LE2: Leic .5C **28**
Victoria Pas. LE1: Leic .6F **5** (3D **28**)
Victoria Rd. LE8: Whet .3H **43**
Victoria Rd. E. LE5: Leic .5G **21**
Victoria Rd. Nth. LE4: Leic .2C **20**
Victoria St. LE4: Thurm .3C **14**
LE7: Sys .6F **7**
LE8: Flec .6B **58**
LE18: Wig .6F **37**
LE19: Nar .3E **43**
Victoria Ter. *LE2: Leic .4D 28*
(off London Rd.)
Victor Rd. LE3: Glen .5B **18**
Victors Cl. LE2: Leic .5G **35**
Viking Rd. LE18: Wig .5C **36**
Villas, The LE8: Kib B .4A **62**
Villers Ct. LE8: Bla .3B **44**
Villiers Hall LE2: Oad .1H **37**
Vincent Cl. LE3: Leic .1F **27**
Vinehouse Cl. *LE7: Thurc .1B 12*
(off Mill Rd.)

A-Z Leicester 101

Vineries, The LE8: Count 2D 54
Vislok Cl. LE16: Mkt H 5D 64
Vitrunvius Way LE19: Brau 1A 34
Vostock Cl. LE2: Leic 2D 28
Vue Cinema
  Leicester 6C 26
Vulcan Bus. Cen. LE5: Leic 6E 21
Vulcan Rd. LE5: Leic 6D 20
Vyner Cl. LE3: Brau 5A 26

W

Waddesdon Wlk. LE4: Leic 5F 21
Wade St. LE4: Leic 2B 20
Wadkins Way LE7: Bush 2G 31
Wagtail Cl. LE8: Flec 6F 59
Waingrove Wlk. LE4: Leic 1B 20
Wainwright Av. LE5: Ham 2C 22
Wainwright Footpath LE5: Ham 2C 22
  (off Sandhills Av.)
Wakefield Pl. LE4: Leic 3F 21
Wakeley Cl. LE19: Nar 4C 42
Wakeling Cl. LE8: Whet 6H 43
Wakerley Ct. LE5: Leic 1F 29
Wakerley Rd. LE5: Leic 4H 29
Wakes Cl. LE17: D Bas 5F 61
Wakes Rd. LE18: Wig 6F 37
Walcote Rd. LE4: Leic 3G 21
Walcot Rd. LE16: Mkt H 3D 64
Waldale Dr. LE2: Leic 5E 29
Waldron Dr. LE2: Oad 4C 38
Wale Rd. LE8: Whet 4H 43
Wales Orchard LE17: Leire 6A 60
Walker Cl. LE9: B Ast 3C 60
Walker Mnr. Ct. LE17: Lut 4H 63
Walker Rd. LE4: Birs 5F 13
  LE4: Thurm 5D 14
Walkers Stadium, The 5A 28
Walkers Way LE7: Sys 5F 7
Wallace Ct. LE2: Leic 6F 29
Wallace Dr. LE6: Groby 6G 9
Wallingford Rd. LE4: Leic 3B 20
Wallis Cl. LE7: Thurc 1B 12
Walnut Av. LE4: Birs 4F 13
Walnut Cl. LE2: Oad 4A 38
  LE9: B Ast 1B 60
  LE67: Mark 3B 8
Walnut Gro. LE2: G Par 5F 35
Walnut Leys LE9: Cosb 3F 53
Walnut St. LE2: Leic 8A 5 (4A 28)
Walnut Way LE8: Bla 5B 44
  LE8: Count 1E 55
Walpole Ct. LE3: Leic 2D 26
Walsgrave Av. LE5: Leic 3D 30
Walshe Rd. LE5: Leic 1B 30
Walsingham Cres. LE3: Leic E 4H 25
Waltham Av. LE3: Leic 5E 27
Walton Cl. LE9: K Mux 3F 25
Walton St. LE3: Leic 4G 27
Wand St. LE4: Leic 4C 20
WANLIP 1A 14
Wanlip Av. LE4: Birs 4G 13
Wanlip La. LE4: Birs 4H 13
Wanlip Rd. LE7: Sys 6B 6
Wanlip St. LE1: Leic 6C 20
Wansbeck Gdns. LE5: Leic 5C 22
Wanstead Rd. LE3: Leic 2G 25
Wanstead Rd. Ind. Pk.
  LE3: Leic 2G 25
Ward Cl. LE2: Leic 2G 35
Wardens Wlk. LE3: Brau, Leic E 4H 25
Wards Closes LE18: Wig 3C 46
Ward's End LE2: Oad 4B 38
Wareham Rd. LE8: Bla 5B 44
Waring Cl. LE3: Glen 4C 18
War Memorial App.
  LE1: Leic 8F 5 (4C 28)
Warmsley Av. LE18: Wig 5E 37
Warner Cl. LE8: Whet 6A 44
  LE67: Mark 2B 8
Warren, The LE7: E Gos 2G 7
  (not continuous)

Warren Av. LE4: Leic 6E 15
Warren Cl. LE3: Leic E 5F 25
  LE5: Leic 5A 22
  LE67: Mark 3C 8
Warren Dr. LE4: Leic 6E 15
Warren La. LE3: Leic E 6E 25
Warren Pk. Way LE19: End 5G 33
Warren Rd. LE19: End 2F 43
Warren St. LE3: Leic 1H 27
Warren Vw. LE4: Leic 6E 15
Warrington Dr. LE6: Groby 3E 17
Warrington St. LE3: Leic 2A 4 (1A 28)
Wartnaby St. LE16: Mkt H 3B 64
Warwick Cl. LE16: Mkt H 1E 65
Warwick Rd.
  LE8: Kib B, Kib H 5F 59
  LE8: Whet 5E 43
  LE9: B Ast 5H 51
  LE18: Wig 6D 36
  LE19: Litt, Whet 5E 43
Warwick St. LE3: Leic 1H 27
Washbrook La. LE2: Oad 5H 37
  LE8: Bur O, G Gle 2F 49
Watchcrete Av. LE7: Quen 4H 7
Waterfield Cl. LE5: Leic 2B 30
Waterfield Pl. LE16: Mkt H 1D 64
Waterfield Rd. LE7: Crop 1H 11
Waterfront, The LE3: Leic 4A 4
Watergate Ct. LE3: Brau 3D 34
Watergate La. LE3: Brau 2B 34
Waterloo Cres. LE8: Count 2D 54
  LE18: Wig 6G 37
Waterloo Way LE1: Leic 7E 5 (3C 28)
Watermead Country Pk. 6A 6
Watermead Way LE4: Leic 1C 20
Watersedge Way LE7: Sys 6C 6
Waterside Rd. LE5: Ham 2A 22
Waterville Cl. LE3: Leic 1A 26
Watery Ga. La. LE9: Thurl 3D 40
  (not continuous)
Watkin Rd. LE2: Leic 8A 5 (4H 27)
  (not continuous)
Watling St. LE1: Leic 1C 4 (6B 20)
Watson Av. LE16: Mkt H 5A 64
Watson Rd. LE4: Leic 3E 21
Watts Cl. LE4: Leic 2E 19
Waudby Cl. LE19: Litt 5E 43
Waveney Ri. LE2: Oad 3D 38
Waverley Rd. LE8: Bla 5C 44
  LE18: Wig 1F 45
Wavertree LE2: Leic 1E 37
Wavertree Cl. LE9: Cosb 1F 53
Wavertree Dr. LE4: Leic 2D 20
Wayfarer Dr. LE7: E Gos 1H 7
Wayside Dr. LE2: Oad 3C 38
  LE4: Thurm 5B 14
Weatherburn Cl. LE3: Leic 4D 18
Weaver Rd. LE5: Leic 6D 22
Weavers Ct. LE19: Nar 3D 42
Weaver's Wynd LE7: E Gos 2H 7
Webb Cl. LE3: Leic E 5H 25
Webbs Way LE9: S Stan 3B 50
Webster Rd. LE3: Leic 3C 26
Weir Cl. LE18: Wig 3H 45
Weir Rd. LE8: Kib B 5A 62
Welbeck Av. LE4: Leic 3A 20
Welbeck Cl. LE8: Bla 5C 44
Welbury Rd. LE5: Ham 1C 22
Welcombe Av. LE3: Brau 6D 26
Weldon Rd. LE18: Wig 6F 37
Welford Ct. LE2: Leic 2D 36
Welford Pl. LE1: Leic 5C 5 (2B 28)
Welford Road 8D 5 (4B 28)
Welford Rd. LE1: Leic 5C 5 (2B 28)
  LE2: Leic 5C 5 (4B 28)
  LE8: Arne 6D 56
  LE8: Bla .3B 44
  LE8: Fost 2B 46
  LE18: Wig 2B 46
Welham Wlk. LE4: Leic 1H 21

Welland Ct. LE16: Mkt H 4E 65
  (Northampton Rd.)
  LE16: Mkt H 2F 65
  (Rockingham Ind. Est.)
Welland Ind. Est. LE16: L Bow 2G 65
Welland Pk. Rd. LE16: Mkt H 4C 64
Welland St. LE2: Leic 3D 28
Welland Va. Rd. LE5: Leic 3C 30
Wellesbourne Dr. LE3: Glen 4B 18
Welles St. LE3: Leic 4A 4 (2A 28)
Wellgate Av. LE4: Birs 3F 13
Wellhouse Cl. LE18: Wig 3A 46
Wellingar Cl. LE3: Brau 5A 26
Wellinger Way LE3: Leic 5A 26
Wellington St. LE1: Leic 5D 5 (2B 28)
  LE7: Sys .6E 7
Well La. LE17: D Bas 5F 61
Wells Av. LE18: Kilby 2D 56
Well Spring Hill LE18: Wig 3C 46
Welton Cl. LE8: Kib B 5H 59
Wembley Rd. LE3: Leic 2H 25
Wembury Gdns. LE4: Leic 1A 20
Wendy's Cl. LE5: Leic 6D 22
Wenlock Way LE4: Leic 2A 22
Wensleydale Rd. LE18: Wig 2D 46
Wensley Ri. LE2: Leic 1C 44
Wentbridge Rd. LE4: Leic 2F 21
Went Rd. LE4: Birs 5G 13
Wentworth Cl. LE8: Kib B 6B 62
Wentworth Grn. LE9: K Mux 3D 24
Wentworth Rd. LE3: Leic 1G 27
  LE8: Flec 6C 58
Wesley Cl. LE6: Ratby 5C 16
  LE9: Sap .6C 50
Wesley St. LE4: Leic 2B 20
Wesley Way LE67: Mark 3D 8
Wessex Dr. LE3: Leic 2C 26
West Av. LE2: Leic 5D 28
  LE18: Wig 5D 36
Westbourne St. LE4: Leic 5C 20
Westbridge LE2: Leic 4A 4 (2A 28)
Westbridge Cl. LE3: Leic 5A 5 (2A 28)
Westbridge Ind. Pk.
  LE3: Leic 4A 4 (2A 28)
Westbridge Pl. LE2: Leic 4A 4 (2A 28)
Westbury Rd. LE2: Leic 6C 28
Westcotes Bowling Club 3G 27
Westcotes Dr. LE3: Leic 3G 27
West Ct. LE1: Leic 7F 5 (3C 28)
Westdale Av. LE2: G Par 1A 44
Westdown Dr. LE4: Thurm 6C 14
West Dr. LE5: Leic 5A 22
WEST END .3G 27
West End LE17: Bitt 2F 63
Westerby Cl. LE18: Wig 5F 37
Westerby Ct. LE17: Lut 5F 63
Westerdale Rd. LE18: Wig 1D 46
Western Av. LE8: Flec 6E 59
  LE16: Mkt H 5C 64
Western Blvd. LE2: Leic 5A 5 (2A 28)
Western Dr. LE8: Bla 4B 44
Westernhay Rd. LE2: Leic 6E 29
WESTERN PARK 2E 27
Western Pk. Rd. LE3: Leic 2E 27
Western Rd. LE3: Leic 4H 27
Westfield Av. LE8: Count 1D 54
  LE18: Wig 5D 36
Westfield Cl. LE16: Mkt H 3B 64
Westfield Rd. LE3: Leic 2E 27
Westgate Av. LE4: Birs 3E 13
Westgate Rd. LE2: Leic 3D 36
Westhill Rd. LE3: Leic 1E 27
W. Holme St. LE3: Leic 2H 27
WEST KNIGHTON 3C 36
W. Langton Rd. LE8: Kib H 6C 62
Westleigh Av. LE3: Leic 4G 27
Westleigh Bus. Pk. LE8: Bla 2B 44
Westleigh Rd. LE2: G Par 2E 45
  LE3: Leic 4G 27
Westley Grange LE18: Wig 6C 36
Westmeath Av. LE5: Leic 1B 30
Westminster Dr. LE2: G Par 2D 44
Westminster Rd. LE2: Leic 6G 29

Westmorland Av. LE4: Leic 3E 21
LE18: Wig 1F 45
Weston Cl. LE2: Oad 5E 39
Westover Rd. LE3: Brau 5B 26
West St. LE1: Leic 7D 5 (3B 28)
LE3: Glen 4A 18
LE7: Sys 5E 7
LE8: Bla 3A 44
LE19: End 1D 42
West St. Open LE3: Leic 3H 27
Westview Av. LE2; G Par 6F 35
West Wlk. LE1: Leic 7F 5 (3C 28)
(not continuous)
Wetherby Cl. LE7: Quen 3H 7
Wetherby Rd. LE4: Leic 1F 21
Wexford Cl. LE2: Oad 5D 38
Weymouth Cl. LE18: Wig 3B 46
Weymouth St. LE4: Leic 5D 20
Wharf St. LE4: Thurm 3B 14
Wharf St. Nth. LE1: Leic ...1E 4 (6C 20)
Wharf St. Sth. LE1: Leic ...1E 4 (1C 28)
Wharf Way LE2: G Par 1B 44
Wheatfield Cl. LE3: Glen 6A 18
Wheatland Cl. LE2: Oad 4D 38
Wheatland Rd. LE4: Leic 6D 12
Wheatlands Dr. LE8: Count 1D 54
Wheatley Rd. LE4: Leic 1H 19
Wheatleys Rd. LE4: Thurm 4B 14
Wheat St. LE1: Leic 2E 4 (1C 28)
Wheeldale LE18: Wig 1D 46
Wheeldale Cl. LE4: Leic 2H 19
Wheeler Cl. LE17: Lut 5G 63
WHETSTONE 3H 43
Whetstone Ct. LE8: Whet 4H 43
WHETSTONE GORSE 5B 54
Whetstone Gorse La. LE8: Whet ...3A 54
Whetstone Gorse Touring Cvn. Pk.
LE8: Whet 5B 54
Whiles La. LE4: Birs 4H 13
Whinchat Rd. LE5: Leic 1E 29
Whinham Av. LE9: B Ast 6H 51
Whissendine Way LE7: Sys 1G 15
Whiston Cl. LE5: Leic 1D 30
Whitby Cl. LE9: B Ast 5A 52
Whitcroft Cl. LE67: Mark 3C 8
Whiteacres LE8: Whet 6G 43
White Barn Dr. LE9: Cosb 2F 53
Whitebeam Cl. LE19: Nar 3C 42
Whitebeam Rd. LE2: Oad 2A 38
White Cl. LE9: B Ast 1C 60
Whitefield Rd. LE4: Leic 2B 20
Whitegates Fld. LE18: Wig 2C 46
Whitehall Rd. LE5: Leic 3B 30
White Hart Cl. LE4: Thurm 4B 14
Whitehead Cres. LE18: Wig 6D 36
White Horse La. LE4: Birs 5H 13
White Ho. Cl. LE17: Leire 6A 60
Whitehouse Cl. LE6: Groby 2E 17
Whiteoaks Rd. LE2: Oad 6C 38
Whitesand Cl. LE3: Glen 4B 18
White St. LE8: Kib B 5H 59
Whitley Cl. LE3: Leic 5F 19
Whitman Cl. LE3: Leic 1B 26
Whitteney Dr. Nth. LE2: Leic 5G 35
Whitteney Dr. Sth. LE2: Leic 5H 35
Whittier Rd. LE2: Leic 2B 36
Whittington Dr. LE6: Ratby 4C 16
Whittington Rd. LE3: Leic 2D 18
Whittle Cl. LE8: Whet 5H 43
Whittle Rd. LE17: Lut 5F 63
Whitwell Row LE2: Leic 4A 36
Whitwick Rd. LE67: C Oak, Ulv, Mark ...1B 8
Whitwick Way LE3: Leic 5G 19
Whixley Rd. LE5: Ham 1C 22
Whixley Way LE5: Ham 1C 22
Wicken Ri. LE18: Wig 5G 37
Wickford Cl. LE5: Leic 4H 21
Wickham Rd. LE2: Oad 5B 38
Wicklow Dr. LE5: Leic 1A 30
Wiclif Way LE17: Lut 3G 63
Widford Cl. LE5: Leic 5A 22
Wigglesworth Ct. LE2: Leic 5H 35
Wightman Cl. LE9: S Stan 2B 50

Wigley Rd. LE5: Leic 5C 22
WIGSTON 6F 37
WIGSTON FIELDS 4D 36
Wigston Framework Knitters Mus. ...1A 46
WIGSTON HARCOURT 3C 46
Wigston La. LE2: Leic 3G 35
WIGSTON MAGNA 1C 46
Wigston Rd. LE2: Oad 5H 37
LE8: Bla 3B 44
Wigston St. LE1: Leic 4E 4 (2C 28)
LE8: Count 1F 55
Wigston Swimming Pool 2H 45
Wilberforce Rd. LE3: Leic 4H 27
Wilkes Way LE7: Sys 1D 14
William Carey Mus. 4E 4
(off Charles St.)
William Peardon Ct. LE18: Wig ...6E 37
Williams Cl. LE19: Litt 5E 43
William St. LE1: Leic 3F 4 (1D 28)
LE19: Nar 4D 42
Willoughby Gdns. LE3: Leic E 4G 25
Willoughby Rd. LE8: Count, Will W ...2C 54
LE17: Ash M 5G 61
Willow Brook Cl. LE3: Glen 3A 18
Willowbrook Cl. LE7: Quen 3H 7
Willow Cl. LE19: Litt 5E 43
Willow Ct. LE2: Leic 2D 28
LE3: Brau 2D 34
Willow Cres. LE16: Mkt H 4B 64
Willow Dr. LE6: Groby 4E 17
LE8: Count 1E 55
Willow Herb Cl. LE2: Oad 5E 39
Willow Pk. Dr. LE18: Wig 6E 37
Willow Pl. LE18: Wig 1B 46
Willow St. LE1: Leic 6C 20
Willowtree Cl. LE5: Ham 3C 22
Willow Tree Cres. LE17: Lut 4E 63
Willow Wlk. LE7: Sys 6D 6
Willsmer Cl. LE9: B Ast 2C 60
Wilson Cl. LE16: L Bow 3F 65
Wilmington Dr. LE2: Leic 1G 37
Wilmington Rd. LE3: Leic 4G 27
Wilmore Cres. LE3: Leic 4B 26
Wilne St. LE2: Leic 3E 29
Wilnicott Rd. LE3: Brau 6D 26
Wilsford Cl. LE18: Wig 3A 46
Wilshere Cl. LE9: K Mux 2D 24
Wilson Cl. LE3: Brau 5B 26
Wilson Rd. LE18: Wig 2E 45
Wilson St. LE2: Leic 1E 29
Wilton Cl. LE2: Oad 4C 38
Wilton St. LE1: Leic 1D 4 (6B 20)
Wiltshire Ho. LE4: Leic 3H 19
Wiltshire Rd. LE4: Leic 3H 19
LE18: Wig 6D 36
Wimbledon St. LE1: Leic ...3E 4 (1C 28)
Wimborne Cl. LE18: Wig 2A 46
Wimborne Rd. LE2: Leic 3F 37
Winchendon Cl. LE5: Leic 6G 21
Winchester Av. LE3: Leic 4F 27
LE8: Bla 3A 44
Winchester Av. Ind. Pk. LE8: Bla ...3A 44
Winchester Rd. LE8: Bla, Count ...4C 44
Windermere Dr. LE9: Crof 1H 51
Windermere Rd. LE18: Wig 6H 37
Windermere St. LE2: Leic ...8A 5 (4A 28)
Winders Ct. LE2: Leic 4H 35
Winders Way LE2: Leic 4H 35
Windley Rd. LE2: Leic 3B 36
Windmill Av. LE4: Birs 3H 13
Windmill Bank LE18: Wig 2C 46
Windmill Cl. LE4: Thurm 3D 14
LE6: Ratby 5D 16
Windmill Gdns. LE8: Kib H 3A 62
Windmill Ri. LE6: Groby 2E 17
Windrush Dr. LE2: Oad 3D 38
Windsor Av. LE2: G Par 2E 45
LE4: Leic 3D 20
LE6: Groby 3F 17

Windsor Cl. LE2: Oad 6C 38
Windsor Ct. LE16: Mkt H 2C 64
Winforde Cres. LE3: Leic 3B 26
Wingates Wlk. LE16: Mkt H 3E 65
(off St Mary's Rd.)
Wingfield St. LE4: Leic 3D 20
Winifred St. LE2: Leic 7B 5 (3A 28)
Winkadale Cl. LE7: Bush 2H 31
Winslow Dr. LE18: Wig 5G 37
Winslow Grn. LE5: Leic 5C 22
Winstanley Dr. LE3: Leic 3D 26
Winster Dr. LE4: Thurm 3C 14
Winston Av. LE9: Crof 1H 51
Winterburn Gdns. LE8: Whet 4H 43
Winterfield Cl. LE3: Glen 6H 17
Wintergreen Cl. LE5: Ham 2C 22
Wintersdale Rd. LE5: Leic 1C 30
Wintersdale Wlk. LE5: Leic 1D 30
Winterton Cl. LE4: Thurm 3D 14
Winton Av. LE3: Leic 5G 27
Winton Wlk. LE3: Leic 5G 27
WISTOW 1H 57
Wistow Cl. LE18: Kilby 2E 57
Wistow La. LE8: Kib H 3E 59
Wistow Maze 6H 47
Wistow Rd. LE8: New H 4H 47
LE18: Kilby 2E 57
LE18: Wig 2B 46
Wistow Rural Cen. 1H 57
Withcote Av. LE5: Leic 1B 30
Withens Cl. LE3: Leic 6E 19
Witherdell LE4: Leic 2E 19
Withers Way LE3: Brau 5B 26
Withington Cl. LE3: Brau 5B 26
Woburn Cl. LE2: Lelc 5G 35
LE16: L Bow 3F 65
LE18: Wig 1C 46
Wodehouse Rd. LE3: Leic 3E 27
Wokingham Av. LE2: Leic 1D 44
Wolds, The LE7: E Gos 1H 7
Wolfe End LE7: Anst 4E 11
Wollaton Cl. LE3: Glen 5H 17
Wolsey Cl. LE3: Leic E 5F 25
LE6: Groby 3E 17
LE8: Flec 5B 58
Wolsey Dr. LE6: Ratby 4B 16
Wolsey La. LE8: Flec 5B 58
Wolsey St. LE4: Leic 5A 20
Wolsey Way LE7: Sys 6D 6
Wolverton Rd. LE3: Leic 5G 27
Woodbank LE2: G Par 1B 44
Woodbank Rd. LE2: Leic 3E 37
LE6: Groby 2D 16
Woodbine Av. LE2: Leic 3D 28
Woodbine Cres. LE17: Lut 5G 63
Woodborough Rd. LE5: Leic 3A 30
Woodboy St. LE1: Leic 1E 4 (6C 20)
Woodbreach Dr. LE16: L Bow 3G 65
Woodbridge Rd. LE4: Leic 2D 20
Woodbury Ri. LE8: G Gle 2E 49
Woodby La. LE17: Bitt 2E 63
Woodcote Rd. LE3: Brau 2C 34
Woodcroft Av. LE2: Leic 3C 36
Wood End LE3: Leic 6E 19
Woodfield Cl. LE19: Nar 3D 42
Woodfield Rd. LE2: Oad 2B 38
Woodford Cl. LE18: Wig 3A 46
Woodford Rd. LE2: Leic 8A 5 (4H 27)
Woodgate LE3: Leic 6H 19
Woodgate LE16: L Bow 4G 65
Woodgate Dr. LE4: Birs 3F 13
Woodgon Rd. LE7: Anst 5F 11
Woodgreen Rd. LE4: Leic 4F 21
Woodgreen Wlk. LE4: Leic 4F 21
Woodhall Cl. LE3: Leic 2B 26
Wood Hill LE5: Leic 1E 29
Woodhouse Cl. LE67: Mark 2C 8
Woodhouse Rd. LE19: Nar 3C 42
Woodland Av. LE2: Leic 6E 29
LE19: Nar 2D 42
Woodland Cl. LE67: Mark 3C 8
Woodland Dr. LE3: Brau 5B 26
Woodland Rd. LE5: Leic 6F 21

Woodlands, The LE8: Count 1D 54
   LE16: Mkt H 2B 64
   LE18: Wig 5H 37
Woodlands Cl. LE2: Oad 5G 39
Woodlands Ct. LE2: Oad 5E 39
Woodlands Dr. LE6: Groby 1D 16
Woodlands La. LE9: K Mux 1E 25
Woodlea Av. LE17: Lut 3E 63
Woodleigh Cl. LE5: Leic 6D 22
Woodley Rd. LE6: Ratby 5C 16
Woodman's Chase
   LE7: E Gos 2H 7
Woodmarket LE17: Lut 5F 63
Woodnewton Dr. LE5: Leic 3D 30
Woodpecker Dr. LE3: Leic E 5E 25
Woods Cl. LE2: Oad 3C 38
Woodshawe Ri. LE3: Leic 4C 26
Woodside Cl. LE4: Leic 4F 21
   LE19: Nar 3B 42
Woodside Rd. LE2: Oad 6D 38
Woodstock Cl. LE4: Leic 1A 20
Woodstock Rd. LE4: Leic 1A 20
Wood St. LE1: Leic 1D 4 (6B 20)
Woodville Cl. LE6: Ratby 4D 16
Woodville Gdns. LE18: Wig 4E 37
Woodville Rd. LE3: Leic 2F 27
Woodway LE8: Whet 3H 43
Woodway Rd. LE17: Lut 5E 63
Woodyard La. LE8: Whet 3H 43
Wooldale Cl. LE7: Anst 4G 11
Woolsthorpe Wlk. LE5: Leic 5G 21
Wooton Ri. LE2: Leic 4H 35
Wootton Cl. LE8: Whet 5H 43
Worcester Av. LE4: Birs 2H 13
Worcester Dr. LE16: Mkt H 1D 64
   LE18: Wig 1F 45
Worcester Rd. LE2: Leic 2H 35

Wordsworth Cres. LE19: Nar 2C 42
Wordsworth Rd. LE2: Leic 1C 36
Worrall Cl. LE3: Leic 3B 26
Worrall Rd. LE3: Leic 3B 26
Worsh Cl. LE8: Whet 6H 43
Worsley Way LE8: Whet 5A 44
Worthington St. LE2: Leic 2E 29
Wranglands, The LE8: Flec 6C 58
Wreake Cl. LE7: Sys 5F 7
Wreake Rd. LE4: Thurm 2C 14
Wreford Cres. LE5: Leic 6E 23
Wren Cl. LE2: Leic 2A 36
   LE7: Sys .5C 6
Wright Cl. LE8: Whet 1H 53
Wright La. LE2: Oad 5D 38
Wroxall Way LE3: Leic 5G 19
Wyatt Cl. LE3: Leic 3A 26
Wych Elm Cl. LE8: G Gle 2D 48
Wych Elm Rd. LE2: Oad 2A 38
Wychwood Rd. LE8: Whet 6A 44
Wycliffe Ind. Est. LE17: Lut 3H 63
Wycliffe St.
   LE1: Leic 4C 4 (2B 28)
Wycliffe Ter. LE17: Lut 4H 63
Wycombe Rd. LE5: Leic 5H 21
Wye Dean Dr. LE18: Wig 1B 46
Wyggeston Hospital LE3: Leic 2G 27
Wykeham Cl. LE8: Bla 5B 44
Wylam Cl. LE3: Leic 5E 19
Wymar Cl. LE4: Leic 2G 19
Wyndale Dr. LE7: Sys 4F 7
Wyndale Rd. LE2: Leic 2D 36
Wyndham Cl. LE2: Oad 2C 38
Wynfield Rd. LE3: Leic 2F 27
Wyngate Dr. LE3: Leic 3F 27
Wynthorpe Ri. LE3: Leic 3E 27
Wynton Cl. LE8: Bla 5C 44

Wyvern Av. LE4: Leic 2F 21
Wyvern Cl. LE9: B Ast 2C 60
Wyville Row LE3: Leic 6E 27

Y

Yardley Dr. LE2: Leic 4D 36
Yarmouth St. LE1: Leic 1D 4 (6B 20)
Yarrow Cl. LE5: Ham 4C 22
Yarwell Dr. LE18: Wig 1C 46
Yaxley Cl. LE7: Thurn 1F 31
Yeats Cl. LE3: Brau 6B 26
Yelverton Av. LE5: Leic 4C 30
Yeoman La. LE1: Leic 3E 4 (1C 28)
Yeomanry Ct.
   LE16: Mkt H 3D 64
Yeoman's Dale LE7: E Gos 1H 7
Yeomans Keep LE17: Bitt 2F 63
Yeoman St. LE1: Leic 3E 4 (1C 28)
Yew Cl. LE3: Leic E 6F 25
Yews, The LE2: Oad 3B 38
Yew Tree Cl. LE17: Lut 4E 63
Yew Tree Dr. LE3: Leic 1A 26
York Pl. LE1: Leic 5E 5 (2C 28)
York Rd. LE1: Leic 5C 5 (2B 28)
Yorkshire Rd. LE4: Leic 4E 21
York St. LE1: Leic 5D 5 (2B 28)
   LE16: Mkt H 3E 65
Y Theatre, The 5E 5 (2C 28)
Yukon Way LE1: Leic 1F 4 (6C 20)

Z

Zetland Wlk. LE4: Leic 6E 13

SAFETY CAMERA INFORMATION

Safety camera locations are publicised by the Safer Roads Partnership which operates them in order to encourage drivers to comply with speed limits at these sites. It is the driver's absolute responsibility to be aware of and to adhere to speed limits at all times.

By showing this safety camera information it is the intention of Geographers' A-Z Map Company Ltd., to encourage safe driving and greater awareness of speed limits and vehicle speed. Data accurate at time of printing.

Printed and bound in the United Kingdom by Polestar Wheatons Ltd., Exeter.